1992

Process and Experience
in the Language Classroom

APPLIED LINGUISTICS AND LANGUAGE STUDY

General Editor
Professor Christopher N. Candlin, Macquarie University

Error Analysis
*Perspectives on second
language acquisition*
JACK C. RICHARDS (ED.)

Stylistics and the
Teaching of Literature
HENRY WIDDOWSON

Language Tests at School
A pragmatic approach
JOHN W. OLLER JNR

Contrastive Analysis
CARL JAMES

Language and Communication
JACK C. RICHARDS AND
RICHARD W. SCHMIDT (EDS)

Learning to Write:
First Language/Second Language
AVIVA FREEDMAN, IAN PRINGLE
AND JANICE YALDEN (EDS)

Strategies in Interlanguage
Communication
CLAUS FAERCH AND
GABRIELLE KASPER (EDS)

Reading in a Foreign Language
J. CHARLES ALDERSON AND
A. H. URQUHART (EDS)

Discourse and Learning
PHILIP RILEY (ED.)

An Introduction to
Discourse Analysis
New edition
MALCOLM COULTHARD

Computers in English Language
Teaching and Research
GEOFFREY LEECH AND
CHRISTOPHER N. CANDLIN (EDS)

Bilingualism in Education
*Aspects of theory,
research and practice*
JIM CUMMINS AND
MERRILL SWAIN

Second Language Grammar:
Learning and Teaching
WILLIAM E. RUTHERFORD

The Classroom and the
Language Learner
*Ethnography and second-language
classroom research*
LEO VAN LIER

Vocabulary and Language Teaching
RONALD CARTER AND
MICHAEL McCARTHY (EDS)

Observation in the
Language Classroom
DICK ALLWRIGHT

Listening to Spoken English
Second Edition
GILLIAN BROWN

Listening in Language Learning
MICHAEL ROST

An Introduction to Second
Language Acquisition Research
DIANE LARSEN-FREEMAN AND
MICHAEL H. LONG

Language and Discrimination
*A study of communication in
multi-ethnic workplaces*
CELIA ROBERTS, TOM JUPP AND
EVELYN DAVIES

Translation and Translating:
Theory and Practice
ROGER T. BELL

Process and Experience in the
Language Classroom
MICHAEL LEGUTKE AND
HOWARD THOMAS

Process and Experience in the Language Classroom

Michael Legutke and Howard Thomas

London and New York

Longman Group UK Limited
Longman House, Burnt Mill, Harlow,
Essex CM20 2JE, England
and Associated Companies throughout the world.

Published in the United States of America
by Longman Inc., New York

First published 1991

British Library Cataloguing in Publication Data
Legutke, Michael
    Process and experience in the language classroom. – (Applied linguistics and
    language study).
    1. Schools. Curriculum subjects : Language skills.
    Teaching
    I. Title II. Thomas, Howard   III. Series
    407.1

    ISBN 0–582–01654–1

Library of Congress Cataloging in Publication Data
Legutke, Michael, 1944–
    Process and experience in the language classroom / Michael Legutke,
    Howard Thomas.
        p. cm. — (Applied linguistics and language study)
    Includes bibliographical references (p.) and index.
    ISBN 0–582–01654–1
    1. Languages, Modern—Study and teaching. I. Thomas, Howard, 1945– .
    II. Title. III. Series.
    PB35.L435 1991
    418'.007—dc20   90–19556
                                                                          CIP

Set in 10/12 pt Linotron 202 Ehrhardt
Printed in Malaysia
by Vinlin Press Sdn Bhd.,
Sri Petaling, Kuala Lumpur.

Contents

General Editor's Preface

There has never been a time when language teaching and learning was more in need of a systematic educational underpinning to its activities. In some curious way, the twin pressures of commercialisation and the often short-term imperatives of research have conspired to make difficult a general reflection on the purposes and objectives of language teaching and learning as part of the personal and cultural experience of teachers and learners. The pressure to publish for what seems at times an inexorable demand by a learning public makes for slicker products constructed for the marketplace whose connections to educational philosophy and curriculum theory seems increasingly tenuous. At the same time, classroom researchers within a tradition of second language acquisition research are, with honourable exceptions, buried in the minutiae of teacher-learner interaction and rarely relate the aims and process of their research or, indeed their findings, to these same intellectual traditions. Both ends of the spectrum, as it were, the products and the research, appear to be operating in a vacuum.

Now of course, this extreme scenario is not all-pervasive; both the European and the North American traditions have such an intellectual resource to hand to be called upon, as do many other cultural and educational environments where language teaching and learning is held in regard. Making the connection, however, is increasingly difficult as the key constructs of the process, the nature of language, the nature of teaching, the nature of learning are naturalised and taken for granted, not open to debate and question.

It is in this context that this innovative contribution to the **Applied Linguistics and Language Study Series** by Michael Legutke and Howard Thomas represents an opportunity for reflection, a chance to explore current practices and identify those which do have that link to educational philosophy and curriculum theory which any public instructional system, and, indeed any responsive private system, should espouse. Such an intellectual enquiry would be sterile, however, if it did not demonstrate a connection to *praxis*, to the reflective exploration, appraisal and creation of theory in action, in the classroom and in the language learning and language using community. This is another kind of connection, as important as the first, and one which teachers in particular will rightly want to see made. It is notable that the authors both reflect the need for these connections in their own work and in their experience can address both the public and the private educational sectors. It is even more important that they come from different intellectual traditions and actual experiences, ones which go a considerable way to breaking down the hegemony of the narrow anglocentric tradition in language teaching.

What then are the motives for the book? At one level it provides a critical history of developments in language teaching and learning in a communicative framework, in terms of content, in terms of teaching and learning and in terms of the *discipline* of language education within the overall curriculum. Helped by the authors' arguments we can see how there has been in the last decade a shift in subject-matter content from a focus on language as sets of formal structures towards one more sensitive (albeit, as Legutke and Thomas point out, still restrictedly so) to contextual variation and pragmatic appropriateness. Even where one hears contemporary cries for 'formal rigour' (as a kind of 'back-to-basics' movement transposed to language teaching and learning) this has not seriously implied a return to mass memorisation of structures as unsituated units. Materials have become more open to individual learner reaction, less directed at the non-negotiable transmission of messages, more responsive to learners' relative engagement, more task-based and increasingly problem-centred. Furthermore, and this will be one of the major themes of this book, although there has still not been any serious comparative exploration of the cultures of the second or foreign language classroom as these might affect acquisition, recent focus on the individual learner has not excluded the society of the learning environment. The focus has begun to be on the varied perceptions, reactions and learnings of the individual learners within their classroom groups, thus implicitly at least raising the issue of learners' personal identities versus their social and cultural identities within the process of language learning.

Such changes of perspectives raise important issues at the macro and the micro levels of curriculum design and implementation, as the authors explicitly acknowledge. At very least they suggest that the disciplinary distinctions within language education among the teaching and learning of the mother tongue, the second (and third) language(s), and the foreign language(s), perhaps owe more to traditional institutional and professional territorial boundaries than they do either to real distinctions in subject-matter, or even to methodology. Indeed, the present authors' exploration of the concept of *project* in language learning and teaching highlights this fluidity of boundary, suggesting some overarching curriculum of language education within which these may best be seen as distinct subject emphases with considerable common ground.

Learners' choice of texts, tasks and roles, and their variable accordance of importance and personal effort to them, invites exploration of the bases of such choices and such emphases. We have become concerned why learners choose what they wish to work on in language learning and why they employ the strategies they appear to. We have begun to ask interesting questions about such processes of choice, the extent to which they are socially and culturally conditioned and the effect on acquisition not just of the distributive context of the classroom (who works with whom on what in which modes) but also of the social context (who, with what social and cultural backgrounds of value and belief, in what roles and with what expected and allowed out-of-classroom opportunity for the realising and testing of what has been learned). All these questions are crucial for a reading of this book. In particular, its Chapter Three offers a central theory, a set of critical principles for the appraisal of language learning theory in the context of classroom activity.

In sum, then, the book shows at this narrative level, how there has been a shift from language to language in context, from the learner as an individual to the learner as a member of social groups, from language teaching and learning as a subject to an educational issue which has become increasingly politicised in the context of mobile multilingual and multi-ethnic societies, from the teacher as a source of classroom learning to a blurring of roles where both teacher *and* learner are objects of the acculturation and learning process.

It would be wrong though to regard the book as merely, or indeed as centrally historical, however reflective and critical. It is intensely practical. It describes how curriculum principles can be actualised and how they can be challenged through reflective classroom practice. It offers concrete examples of the design and realisation of the language teaching process. Chapter Four introduces these examples by an extensive and detailed typology of tasks, the *building bricks* of the communicative curriculum, in the authors' formulation. It is notable how these tasks are defined in a range of ways, partly intellectually, partly affectively, partly logistically, all in the service of what Legutke and Thomas term the 'open classroom'. Bricks, however, imply a building and we can interpret that metaphorically, in terms of language learning *per se* and in terms of learning projects, themselves constituted by this variety of tasks. Project learning has a rich tradition in education, though one which has been less prominent in language learning than in other disciplines in the curriculum. It is, of course, an interesting intellectual question why this should be so. Is it because language learning was seen more as the activity of personal memory and analysis than it was of collective 'doing'? An activity for the closet rather than for the community? One might argue that, and indeed the book takes up this point in its early chapters investigating the intellectual traditions of language teaching. Here, though, we have again a practical but still reflective exposition and exploration of what projects in language learning imply for the parties involved, for the curriculum and for the institution itself. The authors show how the concept challenges received ideas for all these 'participants' in the process, in terms of roles, in terms of expectations, and in terms of organization. There are, then, issues in project learning which need debate and it would be foolish to pretend that a decision to adopt such an orientation to language teaching can be taken without thought for its implications. This is precisely the value of this book, that it does not utter slogans but looks at their consequences. In doing such, of course, it works against the unreflective promotion characteristic of the undertheorised and underconceptualised industry which language learning has too readily become.

We return, then, to the theme at the outset of this Preface, one which is given its focus in this book in Chapters Seven and Eight with their concentration on learner education and teacher education. The terms are not adventitious. In these two Chapters we have in one place a rationale for language education, not ahistorical, not asocial, but one which demonstrates tradition and places the curriculum process where it should be at, in the reflective *praxis* of the informed teacher and the informed learner. Readers of this book will be aware of current calls for teacher *education* as opposed to teacher *training*, as if the concepts were always distinguishable in practice or as if the idea of *education* had just been cracked out of some intellectual egg: read the literature the authors would argue, and you would see that it has always been alive and well, despite the countervailing winds. What is more important is their emphasis on educating *learners*. That is more original, and more dangerous, since it implies the potential for learners' independent action borne out of a critical awareness of the issues involved in learning a language: who am I, what is s/he, why is this process as it is, what is it for? Here, of course, teachers of adult learners, especially migrants or professionals, have always had these questions to answer, less so their colleagues in the school system. What is challenging about this book is how Legutke and Thomas combine their experience of learners across these sectors to create a perspective on language education which, as so often in this book, traditional boundaries are crossed. In sum, I suppose, this book *is* about crossroads, points of contact and points of departure in language learning and teaching, but always points that have been reached along paths from somewhere and are directed at a multiplicity of objectives. Tracing those paths and discovering those objectives is what **Process and Experience in the Language Classroom** has as its theme.

Professor Christopher N Candlin
Macquarie University, Sydney
January 1991

Acknowledgements

The publishers are grateful to the following for permission to reproduce copyright material:

Warner Chappell Music Ltd./Polygram/Island Music Publishing Group to reproduce the lyrics of the composition 'Soldier's Things' by Tom Waits, © Warner Chappell Music Ltd./Copyright © 1983 Jalma Music, Worldwide rights controlled by Ackee Music Inc., International Copyright Secured, All Rights Reserved; Peters Fraser & Dunlop Group Ltd., Jonathan Cape Ltd. and Roger McGough to reproduce the poem 'First Day at School' from *In the Glassroom* (1976) by Roger McGough; Verlag Ferdinand Kamp GMBH & Co, KG Bochum for pages 151–154, 177 and 228–232 from *Lebendiger Englischunterricht* (1988) by M. Legutke, pages 56 and 92 from *Encounters with American and British Culture: Confidence* (1984) by L. Bredella and M. Legutke, and pages 245 and 256 from *Schuleraktivierende Methoden im Fremdsprachenunterricht* (1984) by M. Legutke; F. de Reuver for Self-assessment of Skills for Office Skills Course from *Office skills and English course*, National Curriculum Project documentation (1987), Sydney Adult Migrant Education Service; Heinemann Publishers (Oxford) Ltd. for a task by M. Rinvolucri in chapter 4 of *Towards the Creative Teaching of English* (1981) ed by Spaventa; The Bell Educational Trust, Cambridge, for Figures 6.5.(1) and 6.3.2.(1); The Bell School, Bath, for Figures 4.2.1.(1), 4.2.9.(3), 5.3.2., 5.3.3.(1), 6.2.1. and 6.6.4.(2); Colin Oakley for Figure 4.2.3.(1).

Acknowledgements

Like much learning and teaching in the communicative language classroom this book owes a great deal to international cooperation. We are grateful therefore to a wide circle of colleagues whose work we have drawn on directly and indirectly. They come from many countries: Australia, Austria, Denmark, Finland, Great Britain, Holland, India, Italy, Portugal, the Soviet Union, the USA, Switzerland and West Germany, and represent many sectors of education: secondary/high school, adult, university and teacher in-service.

Individually we would like to thank: Chris Candlin for his constructive editorial comments and enthusiastic support and Keith Morrow for his critical insight. We are also grateful to our colleagues at the Bell School, Bath, and in particular to Graham Carter, John Roberts and Judy Hallam for their innovatory work in the project classroom, and Steve Walters who had the vision to promote project work institutionally. We would also like to acknowledge the contribution of the foreign language teachers in the Pacific Northwest of the USA, in particular, the teachers of German in Washington, Oregon, Idaho, Montana and Alaska who inspired us with their commitment to innovation. Not least, we owe a debt to the countless students worldwide who have enriched our understanding of the experiential classroom through their enjoyment and their helpful criticisms of it.

Our thanks are also due to Linda Harrison, Bernice Ege-Zavala and Stefanie Duncan who helped in the difficult process of completing the manuscript, and to Richard Tiley who conjured up a Apple Mac SE when all hope seemed lost.

For Claire, Janna, Isabel, Regine, Ruth and Sally

1 The modern language classroom: the case of the outmoded paradigm

> The ideal of using the present simply to get ready for the future contradicts itself. It omits, and even shuts out, the very conditions by which a person can be prepared for the future. We always live at the time we live and not at some other time, and only by extracting at each present time the full meaning of each present experience are we prepared for doing the same thing in the future. This is the only preparation which in the long run amounts to anything.
>
> (Dewey 1963, p. 49)

1.1 The challenge of Communicative Language Teaching (CLT): shifts of paradigms

The last two decades have seen a major shift in paradigms in the debate over foreign language learning. We have witnessed an exciting time in the development of programmes for language teaching and learning and for the consequent training and education of teachers. One of the key concepts that has emerged is the notion of communicative competence. Ideas relating to and deriving from this concept which were speculation in the late 1960s and early 1970s have gained the increasing support of philosophical investigation and – as we will see – classroom experimentation and experience.

In 1980 the newly founded journal *Applied Linguistics* immediately joined the debate by publishing two programmatic articles in its first volume. Both of them dealt critically with the notion of communicative competence and with 'communicative approaches' which had emerged in the 1970s and rapidly gained prominence among theoreticians, textbook authors and practitioners in Europe, Canada and to some extent in the USA (see Howatt 1984; Jäger 1984). In the first article, Canale and Swain (1980) presented a critical framework for the consideration of 'communicative competence', which led them to identify various shortcomings of the emerging 'communicative approaches'. They concluded that the many aspects of communicative competence had to be investigated in

1

a more rigorous manner before a communicative approach could be fully implemented in second language teaching and testing. They called for classroom-based research which would have to investigate – among others – several immediate and long-term research issues. Some of the immediate issues were:

(1) the manner in which and extent to which communication is focused on in different second language classes in 'current' general programmes (e.g. the function, scope and limitations of communicative activities);
(2) the suitability of CLT for young learners;
(3) how to interpret the significant differences between and among groups of learners with reference to implementing a communicative approach and testing its outcomes;
(4) the relationship between CLT and learner motivation.

The second programmatic article in this initial volume of *Applied Linguistics* by Breen and Candlin (1980) presented the potential characteristics of CLT in terms of a curriculum framework. The authors called for a radical departure from objectivist curriculum models which had dominated foreign language teaching and classroom practice. By aiming at the operationalization of predetermined goals, the objectivist models had turned the classroom into a hierarchically structured, teacher-dominated arena of knowledge and skill transmission whose procedures and forms of interaction were neither compatible with what we had come to know about learning, nor with educational values of democratic societies. The objectivist model *sui generis* could not provide for the development of a responsible and participatory citizenry.

Just as the language classroom is the main focus of Canale and Swain's rigorous research agenda, so the classroom is at the heart of Breen and Candlin's curriculum framework. The classroom is understood as a unique social environment with its own human activities and its own conventions governing these activities. It is an environment where a particular cultural reality is constructed, which implies a communicative potential to be exploited for learning rather than constraints which have to be compensated for:

> Within the communicative curriculum, the classroom – and the procedures and activities it allows – can serve as a focal point of the learning–teaching process . . . . It can become the meeting place for realistically motivated communication-as-learning, communication about learning, and metacommunication. It can be a forum where knowledge may be jointly offered and sought, reflected upon, and acted upon.
>
> (Ibid., p. 98)

In short, a curriculum with its emphasis on learning and teaching of communication highlights a process whereby the interrelating curriculum components are themselves 'open to negotiation and change' (ibid., p. 106). This framework of a negotiated curriculum has far-reaching consequences for:

(1) the classroom process itself where and through which negotiation takes place;
(2) the definition of teacher and learner roles;
(3) the provision of learning content from both teacher and learner;
(4) the structuring of the learning process for which both teacher and learner take responsibility;
(5) the methodology exploiting the classroom as a genuine resource with its own communicative potential.

Ten years later, *Applied Linguistics* (**10**: 2/1989) published a special issue reporting proceedings of a British/American gathering of researchers and theoreticians to 'take stock', so to speak, of what had become of communicative competence. The papers focus on the development of the construct, the various sources from which it was correctly or wrongly derived, the impacts these derivations had on the theory of language acquisition and learning, etc. It is not our intention to devalue the contributions of this conference. Nevertheless we believe it omitted to address two crucial areas.

The first is that no reference is made to the non-English speaking voices during twenty years of intensive debate. In particular the continental European contributions, which unfortunately are written in French, Dutch, German, Danish, Portuguese or Polish, needed to be taken into consideration. In this respect the attempt at stock-taking remained parochial (see van Essen 1989).

The second, and more important, fact is that the social reality of the language classroom on both sides of the Atlantic is not only ignored from a systematic perspective, but also from a historical point of view:

- What do we know – after two decades – about the psycho-social nature of the L2 classroom, its culture and the impact it has on L2 learning?
- What has happened in L2 classrooms since the introduction of the construct of communicative competence, since curriculum developers and textbook authors have begun to use it – even if applications seem to have been 'too extensive and premature' (*Applied Linguistics* **10**: 2/1989: 114)?
- What do we really know about implementation efforts at secondary

and tertiary levels, and what were their outcomes? What kind of evidence, for example, do we have about the effects of the Council of Europe's Modern Languages Project No. 12?

– What has become of Canale and Swain's call for a rigorous research programme? Has it been carried out? What would be its contribution towards helping, directing or even correcting the implementation of communicative approaches?

– In which way has the investigation of the L2 classroom following Canale and Swain, Breen and Candlin, or any other framework enriched or even changed the construct of communicative competence itself?

– How has the construct – even if it was often diluted, misunderstood, or not clearly defined – challenged teachers to rethink and ultimately reorganize their teaching?

– How do teachers teach at the end of the 1980s, and how do L2 learners learn? In which way do both their activities differ from those of the early 1970s? Have there been any specifiable changes in the roles of teachers, learners, content and process?

– What do teachers, who do not have the time to write research papers nor the money and sabbatical options to attend language-acquisition conferences, have to say about their own attempts at implementing innovation in their classrooms? Should the teachers (and if so, in what way) be part of the research process itself?

– Do we have any accounts of negotiated curricula in action, and what do we learn from them?

Since none of the above questions is addressed in this special issue, it comes as no surprise that Canale and Swain's research programme seems to have fallen by the wayside, and that Breen and Candlin's call for radical curriculum renewal is not even mentioned.

Before we return to the issues relating to the L2 classroom, we will take a brief look at some of the shifts of paradigms we mentioned above. Without making any claim for completeness with regard to the overall debate (see Morley 1987 for survey), we hold the following shifts to be of crucial relevance for the argument of this book:

(1) We have seen a shift from language as form to language in context and as communication (Piepho 1974; 1979; Widdowson 1978).

(2) We have experienced increased attention on the construct of task as the pivotal component of classroom design and implementation (Prabhu 1987; Candlin and Murphy 1987; Legutke 1988a).

(3) Connected to the focus on task and meaningful activities in which

learners engage in an effort to cope with communication has been the shift from the learner as a passive recipient of language form to an active and creative language user (Kramsch 1984; Puchta and Schratz 1984; Bredella and Legutke 1985a).

(4) There has been a clear shift from the learner as individual to the learner as member of the social group actively involved in co-managing the learning process (Schwerdtfeger 1977; Dietrich 1979b; Martin 1985; Allwright 1984).

(5) With the growing interest in meaningful encounters there has been a noticeable rediscovery of literary texts for L2 classroom use as an important means of authenticating communication. After being neglected in the early phases of notional and functional teaching literary texts are now considered essential for the teaching and learning of language-in-culture (Hunfeld 1982; Bredella 1985; 1989; Kramsch 1985).

(6) The curriculum is no longer exclusively understood as a list of items to be completed, but as something which also requires a process of negotiation in which both the teacher and the learner participate (Breen and Candlin 1980; Nunan 1987).

(7) Consequently, the roles of teachers and learners have not just been expanded in scope, they have received new definitions (Wright 1987a).

(8) In keeping with the emphasis in communicative curriculum models on the learning process as opposed to learning outcomes, assessment 'now tends to be regarded . . . not merely as a means of measuring outcomes, but also as an aid to learning' (Brindley 1989).

(9) Finally, we are witnessing a rediscovery of the *educational* values of language learning – not only for the elites as in the past, but for all citizens. The shift from language instruction to a holistic, critical and explanatory pedagogy is immensely political (Bach and Timm 1989; Candlin 1989; Kohonen 1989).

1.2 CLT: a 'glimpse' at classroom reality

Whereas the quantity of books and papers heralding these changes and propelling the debate forward has now reached proportions which can no longer be grasped by the individual researcher, investigations of the dynamics of the L2 classroom's culture *itself* have remained scarce. We have, as van Lier points out, so far failed to consider and investigate its communicative potential 'and the authentic resources for interaction it has to offer' (van Lier 1988,

p. 30). Our insights are still rather limited as to whether the aforementioned changes mirrored in academic works are matched by respective modifications of classroom practice. The little we know gives rise to some well-founded scepticism.

In a comparative study of forty different English classes from different West German high schools between 1971–73 and 1981–83, G. Solmecke (1984) takes the shift in paradigms as the starting point for his investigation. He argues that if one takes into account what has been published in the last decade one could assume that far-reaching changes must have occurred at classroom level, especially in the forms of learning management and learner–teacher interaction. However, his study leads him to the well-founded assumption that the basic structure of classroom interaction has changed very little. It is no exaggeration to characterize it as a largely ego-impoverished and teacher-centred one-way street, in which display questions still dominate, concerns of accuracy by far outnumber fluency attempts, and where communication is hard to find.

Solmecke does not claim general validity for his findings. However, if we add further studies by Schratz et al. (1983), Dinsmore (1985) and Nunan (1987), and if we also take into account our own – admittedly personal – observations of many language classes, which we visited as language consultants and teacher trainers in Britain, West Germany and the USA, we feel inclined to report a striking discrepancy between what is proposed and written by academics, between what is claimed by gurus descending into conference assemblies of language teachers – and what actually happens in L2 classrooms. Nunan (1987) for example, analysing classes which were taught by experienced teachers claiming to teach according to communicative principles, found that communication rarely happened, form was more important than message conveyance, accuracy issues always dominated fluency concerns. There were no signs of curriculum negotiation. More radical than Solmecke, Nunan summarizes:

> Given the fact that all but one of the teachers in the study reported here were highly skilled and experienced, and were knowledgeable about and committed to the concept of a communicative approach to language teaching, it is reasonable to assume that the results are not unrepresentative of a much wider range of language classrooms.
>
> (Ibid., p. 141)

There are – as we will demonstrate in chapters 5 and 6 – encouraging exceptions presenting powerful alternatives to what we – with all caution – can describe as 'main stream' L2 classrooms. In full awareness of the limitations of our view we see good reasons to characterize the latter as follows:

(1) *Dead bodies and talking heads* Time and again we found a disquietening progression of lifelessness especially in state schools on both sides of the Atlantic. In a first-year FL class you will perceive a lot of animated and expectant faces, and a forest of hands signalling the willingness to embark on the exciting venture of exploring new territories. Learners are still involved with their whole personalities: they act, sing, perform, simulate, play, draw and write. On returning two or three years later the observer will quite often find that the excitement has vanished. Learners have become progressively more passive and bored as they work through texts, structures, grammatical items, drills and, of course, tests. They seem to have gradually turned into mostly dead bodies with talking heads. The more 'academic' or 'adult' the orientation of the course, the more learning seems to take place 'from the neck up' (Rogers 1983, p. 19). This contradicts what we have come to know about language acquisition, about motivation and ego-involvement, about whole language learning.

Question 1: Is it possible and feasible to turn L2 classrooms into whole-person events, where body and soul, intellect and feeling, head, hand and heart converge in action? We will suggest some answers in chapters 4, 5 and 6.

(2) *Deferred gratification: the loss of adventure* The Latin saying *'non scholae, sed vitae discimus'* certainly requires clarification in view of Dewey's comment with which we started this book. No doubt, formal L2 learning needs to be future-oriented. However, the distant future alone cannot guarantee learner commitment and successful language learning because, first of all, we live in the here and now. Therefore, the emphasis of our educational work should be on the actual learning process. It seems to us, that what happens on the day-to-day basis in schools is still overpowered by and predominantly oriented towards future achievements: tests, university placement and career qualifications. They seem to smother curiosity and heuristic procedures, which are of course necessarily bound to uncertain outcomes. This is in contrast of what has been suggested regarding the value of exploring the authentic reality of the L2 classroom's culture, what we know about the adventures of learning (Vester 1978; 1980) and the dialectics of present experiences and future action.

Question 2: Can L2 learning be a satisfying activity in itself, in the here and now of the classroom? What do we need to do to exploit the psycho-social reality of the L2 classroom and its immediate significance for both teacher and learner? What adventures and challenges are possible under the very conditions of L2 learning? We will provide some suggestions.

(3) *Lack of creativity* Apart from a lack of sensuality (learners do not read with their noses, listen with their eyes or speak with their bodies) and pleasurable experience in the here and now, a lot of language classes lack productivity and creativity. Instead of being workshops for the cooperative production of learner texts, classrooms often generate output which is simply boring, uninspired and noncommittal.

Research into youth sub-cultures for instance carried out in the UK (Hebdidge 1979) and the Federal Republic of Germany (Jugendwerk der Deutschen Shell 1982; 1983; Fischer et al. 1985) provide some interesting insights in relation to the creativity issue. The findings have highlighted a significant discrepancy between the often rather dull and colourless products which adolescents are obliged to produce in school and the aesthetic 'practice' of young people outside the confines of organized learning. Through the creative transformation and rearrangement of what is given (or 'borrowed') into patterns which carry new meanings, large numbers of young people have generated distinctive individual styles which display a high degree of expressiveness and artistic inventiveness. These can not only be seen in exotic hairstyles and the adaptation of fashionable accessories such as badges, stickers, ties and all sorts of cheap jewellery but also in the way cars and motor-bicycles are transformed, and rooms are decorated with posters and advertisements, and indeed in the 'subterranean culture' of schools. For certain groups of young people this goes hand-in-hand with a highly sophisticated and emotionally committed writing practice, including diary and letter-writing as well as the writing of poetry.

Question 3: What needs to be done to regain some of this creative potential in the L2 classroom? Can we assume a similar potential for adult learners? Do we have to consider individual and cultural differences? Throughout the book we will return to these issues, both from a conceptual and a practical perspective.

(4) *Lack of opportunities for communication* In spite of trendy jargon in textbooks and teacher's manuals, very little is actually communicated in the L2 classroom. The way it is structured does not seem to stimulate the wish of learners to say something, nor does it tap what

they might have to say. Fenced in by syllabus demands, often represented by the total dominance of a textbook, learners do not find room to speak as themselves, to use language in communicative encounters, to create text, to stimulate responses from fellow learners, or to find solutions to relevant problems. Topicality is still sacrificed for the benefit of grammar and structure. Silent or aside communication, fantasies, imagination, dreams do not happen in the target language.

Question 4: What needs to be done to create situations and scenarios where communication in the target language could be more meaningful? What are the roles of teacher, learners, topic and input in such scenarios? Could even inter- and intra-student discourse be carried out in the target language? We will explore these issues in detail when discussing the notion of communicative tasks in chapter 4 and project scenarios in chapters 5 and 6.

(5) *Lack of autonomy* There seems to be a striking lack of learner autonomy or self-direction. Democratic principles appear alien to L2 classrooms. Learners do not participate in the management of their learning and teaching as actively and as comprehensively as they could. Most of the responsibility for decision-making, content and process determination rests with the teacher alone. This is not only incompatible with recent claims of learner-centred methodologies, but also constitutes a major discrepancy with the overall educational goals of democratic societies.

Whereas for instance adolescents are expected to make responsible choices outside the classroom, they are seldom encouraged to experiment with such behaviour under the conditions of L2 learning. The teacher, or better the textbook, seems to set the tone, define the type and scope of activities, and prescribe what and how is to be learnt. A capacity in learners for critique of content and process is not developed or focused upon.

Question 5: What needs to be done to develop in learners such a capacity for critique? How can they become co-managers of their learning and participate in their own teaching? What are the limitations of learner autonomy and self-direction with different groups in different settings? How do we create the learning space so that learners can take initiatives to pursue their own learning for their own benefit, and to discover their own learning styles? Through an analysis of retrospective syllabus accounts we will try to describe some passages towards learner autonomy in chapters 6 and 7.

(6) *Lack of cultural awareness* In spite of a growing body of publications on intercultural learning, culture very often appears as some kind of additional input to be learnt and not as an integral part as language-in-culture (Candlin 1989). Thus it does not affect learners as persons and has no critical impact on their perception of the world. Cultural awareness, however, as several classroom projects discussed in chapters 5 and 6 show, involves a complex dialectic between one's own experiences and those of people from the L2 culture. It requires constant negotiation of meaning. Thus, intercultural understanding is not achieved when we learn only facts about the foreign culture. It is when we become aware of other equally possible ways of doing and seeing things, and when we begin to ask questions and try to explain, that intercultural understanding is achieved. Such a critical and explanatory pedagogy is a necessary way of overcoming ethnocentrism and cultural chauvinism (Bredella 1988; Candlin 1989).

Question 6: Can cultural awareness be taught? What forms of teaching and learning would be most suitable for such an endeavour? The experiential and process-oriented mode, especially in its forms of encounter projects, will be presented as one way of teaching and learning language-in-culture (see chapters 5 and 6).

1.3 CLT: missing links

How do we explain this disparity between academics' claims, and classroom reality? There are, of course, no easy answers. And we – by no means – contend that the following chapters will provide solutions. What we hope we can do is at least point to a number of missing links which we want to conceptualize and elaborate upon in the light of documented classroom experiments.

One missing link results from the breakdown in communications between researchers and teachers. The fundamentally hierarchical and prescriptive discourse between those who advance theories and teaching methods and those who are asked to 'apply' concepts to practice (Clarke and Silberstein 1988), has led to understandable scepticism and mistrust on the part of the teachers. With good reason the latter have remained resistant towards innovations in general and 'innovative methods' in particular (such as Total Physical Response, Natural Approach, Humanistic Approaches, Community Language Learning and CLT in its reduced version as 'method'). These 'innovations' were often promulgated by means of dogmatic and prescriptive concepts which limit the educational practice of teachers (Pennycook 1989). We hope to contribute to a more fruitful and critical discourse, i.e. a reciprocal relationship of practice and theory, and thus make a new attempt at classroom innovation. Many teachers have contributed to this book. Our notions of process and experience, within the overall framework of a participatory model of L2 teaching and learning has been informed by numerous classroom projects of others and our own. These classroom projects – retrospective syllabus accounts – constitute our data base. A survey of our data is presented in chapter 5.

To begin with, however, we will focus in chapter 2 on a missing link in the theory of CLT: the interaction potential of the L2 classroom – a concept which needs clarification. By synthesizing existing models of the communicative classroom and a model of theme-centred interaction we will try to conceptualize the complexity of both the structure and the process of interaction in L2 classrooms. This will allow us to define the reservoir of communicative action – as pedagogic, experiential and experimental endeavour.

In chapter 3 we will utilize the construct of theme-centred interaction as a critical instrument to discuss some of the implications of 'alternative methods' for such a pedagogy. Our critique of Humanistic Approaches and Confluent Education will lead us to propose a set of criteria. These could guide teachers' decisions when selecting and evaluating methodological options for the exploitation of the communicative potential of the L2 classroom's culture.

The critical criteria and the concept of the interaction potential also provide the framework for discussing function, scope and limitations of communicative tasks in chapter 4. Tasks will not be presented as neutral or motivational gambits, nor for the pursuit of individual introspection, but as pivotal forms of action in an educational process. Although very practical, chapter 4 does not contain recipes and ready-made techniques, but offers a typology of communicative tasks in contexts of different L2 classes. The primary responsibility for orchestrating these tasks lies with the teacher.

In chapter 5 we will then shift the focus to the learners' contributions to the learning process where they are given a chance of determining their own learning. We will approach our task historically by drawing upon traditions of the educational reform movements of the 1920s mainly on the Project Method of Dewey and Kilpatrick and on documented FL classroom experiments since the early 1970s which deserve to be called projects.

Chapter 6 draws attention to a number of areas relating to conceptual and practical matters in the process and project-oriented classroom. Informed by the experience of the data, this chapter will identify a number of questions which require further enquiry and research for learner education and pre/in-service teacher development.

Consequently, we will conclude our investigation of process and experience in language learning by addressing the crucial issues of learner and teacher education (chapters 7 and 8). In chapter 7 we propose a broadening of the traditional concept of communicative competence by adding the domain of process competence. This will lead us to confront popular concepts of learner training. We will point to the somewhat disquietening lack of an educational framework within which to train the learner instead of the resurrection of any decontextualized and arbitrary training (from which the L2 classroom of the past has suffered under the dominance of structures and grammar) we will propose a holistic L2 pedagogy.

In short, this book seeks to make concrete, both from a theoretical and a practical point of view, what has become known as a 'strong' version of CLT. Whereas the weak version attempts to integrate a communicative component into a traditional language programme, the strong version 'advances the claim that language is acquired through communication, so that it is not merely the question of activating an existing but inert knowledge of the language, but of stimulating the development of the language system itself. If the former could be described as "learning to use" English, the latter entails "using English to learn it".' (Howatt 1984, p. 279)

2 Theme-centred interaction in the L2 classroom

2.1 The 'culture' of the L2 classroom

Our commitment to a strong version of CLT does not in any way imply an interest in advancing a new 'method'. Rather, our concern is to develop and discuss an educational framework which can guide principled decisions of teachers and researchers. Our starting point is the social reality of the L2 classroom as a reservoir for teaching and learning – its interactive and, respectively, communicative potential. Two main sources have helped and enriched our efforts. The notion of theme-centred interaction, which we will elaborate upon in this chapter, draws, first of all, on the work of the educational psychologist Ruth C. Cohn (1975; 1984). From her we have not only derived the term 'theme-centred interaction' but also adapted the basic components of the model, which as we will show, captures both the structure and the dynamic process of interaction in educational groups.[1]

In applying Cohn's model to language learning we are indebted to Breen (1983; 1985a) and Breen and Candlin (1980) whose notion of a communicative classroom comes very close to a model of theme-centred interaction. In particular, Breen's insistence – in a similar way to Cohn's – on the fundamental equality of process and content in learning situations has proven to be a stimulating challenge in our search for an alternative to a text- and teacher-dominated classroom.

In an exploration of the specific contributions of the social reality of the classroom to the process of language development, Breen (1985a) offers a metaphor of classroom as culture. It is an 'arena of subjective and intersubjective realities which are worked out, changed, and maintained. And these realities are not trivial background to the tasks of teaching and learning. They locate and define the new language itself ... and they continually specify and mould the activities of teaching and learning' (ibid., p. 142).

Breen goes on to describe eight essential features which characterize this culture. Since we will return to all of them throughout the book from various perspectives, we will mention them here briefly. The classroom's culture is:

(1) *interactive*;

(2) *differentiated* (i.e. although the classroom appears as one social unit it is always a composition of many social realities with often conflicting views of the world, of language and of learning);

(3) *collective* (i.e. it constitutes itself in the constant interplay between individual and collective processes);

(4) *highly normative* (i.e. any formal and institutionalized L2 learning situation cannot escape the fact that it is evaluative in nature, engaging teacher and taught in continually judging each other in various respects and on various levels);

(5) *asymmetrical* (i.e. asymmetrical relationships with respective roles and role expectations do not only exist between teacher and taught, but also between groups and sub-groupings; in institutionalized settings there is a clear connection between asymmetry and power relations, which have a decisive impact on the learning process);

(6) *inherently conservative* (i.e. as with any group, language classes have a tendency to establish their own rules, develop their own rituals and styles, which may become quite resistant to innovation and change);

(7) *immediately significant* (i.e. the learning experience itself takes place in the here and now);

(8) *jointly constructed*:

> What someone learns in a language class will be a dynamic synthesis of individual and collective experience. Individual definitions of the new language, of what is to be attended to as worth learning, of how to learn, and personal definitions of progress will all interact with the particular classroom culture's definitions of each of these things . . . . The language I learn in a classroom is a communal product derived through a jointly constructed process.
>
> (Ibid., p. 148–9)

Given these complex conditions and inter-relating variables the question we want to address in the following pages is how to conceptualize the interactive potential of this 'culture'. We will do this with the intention of demarcating more clearly the scope and space for communicative action which teacher and learner have at their disposal.

2.2 The interaction potential of the L2 classroom

2.2.1 Content and process materials in classroom interaction

Natural and spontaneous, that is, unintended or unplanned interactions are part and parcel of a communicative learning process
which is open to learner contributions of all kinds. By allowing
learners to lose themselves in themes, texts and group experiences,
open classroom procedures encourage the emergence and pursuit of
goals independent from those set by the teacher. Several authors
have pointed to the central significance of such spontaneous
interaction as part of the communicative process (e.g. Brumfit 1984;
Stevick 1980; 1982; Rivers 1983; Puchta and Schratz 1984; Nunan
1988). For our discussion for the moment, these spontaneous
interactions, however, are of secondary importance. This is because
the central methodological challenge, for both teacher and student,
consists of creating the learning space (Stevick 1980) within which
interaction is to unfold. To mobilize the interactive potential of the
classroom learning situation, they do not only need to be aware of its
dimensions, they need to be able to set up points of encounters for
the components and participants in the interaction (the person, the
group, the theme, and the external factors and constraints). Only
through such encounters is a process of balancing out, of negotiating
together, and of learning set in motion. Since such points of
encounter have to be specified according to different educational
disciplines and subject areas, there will be different answers
according to different subjects within a curriculum even if they all
begin with the theme-centred interaction starting point.

Within the modern language classroom such points of encounter
depend on events set up by both teacher and learners. They result
from conscious interventions from the teacher and learner but also
from semi-conscious or implied strategies and steering mechanisms.
Allwright (1984) has pointed out that even in teacher-centred
language teaching, learners participate indirectly in interaction
scenarios by asserting influence on five different areas of interaction
management. They are Turn, Topic, Task, Tone and Code
(Allwright 1984, p. 161). Management activities or scenarios such as
these set up a relationship between two components of materials,
process materials on the one hand and content materials on the other
(Breen 1983).

What we mean here by *content materials* are L2 texts which

thematize and represent particular aspects of the target culture and its language. They can be made available both by the teacher and by learners. We also include here texts which focus on the language from a semantic (notions, concepts, logical relationships), linguistic (grammar, phonology, lexis, kinesis) and pragmatic (speech acts, conversational principles) point of view. Content materials appear in the form of various types of texts in various media forms. Because of the nature of the classroom as a community of readers and learners, we prefer to speak of texts rather than data materials, as Breen suggests (Breen 1983), a term we find reductionist and misleading. As we know from research into reading and from hermeneutics, the comprehension of texts requires much more of learners and teachers than the ability to manipulate, store or recall data. The comprehension of texts, and in particular the interpretation of literary texts[2] is a complex process of negotiating and creating meaning, which, under classroom conditions, depends on a collective effort to relate the (aesthetically) encoded reactions of the writer/author/poet to the world around him/her, to the world view, experience and knowledge of the reader. Kramsch has characterized the challenge of this process as two-fold: 'On the one hand, a dialogue must be constructed between the text and its readers . . . . On the other hand, a reception must be created among the readers' (Kramsch 1985, p. 358). Thus the multi-intertextuality (Kramsch, ibid.) of a classroom situation represents important interaction potential in itself, which can be tapped and mobilized so that communication can take place. We have deliberately omitted here the question of how one defines areas of content of knowledge for the modern language classroom and how one grades and sequences them in units within the negotiated curriculum, as this is a major component of future work for the field. Furthermore, we do not deal here with the question of text selection or the issues of prioritizing certain text-types according to phases and stages of the teaching-learning process.

Apart from the text types mentioned above, content materials also include texts which have as their theme the learning process itself and which help reflection, evaluation and the optimizing of learning and teaching processes (individual learning diaries, diary studies, audio and visual documentations of particular phases in the learning process, observers' minutes/remarks). Our notion of content materials also includes L2 texts which learners produce themselves and which therefore make available their own knowledge, the knowledge of the group, the experiences of the world in which they live and their reactions to representations of the world of the target culture. They give evidence of their collective attempts to make sense of their experience. Learner texts come likewise in many different types and make use of all forms of media. They are the representations of student-contributed content.

A particular subsection of content materials are those *support* materials which make available information *about* the target language and its use in various communicative contexts (Breen calls them information materials). They include various grammars – descriptive and pedagogic – vocabulary books, dictionaries, topic-based word lists and word-fields written by students during their course work, but also learner-produced descriptions of successful ways of decoding texts, etc.

Whereas content materials serve the primary purpose of providing input for communication and meta-communication in the target language, *process materials* are the moving force of the teaching-learning process. They are designed with the explicit intention of stimulating interactions in the classroom group, to set in motion investigative and research activities and to open up opportunities for learning and practice. They are, as we will discuss in greater detail later, *language-learning tasks* which aim at training particular language skills (see 3.1); *pre-communicative tasks* such as those made available by the exercise typology for the communicative classroom (BAG 1978; Candlin 1981; Neuner 1981); *communicative tasks proper* (see chapter 4); and finally *instrumental and management tasks*, which enhance learners' managerial and procedural capacities. Tasks and exercises can, according to character, intention or negotiated aims be language-related, content- or process-related. They can give prominence to the knowledge and experience of the individual or concentrate on the group and the knowledge of the group. They may smooth the path towards a differentiation and an unfolding of the theme. Just as with content materials, process materials may be introduced by anybody involved in the learning process (by the teacher whose job it is to be responsible for guiding the process, by the learner who gradually develops a didactic competence and takes over classroom leadership and management and thus functions as a participating manager, and by classes or groups who collectively prepare and lead learning processes). Allwright describes this as follows: 'We are no longer talking of teachers teaching and learners learning, but of everyone contributing to the management of everyone's learning (including their own, and including the teacher's, of course)' (Allwright 1984, p. 166).

The degree to which participants share the guiding of a learning process depends on how far their ability to participate has developed, their degree of independence, their willingness to take risks, and of course also on the ability and the willingness of the teacher to allow a part of her own responsibility to pass to the learners. Taking responsibility for one's own learning is not simply something which can be achieved by advanced learners of a language (Carter and Thomas 1986), it can in fact be undertaken in the very early phases of language acquisition, as we will show in chapter 5 by means of the Airport project (see fig. 2.1).

2.2.2 The learner and the teacher in the interactive process

We look now at the personal and the group factor, the 'I' and 'we' dimension of interaction within the specific framework of FL classes. To do this we distinguish, as Breen (1983) suggests, between implicit and explicit contributions to the teaching/learning process. With regard to the learner, implicit contributions denote those moments which are at play in any organized language-learning situation and which, at the same time, make for the variety and uniqueness of any given group of learners. We refer here, to what the learners bring to the classroom, their prior knowledge in its broader sense, their experiences of the world in which they live, their experiences of and with the world of the target language and its culture, their social, cultural and ethnic background and value systems; but also their preferences with regard to other people, to themes and ways of working; their knowledge of learning strategies and their expectations with regard to how learning should best be organized; their attitudes towards the subject of the school, to the teacher; their willingness to communicate, their readiness to take risks, their openness and ability to empathize; and not least their inhibitions and idiosyncrasies which may derive from sources not involved with the learning process (feelings of alienation, anxiety and fear of rejection, feelings of distance) – all of which may oppose the unfolding of the learners' potential. Although these implicit contributions are always 'at play' in the learning process, where they determine the concrete – explicit – actions of the learner, the latter may only partially reveal the former. Since explicit contributions, by setting up interactions and resulting from such interactions, bring to the surface what the learner implicitly means and feels, they have three functions in the communicative classroom:

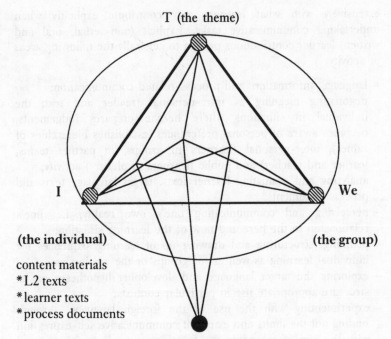

T (the theme)

I

We

(the individual)

(the group)

content materials
* L2 texts
* learner texts
* process documents

Points of encounters

support materials
* dictionaries
* grammars
* word-lists
* word-fields
* resource books of tasks

process materials
* language-learning tasks
* pre-communicative tasks
* communicative tasks
* instrumental tasks
* management tasks
* project materials

Figure 2.1 Theme-centred interaction (a)

First, to activate and focus those implicit contributions which we have already identified. Second, to reveal and socially share individual contributions for the potential benefit of all learners in the group and to inform the teacher of the *actual* needs, expectations and preferred ways of working of the learners. And thirdly, such explicit contributions serve as important means to facilitate classroom learning.

(Breen 1983, p. 9)

For the moment we will only briefly specify the scope of the explicit contributions learners can make within an interaction process. As far as the implicit moments in this process are concerned, the discussion will be resumed in chapter 3, whereas chapter 4 will deal extensively with what learners may contribute explicitly when undertaking communicative tasks. Explicit (non-verbal, oral and written) learner contributions pertain to generally the following areas of activity:

– language, information, and process-related communication;
– negotiating meaning as intra-personal (reader and text; the individual in situations where he/she prepares judgements, becomes aware of personal preferences, establishes hierarchies of values), inter-personal (learners in groups, in partner teams, learner and teacher) and public (learners in plenary) activity;
– analysing and evaluating learner texts, target language texts and process documents;
– perceiving and communicating one's own reality, i.e. one's relationship to the here and now of the learning situation;
– planning, structuring and drawing up of learning sequences for individual learning as well as for groups or the whole class;
– exploring the target language and developing hypotheses on its structure appropriate use in particular contexts;
– experimenting with the use of the foreign language, through finding out the limits and extent of communicative self-expression with the aim of extending the frontiers of one's knowledge and expertise;
– experimenting with and researching possibilities for optimizing learning and creative play.

In contrast to Breen, who makes this distinction of implicit and explicit contributions solely with regard to the learner, it is also sensible to make the same distinction for the teacher. For through her own explicit contributions, whether it be in the role of presenter and coordinator of the learning process, or as informant making materials available, or whether as someone who opens new doors and windows for learners to experience themselves by means of experimenting in the target language, or whether as a guide through the difficult terrain of intercultural encounters; whether it be in the role of researcher whose role it is to investigate the learning process to see if it can be improved or whether it can realize a collectively negotiated curriculum as a way of meeting social needs and individual wishes – they will always give shape and expression to whatever her implicit contributions are: preferences, attitude towards the subject, professional and methodological ability, degree of self-knowledge, ability to empathize, willingness to be flexible and last, but not least, her present relationship to the learning situation at hand.

This basic identity of learner and teacher as individuals in the interactive process, however, does not remove the structural asymmetry which governs any learning group. In terms of roles, for instance, of the participants in relation to completing learning tasks or structuring learning space, responsibility and/or capabilities may be distributed unevenly among the group members. Yet, learners are never simply learners, nor does the teacher simply lead and manage learning. As a participant she shares with the learners their role, e.g. when the learners may very well assume leadership of many stages of learning and even teaching. In any case, it is the subtle and complex interplay of implicit and explicit contributions of all individuals involved which make up the interactive potential to be exploited for learning/teaching a second language (see fig. 2.2).

Learning in schools takes place within the framework of a group, which in itself is composed of a web of inter-related sub-groupings. which in itself is composed of a web of interrelated sub-groupings. Therefore, the notion of negotiation as an inter-personal and public element is always connected with group processes. This rather obvious insight supported by the research findings of sociology, of group dynamics, and the psychology of groups (Brocher 1967; Schwäbisch and Siems 1974), is widely ignored when it comes to exploiting the interaction potential of the classroom situation, or to catering for the specific limitations it imposes (Seletzky 1989). Since the group, whether as a collection of sub-groups or as a complete entity, is subject to its own laws and makes available specific opportunities for learning and action, we must also recognize that this has a particular significance for language teaching. We need to note that group fantasies, group anxieties and taboos, group rejection, but also group power and commitment are at play. Therefore, group aims and agendas, cooperation and rivalry may appear in ever changing and various complex constellations (in the group as a whole, in sub-groups in relation to each other and to the whole group, in mini-groups which include the teacher, etc.). All these group constellations contain inherent potential and offer space for learning and action which could have concrete significance within the classroom. They could, for example, function as a source of self-perception, as a stimulus for the exploration of knowledge and experience, as an opportunity to talk about oneself, as a data bank for the production of texts or as a source of energy in situations of insecurity when one is researching or experimenting. The potential power of a group can also hinder learning, slow it down or in due course make it impossible (see fig. 2.3).

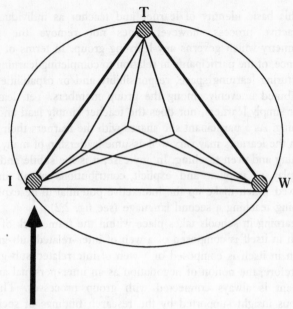

The 'I' dimension: learner and teacher
* prior knowledge
* world experience
* expectations
* social and ethnic background
* values and preferences
* prior learning experiences
* skills and abilities
* empathy
* courage
* . . .

Figure 2.2 Theme-centred interaction (b)

2.2.3 The thematic dimension: theme and topic

We have already referred to the thematic component in connection
with content materials. During the 1970s, theme-oriented English
teaching became a critical programme of curriculum renewal among
communicative circles in Europe (e.g. see BAG 1978; Candlin 1981).
The classroom was no longer understood simply as the institutional
location for the transmission of a foreign language system. The
specification of meaningful content and of topics relevant for the

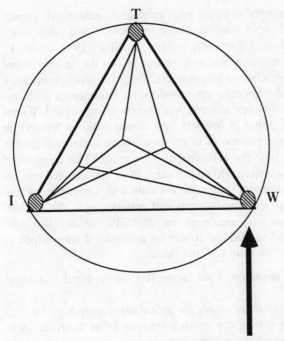

The 'we' dimension: the group
* small group/small group
* small group/whole class
* small group/small group/small group
* . . .

group fantasies
group anxieties
group energy
group goals/agendas
group protection
group projection
group rejection
. . .

Figure 2.3 Theme-centred interaction (c)

learners was considered to be the basic curricular decision. All further decisions, for example what language to choose, and what tasks needed to be derived from that priority (Edelhoff 1981, p. 50–1). Relevant as this argument was as a critique of – at the time dominant – structural approaches to language teaching, the assumption that a well-selected and interesting topic would solve motivational problems and increase a willingness to learn, was possibly short-sighted. Within the interactional group of learners, any theme 'task' or 'project' at hand is linked to a process of negotiation before it can become the driving force for both the individual and the group. The theme itself represents a dynamic element taking shape in an interactional process which mediates learners' interests, not only with societal/curricular demands, but also with the interests and preferences of the teacher. The theme, therefore, needs to be constantly made clear and concrete. We need to distinguish here six interrelated areas which in principle provide the source of the theme:

(1) *The world of knowledge of the learner* (his own cultural and social experience).
(2) *The world of the target culture* (target culture experience).
(3) *The processing of these two worlds* when one seeks to create sense and meaning within the classroom.
(4) *The language of the target culture.* It can be the thematic focus not only from the point of rules of usage (semantics, phonology, syntax, and grammar), but also with regard to rules and conventions of use which determine language as social behaviour and communication.
(5) *The procedure of learning itself* taking into account process and product. The process becomes the theme when it is a question of making it conscious and reflecting upon it with regards to the planning direction and possible alternatives during its course. One would undertake this in order to make improvements and at the same time to develop the didactic confidence of learners.
(6) *The results of the process.* These are the thematic focus when one is concerned with recorded oral work and language behaviour in particular situations, learner texts, presentation of project displays for the purposes of evaluation (see fig. 2.4).

Learning in schools does not take place in isolated educational contexts free from exterior constraints. In the case of modern languages, Ruth C. Cohn's global category would have to take account of several factors which have an effect on how one exploits the interactive potential. The teaching/learning process has to deal

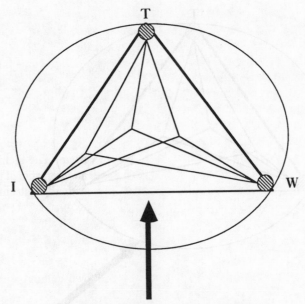

The thematic dimensions: theme and topic
* world of the learners
* world of the target culture
* reactions and responses to the world of the learner
* reactions and responses to the world of the target cultur
* the target language
* the learning/teaching process

Figure 2.4 Theme-centred interaction (d)

with tensions created between institutional/societal demands and individual and group needs and interest. Social requirements concerning academic qualifications and professional skills may appear in form of ministry guidelines, school curricula and textbook material. What is important, though, is not only how the social requirement of individuals' competence is defined under political and economic pressures and ideological positions held by school and communities, but also how the representatives of various layers within institutions and bureaucracies are in a position to, or are prepared to, realize these requirements at classroom level. There are, of course, both objective factors here such as the equipment in the school, material and textbooks available, media resources, etc., and also subjective conditions such as the teacher's qualifications, attitude towards the

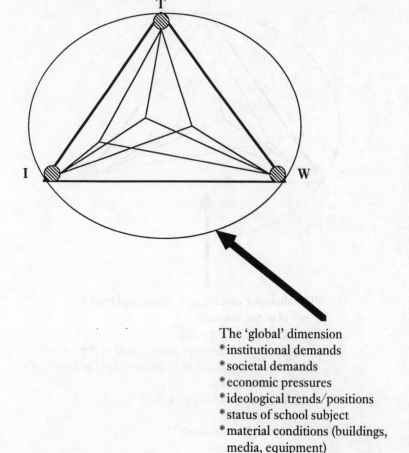

The 'global' dimension
* institutional demands
* societal demands
* economic pressures
* ideological trends/positions
* status of school subject
* material conditions (buildings,
  media, equipment)
* . . .

Figure 2.5 Theme-centred interaction (e)

subject, to the learners, etc. – some of which we have mentioned above. Status and value, attached to language learning by communities and the society as a whole, would be relevant from a global point of view, as well as the position of the subject to the other subjects in the school. Is foreign language learning considered to be of such educational value that it is given mandatory status or is it simply an elective subject with little or no consequence for learners' academic and professional careers (see fig. 2.5)?

2.2.4 Domains of communication

If one overlaid the four versions of the model we have presented in the previous sections, one would arrive at a graphical representation of the interaction potential which, we believe, resides in the language classroom. Such a model would, of course, require further refinement in all four sub-areas. However, in its present form it achieves at least three things:

(1) Firstly, it allows us to define more accurately the scope of class-room discourse under language-learning conditions. Following Piepho (1979) and Kohonen (1989), we would characterize it as communicative actions of learners who are and become themselves, i.e. who develop a self-concept while gradually appropriating the target language, thus expressing, implying and creating meaning.
(2) Secondly, the model forces us to face up to the consequences that ensue for the planning of courses, the preparation of inventories of topics, notions and functions, and the training of non-linguistic skills.
(3) And thirdly, we need to decide which teaching methods will be best suited to mobilize the classroom's potential, so that learning through discourse can unfold.

Because of its psycho-social nature, we regard the classroom – in harmony with Breen (1985) and Martin (1986) – as a genuine source of communicative activity. That means that learners in the role of creative language-users and researchers (as individuals and in small groups) pursue tasks through which they learn about themselves while attempting to understand what lies beyond them, what is strange, new, different and challenging. As individuals and members of groups, they engage in communicative self-expression while experimenting with the target language. Such experimentation with language embraces not only its creative expressive use, but also the conscious understanding of its structures and rules. This view of the classroom further entails that learners investigate the learning process itself as it unfolds its potential – taking into account the challenges of the theme and the project, as well as the needs of the individual. While engaging in such multifaceted activities they interact with a wide range of textual representations of the target culture and its language. They would use the same text media (print, visual, audio-visual) to publish their own text experiments. The interaction with process materials and the responses to teacher/fellow learner interventions will propel the process.

We have tried to demarcate the scope and space of action learners have at their disposal when learning a foreign language. While accepting the fundamental asymmetry of any learning situation, the model does not go on to derive from it a fixed acceptance or monopoly of roles, as is the case in the traditional transmission model of learning. Rather, it provides for role-related responsibility and accountability. The model further assumes that learners not only want to learn, but that they are capable of independent, self-directed action, even in the language classroom. Consequently, the model allows for all participants to contribute content and provide process materials, to coordinate research processes, to lead and supervise tasks, to learn and to lead learning. With the interactive potential of the language classroom we have defined the reservoir of communicative action – as pedagogic, experiential and experimental endeavour. In summary, we can abstract from this the following areas of possible language use in class:

(1) encoding of and communicating about self-perception and processes of learning about oneself;

(2) encoding and communicating perceptions of how groups and group members interdepend in their attempts to understand and create meaning;

(3) encoding of and communicating about experiences with and reflections upon the process of learning;

(4) verbalizing and communicating one's perceptions of disturbances and breakdowns in group harmony and efficiency, and how they are processed and dealt with;

(5) responding to representations of the world of the target language and participating in collective processes of creating meaning (see above: the notion of multi-intertextuality);

(6) defining and communicating goals to be followed (finding themes, structuring themes, project plans, ideas for research, etc.);

(7) choosing and where necessary modifying/redefining original process materials, and participating in classroom management;

(8) communicating criteria for evaluation with the intention of assessing learner utterances, learner texts, project presentations, oral and written performance;

(9) encoding of and communicating about process documents to make clear learning procedures and to reflect on the experiences of learners;

(10) negotiating responsibility for particular sequences within the learning process, for planning, leading and evaluating;

(11) choosing, developing and testing ways of working in order to optimize individual learning and to set free individual creativity and willingness to communicate;

(12) developing, testing, and transposing leadership tasks undertaken by learners (the learner as a participant who leads).

In the 1970s, Black and Butzkamm (1977a; 1977b) conducted an extensive study of classroom interaction in early high school language learning in West Germany. Using Sinclair and Coulthard's framework of *classroom discourse* (Sinclair and Coulthard 1975) as a starting point, they assumed that the classroom situation itself must provide the nourishing ground for the development of communicative competence through experimentation with and realization of real communication. Their findings led them to distinguish between language-related and information-related interaction. By language-related interaction they understand basically a one-dimensional, teacher-guided exchange, principally concerned with formal aspects of the language and the manipulation of particular language elements. Within the evaluative framework of schooling, language-related interaction is largely characterized by the intention to test what has been learnt, and on the part of the learner, by the consciousness and expectation of being tested (Black and Butzkamm 1977b, p. 117). Information-related interaction on the other hand comprises verbal and non-verbal responses and contributions which are primarily directed towards expressing and realizing particular communicative intentions. Both of these basic forms of interaction occur in various forms and mixtures.

Black and Butzkamm propose that, in the interest of developing communicative competence, the area of information-related interaction should be extended. In order for this to be successful, learners should be systematically taught new means of expression, which the traditional coursebook does not provide. After controlled practice of these new means, it is hoped that in the long term learners would be able to use them spontaneously.

No doubt, this clear and simple distinction has extended the scope of meaningful language activities decisively because it uses existing elements of the interaction potential in the class as possible content for communication (ibid., p. 124). Following Black and Butzkamm's work, textbook authors began to offer lists of functions entitled 'classroom discourse' or 'phrases for the classroom'. However, since Black and Butzkamm maintained centrally controlled and teacher-directed instruction with materials that allow for virtually no learner-contributed content, their suggestions did not call for a radical change in the teaching/learning situation. All they were doing was making a case for including communicative elements into an essentially non-communicative classroom. In this, they are in company with many other reformers of language learning (cf. Taylor 1983).

In order to exploit the great interaction potential of the foreign language classroom with the intention of bringing about, nourishing and developing communication and learning, much more is required than the incorporation of a communicative element into the teaching/ learning process (Taylor 1983). We need to consider implications on at least three levels:

(1) At the level of *content*. Content needs to be specified and systematized not only according to factual categories of target culture experiences. What is required at the same time is a specification of content in terms of experiential categories which define the continually interchanging reality of teacher–learner, learner–learner, group–group in theme-centred interaction. Such undertaking would have to deal with issues of the design and implementation of an experience-oriented syllabus model, which neither ignores the need for planned and sequenced content, nor perpetuates the common fallacy of imposing a step-by-step programme on teachers and learners (Candlin 1984).

(2) At the level of *target language vocabulary and discourse inventories*. These would need to be systematically drawn up and described not only in grammatical, and generally functional and notional categories, but also according to specific discourse conditions and opportunities for communication in the target language particularly under the conditions of classroom language learning.

(3) At the level of *methodology*. Methods would need to be specified and critically evaluated in practice with regard to their range and limits in order to mobilize the interaction potential of the learning situation.

2.3 The 'dynamic balance' in theme-centred interaction

The following chapters of the book will be primarily devoted to dealing with issues of methodology, i.e. with ways of unlocking the interaction potential and structuring the communicative process. We will approach our task from a broad educational perspective. Our efforts will be guided by Cohn's notion of a dynamic balance of

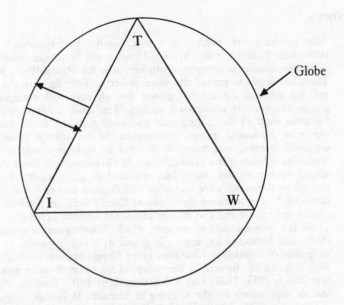

Figure 2.6 Theme-centred interaction (f) (Cohn, R. 1984)

theme-centred interaction which she represented by an equilateral triangle in a multi-layered and transparent circle.

Since in the process of learning this idealized balance is constantly shifting towards a greater emphasis on one pole over other poles, the teacher is, according to Cohn, faced with the challenge of becoming aware of imbalances, and re-establishing the equilibrium. In her efforts to create a learning space within which theme-centred interaction can unfold and thrive the teacher can employ communicative tasks and task scenarios. For this reason chapters 3 and 4 will focus more on the teacher, who, while participating in the process, functions in the role of manager and leader with the right and responsibility to structure, suggest and intervene. In chapter 5 we will then shift the focus to learners' contributions to the learning process. Taken as a unit, the following three chapters will argue that the teacher's right and responsibility to intervene, structure and balance the process, and the learner's autonomy are not only compatible but mutually supportive.

Notes

1. After receiving her training as a psychoanalyst in Switzerland, the Berlin-born Cohn emigrated to the USA where she became instrumental in the development of group psychotherapy after the Second World War. There she began to expand the scope of her activities and research by applying some of the insights gained through work with therapeutic groups in primarily educational settings. Her main concern was to transpose some of the commitment and excitement she found among clients in therapeutic groups to education. In her attempt to imbue organized learning with new life she was an early representative of humanistic education (see below, chapter 3). On returning to Switzerland several of her articles which had appeared in psychoanalytical and psychological journals were translated into German and edited in book form (1975). For a critical discussion of Cohn's work, its potential for educational reform and also its limitations, see Legutke (1988a).
2. There is a growing body of research, which, following reader-response theory and hermeneutics, argues in favour of a new approach to the integration of language and literature in the foreign language curriculum. Such research has focused on the nature of the comprehension process (e.g. Bleich 1975; 1978; Fish 1980; Rosenblatt 1978; Tomkins 1980) and its implications for the teaching of literature in foreign language classrooms (e.g. Bredella 1985; 1989; Brumfit and Carter 1986; Hunfeld 1982; Kramsch 1985; Swaffer 1988).

3 From 'Humanism' into the classroom: critical criteria

3.1 Classroom activities: towards a definition

In the last chapter we sought to demarcate the room for action which the protagonists in a communicative classroom, the teacher, the learner and the group, have at their disposal when they engage in theme-centred interaction to learn a foreign language. This and the following chapter are concerned with aspects of methodology – more specifically with tasks which claim to initiate and foster meaningful communication through various forms of interaction. A great number of these tasks have appeared in the literature as part and parcel of teaching/learning procedures which are fashionably known as 'Alternative Methods' to language teaching (Schwerdtfeger 1983; Dietrich 1983; Thomas, U. 1987). The last decade has seen an ever growing number of publications offering such tasks to teachers. Equally numerous are the labels which have been given to these tasks. They have been called variously: *language games*, *drama events*, *simulations*, *awareness and fluency activities*, *value clarification tasks*, *encounter games*, *structured experiences*, *confluent growth strategies* and often they are referred to generally as *humanistic techniques and methods*. The claim made is 'that they work' (Oller 1983; Olliphant 1986). What do *we* mean, when we speak of tasks? Following Candlin (1981; 1987), Piepho (1981), Dickinson (1987) Sheils (1988) and Legutke (1988a) we distinguish four main types of classroom tasks:

(1) First of all, there are LANGUAGE LEARNING TASKS, which through *controlled and guided practice* aim at developing *discrete language skills* in areas of grammar, phonology, lexis and semantics. Although language skills are prerequisites of any form of linguistic communication, this does not imply that language learning tasks have to precede all other types in the classroom. As we will argue in the following chapters, they can appear at any point in the learning process.

(2) The second group of classroom activities can be best summarized as PRE-COMMUNICATIVE TASKS, the purpose of which is to enable learners to react to and deal with different kinds of input data, mainly in form of texts. By engaging learners in *controlled*

and *guided practice*, chains or sequences of such tasks aim to enable them gradually to express their own views and meanings. This is achieved by preparing, structuring, developing and simulating communication with the intention of replicating important aspects of real-life language use in the classroom (BAG 1978; Candlin 1981; Neuner et al. 1981).

(3) The third group comprises the COMMUNICATIVE TASKS proper. They initiate and frame *exploratory practice* where discourse emerges from genuine communicative needs and interaction. They call upon the *interplay* of linguistic, strategic, subject matter, personal and interpersonal skills. We will focus primarily on these tasks in this and the following chapter.

(4) Finally classroom activities can be grouped as INSTRUMENTAL AND MANAGEMENT TASKS. These are intended to enhance, through *controlled and guided practice*, learners' managerial and procedural capacities, which make up an essential part of what we will address as process competence later in this book (see chapter 7). Management capacities for language learning require media skills, organizational skills, self-access skills, and, last but not least, didactic skills.

As will become clear in the following chapters, there is a great deal of overlap and interdependence between the various types of activities when seen in process terms. A communicative task may presuppose a specific skill-training activity, i.e. a management task, or might lead to the investigation of specific language items, which, in turn, may require special training for individuals or groups of learners. However, we will begin by focusing on communicative tasks alone. This chapter will argue that a detailed examination of communicative tasks, their underlying educational and psychological assumptions will help to provide a basis on which one can construct a principled methodology for a task-based and interactional approach to modern language teaching. As Scovel points out:

> . . . there is no one method, no single package of techniques and procedures, which can be used effectively in any situation. Just as obvious, however, is the impracticality of mixing a little bit of each method together into one pot, as if you were preparing a soup from all the leftovers available in the kitchen! The compromise between the two extremes is the careful construction of an eclectic method which suits the need of the students, the teachers, and the society at large.
>
> (Scovel 1983, p. 11)

We take this to mean that there is no value in looking at examples of individual learner-activating processes merely to add them to the already extensive list available to the teacher. Our examination of examples of tasks and processes on the other hand will explicate criteria from which it will be possible for teachers to evaluate tasks (including those which derive from non-language-teaching backgrounds), to make choices for their own situations, adapt them according to the specific demands of their learners and to be able to invent their own. We will use the model of the interaction potential from the previous chapter as a framework in which to develop these criteria. There is no guarantee, however, that the existence of selection criteria will ensure that task-based language learning will take place, or that teachers will use this instrument to create space for communication in theme-centred interaction. We would also underline that, whatever is available to teachers in terms of tasks, techniques, or principles, there is no substitute for personal warmth, tolerance and a positive attitude to people: to oneself and to others.

3.2 Humanistic language teaching

In the wake of the 1981 TESOL convention in Detroit, the British Council (1982) published a collection of papers to begin an 'Anglo-American dialogue' on the wider implications of the 'humanistic approaches' which had surfaced and had been written about extensively in the USA since the mid-1970s (Galyean 1975; 1976; 1978; 1979; Moskowitz 1978; Stevick 1980; Curran 1976; LaForge 1975). For some scholars the US movement promised a new and 'Golden Age' or 'Renaissance' in language-related disciplines (Yosihikawa 1982, p. 391).

At the same time, the Goethe-Institut in Paris decided to make 'Alternative Methodological Approaches in FLT' the theme of an international conference, which was attended by experts from Britain, France, West Germany and Portugal: 'the rise of more and more exotic blooms on the borders of institutionalized teaching, and sometimes cavalier treatments they receive, persuaded them [the scholars, M.L.] that they should, at last, grasp the nettle' (Goethe-Institut et al. 1982, p. 2). Both publications were followed by a number of similar attempts all over Europe to come to terms with the new approaches (Bolte and Herrlitz 1983; Schwerdtfeger 1983), which added to American survey articles and critical appraisals (Yoshikawa 1982; Scovel 1983; Richards and Rodgers 1982; 1986).

Among these approaches under discussion were the interpersonal methods, Community Language Learning and Humanistic Approaches or Confluent Language Teaching, both of which had developed in direct relationship to what became known in psychology as the 'Third Force' between Behaviourism and Freudianism: Humanistic Psychology (see below 3.3). The discussion also focused a great deal on the growing interest in Suggestopaedia, which although it had been in existence for some time, suddenly gained prominence in a generally revitalized climate of cultural transformation. The time was ripe for these theories to be put into action with particular regard to the conscious and unconscious potential of the learning individual.

While scholars in Europe were still debating what the implications of these new approaches might be, methodologists and practitioners had already began to glean ideas for classroom techniques provided by proponents of these approaches such as Moskowitz and Galyean. Humanistic tasks and strategies began to trickle into European language classrooms mainly through the innovative initiatives of such organizations as the Pilgrims' English Language School in Canterbury, represented by Rinvolucri and his colleagues (see Bibliography). They were also quickly absorbed by those communicative methodologists who had been working on the role of games in language learning (Löffler 1979; Klippel 1980) or who had shown an interest in learner identity formation and emotional development in language learning (Schiffler 1980; Schratz 1983).

Humanistic language teaching reflects the wider educational debate of the late 1960s and early 1970s which took a radically new direction. In the aftermath of anti-establishment movements with explicit anti-institutional implications (above all the free school movement), educational approaches which called for the de-schooling of society (Illich 1970) or, in its less radical forms, for a basic humanizing of technocratic and de-humanizing schools, had gained ground. To humanize schools would require an orientation towards 'holistic' education, which aimed to promote growth in intrapersonal awareness and interpersonal sharing as well as intellectual development. Concern for the former had been ignored by traditional education which was in turn blamed for failing to develop the full potential of students.

Stevick has identified four forms of alienation which are possibly responsible for failure in modern language teaching. These are: the alienation of the learners from the material, from themselves, from the class and from the teacher (Stevick 1976b, p. 225). This alienation is also the educational starting point of the proponents of humanistic approaches and the hidden agenda of many resource books offering communicative tasks. Their suggestions for the classroom claim either to overcome or minimize these alienations. In Galyean's view this can be accomplished if the following four components are able to play an equal part in determining classroom events:

(1) *Learning in the here and now* (Galyean 1977). By this is meant that themes and procedures must be significant for all learners at the time that the teaching takes place and not rely for their relevance on some possible future application. Engaging in the here and now takes place when the learner himself becomes the theme. As a result the second component is:

(2) *Student offered material as the basis for learning and practising language structures* (ibid.). Here the learner becomes the most important source for learning which in turn is conditional on the third component:

(3) *Interpersonal sharing* (ibid.). Here, following Humanistic Psychology and pedagogy, Galyean makes the assumption that learners bring to the learning situation a basic need and willingness to communicate and the desire to experience themselves. 'The important thing is that the students will want to communicate as these personalized activities are excellent motivators' (Moskowitz 1978, p. 30). Both communication and experience of self occur in encounter situations in which ideas, fantasies and everyday life experiences are being listened to and shared in various social formations (pairwork, small group work, circle discussions). Such interpersonality requires consciousness of one's own situation and that of one's partner. The fourth component is therefore:

(4) *Self-awareness and realization* (ibid.).

In order to introduce these four components into a learning situation proponents of humanistic approaches resort to a wide range of activities, often referred to as 'growth strategies' developed by Humanistic Psychology (see 3.3). They claim that these activities 'when practised by both teachers and students, allow deliberate self-reflection and understanding to flourish. Participation in these specially designed 'growth' strategies enables one to focus on his/her inner worlds of need, feelings, concerns, interests, and subsequent values, and to express these to others' (Galyean 1977, p. 145).

Or in the words of Moskowitz, they are intended to foster 'self-discovery, introspection, self-esteem, and getting in touch with the strengths and positive qualities of ourselves and others' (Moskowitz 1978, p. 14). They will make communication happen, which in

Galyean's words 'is you and me interacting, becoming one with each other, seeing ourselves reflected in others' responses to us' (Galyean 1976, p. 1).

By making the development of self–other awareness through communicative tasks the overall purpose of the language class, a primary self-reflective function is attributed to the target *language*, i.e. language learning *per se* now is of secondary importance because the language acts as a vehicle for experience (Stevick 1980, p. 115). It becomes 'the necessary tool for self-discovery. Students in humanistic language classes employ the language matrices to help them explore their own meaning nodes and to share them with others' (Galyean 1979, p. 123). Language will emerge *from within*, as the title of Galyean's pioneering study programmatically indicates (Galyean 1975). The *learners* are seen to thrive in a climate of togetherness and trust, which is claimed to evolve in direct relation to the growth of self-concept and the increase of social cohesion among students. The *teacher's* role, on the other hand, is to build this sense of social cohesion and structure the space conducive to learning. Her main instruments for guiding students to self-experience are humanistic techniques.

How are we to evaluate these approaches, promulgated with great enthusiasm in the 1970s and early 1980s? Are the techniques suggested the long-awaited tools for meaningful discourse as the title and sub-title of Moskowitz's 1978 publication *Caring and Sharing in the Foreign Language Class. A Sourcebook on Humanistic Techniques* seem to indicate? Although they may seem attractive as a way of introducing real communication into language classrooms in view of what had gone on before, e.g. the alienating classroom and the failure of audiolingualism to produce results, these approaches also give rise to several crucial questions, which the following discussion of the criteria will address:

– What does it mean 'to express oneself' from the point of view of learner language acquisition?
– What are the possible dangers of transferring into educational contexts processes which were primarily intended for the therapeutic revealing of self-experience?
– Are any of these ideas at all feasible with groups of learners in compulsory schooling where, for example, the assessment-dominated environment of the school requires the testing and ranking of learners?
– How does a learner acquire in conditions such as these the

openness, willingness and trust to participate in processes which –
because they require a great deal of risk-taking and self-disclosure
– would leave him at least partially unprotected within his learning
group?
- Is the teacher not completely out of her depth if she has to become
involved with the emotions of learners, even to the point of
introducing her own into the classroom?
- Finally why should the modern language classroom be the place
within the confines of a school where self-experience takes place?
Are there not enough problems already, e.g. the demands of
organized language acquisition and the commensurate limited
ability to express oneself in the language; insufficient available
knowledge of vocabulary and language functions, which would
place a fundamental question mark against such thinking?

However, before we address these questions we need to be aware
of the educational and psychological assumptions which underlie
Humanistic techniques. This is necessary for two major reasons:

(1) The way the tasks function presupposes particular views of the
individual, of awareness, communication and learning, all of
which derive from non-language-learning disciplines. Indeed, a
substantial number of them have simply been transferred to the
language class from psychotherapy practice.
(2) The underlying philosophy, which originated in self-awareness
groups and therapy has become blurred or even lost among the
proliferation of tasks in resource books, whose authors creatively
borrow from one another or plunder the same handbooks for
group therapy techniques.

A striking example of the second issue can be derived from a
comparison between the first and second edition of the resource book
Look Who's Talking by Christison and Bassano (1981; 1987). Whereas
the first edition still makes explicit reference to the origins of the
activities '. . . other activities come to us from experiences in general
communication-skill classes, self-awareness groups and psychotherapy
practice' (1981, p. vii) and implicitly quotes the notion of Humanistic
Education that learners are asking for more of an opportunity 'to
become themselves' in the new language (1981, p. xv), the second
edition presents more or less the same material without any further
explanation or reference than 'meaning-based activities for language
learning' (1987, p. v).

3.3 Humanism and education: a brief historical perspective

3.3.1 Humanistic psychology and the climate of change

Although Humanistic Language Teaching did not gain prominence until the late 1970s, its philosophy and concept of learning relates to the active debate of the late 1960s and early 1970s, when educational and social institutions were under attack. Carl Rogers, who had become one of the major contributors to this argument, expressed his concerns as follows:

> Each year I become more pessimistic about what is going on in educational institutions. They have focused so intently on the cognitive and have limited themselves so completely to 'education from the neck up', that this narrowness is resulting in serious social consequences . . . . As a consequence of this overstress on the cognitive, and of the avoidance of any feeling connected with it, most of the excitement has gone out of education.
>
> (Rogers 1975, pp. 40–1)

In 1971, George Isaac Brown presented a study which was to set the stage for a significant change. This study, *Human Teaching for Human Learning*, which arose out of a pilot project at the Esalen Institute in Big Sur, California, proposed a new educational movement, *Confluent Education*, the pedagogic vehicle for humanistic thinking. The pilot project's aim was two-fold. First, it tried to explore ways of adapting approaches and concepts in the affective domain, which had gained attention on the fringes of established psychotherapy, to educational theory and curriculum development. It drew principally on Rogers' work in client-centred psychotherapy and person-centred learning (1951; 1961), Maslow's psychology of self-actualization (1962), and, most importantly on Perls' Gestalt Therapy (Perls, Hefferline and Goodman 1951). The project also incorporated developments in fields as diverse as creativity training, eastern philosophies and meditation, dance and even physical education 'to renew the central tradition of western education' (Castillo 1973, p. 3).

The Ford–Esalen project itself was not restricted to conceptualization and theory. From the outset it included an intensive teacher-training component which consisted of awareness training under the guidance of several therapists (among them Perls), research work, lectures and, interestingly, feedback on and evaluation of classroom experiences. Teachers from all levels of education became involved in working for the 'integration and flowing together of the affective and cognitive elements in individual and group learning' (Brown 1971, p. 3). Several participants in these early training experiences such as Castillo and Galyean were to become proponents of Humanistic Education through their own publications.

As Bach and Molter (1976) point out, the various branches of Humanistic Psychology exercised a considerable influence on the psycho-therapeutic practice in Western industrial societies in the 1970s. That this is indeed the case is certainly not attributable to the achievements of their theory, which remained sketchy and aphoristic, but rather to a wealth of therapeutic techniques which seemed to satisfy the insatiable hunger of the educated middle classes in the US and Western Europe for self-awareness training and therapy. It was this desire which found a practical expression through the Human Potential Movement and caused the main work of Gestalt therapy – which had already been written by 1951 – to become known among parts of the counter culture. It was also within this context that the Esalen Institute thrived.

These initiatives of the counter-culture (the heterogeneous movement of drop-outs, drug-freaks, hippies, yippies, representatives of the new Left, country communards, poets, women's groups, ecological action committees, various spiritual and neo-religious groups and human potential movements or growth movements with their encounter and awareness-raising groups) were attempts to react to a crisis in American society which was representative for all advanced industrial states. This was a crisis whose main character-istics were the deadening of human communication within techno-cratic and bureaucratic institutions, the progressive destruction of liveable space in the cities, the aggravation of spiritual impoverishment and poverty in spite of a rapid growth of affluence, the obvious chauvinism of the so-called civilized world and its democracies towards the countries of the Third World and the exploitative relationship with nature which led to a progressive reduction of the quality of life in the name of progress.

While sections of the counter-culture which were concerned with the politics of ecology had developed theories and projects to liberate the second nature of man from technocratic and industrial subjection (Roszak 1972), the human potential or growth movements – as they were also called – concentrated on rediscovering man's first nature as a free and uninhibited organism. The notions to which these groups drew particular attention, i.e. expansion of awareness, the experience of one's body, relaxation, self-perception and a new togetherness, were, at least in the beginning of the movement, always meant as a criticism of social institutions and established forms such as schools, universities or hospitals. As a result the human potential movement thought of what it was doing as a contribution to social transformation because it proceeded from the premise that this could not take place without the transformation of the people involved.

3.3.2 Key concepts of Gestalt Therapy

It was Gestalt Therapy – in particular its emphasis on body-awareness, on direct emotional expression with a plea to liberate oneself from social pressures in order to develop the full potential of the individual, which offered concepts and a practical way of activating a shattered sensitivity. It achieved this goal by recognizing dead clichés and norms, and discarding them. It granted 'permission' to be free and it opened up ways of discovering oneself. What fascinated Perls' collaborators and students at the Esalen Institute in Gestalt therapy were concepts such as the organism-as-a-whole, organismic self-regulation as the basis for all learning and growth, of awareness in the here and now, and of learning through contacting, sensing and experiencing (Perls et al. 1951). Most attractive of all was the key notion of responsibility with its deliberate duality of meaning: 'But responsibility can also be spelt response-ability, the ability to respond, to have thoughts, reactions, emotions in a certain situation. Now, this ability to be what one is, is expressed through the word "I" ' (Perls 1971, p. 70). Confluent educators were particularly concerned about making what were in reality initiatives for therapy useful and productive for a new pedagogy. This thrust, along with Perls' work, drew heavily on Rogers' (1970) observations of inter-person learning and self-directed change, and on the theories of self-actualization and creativity by Maslow (1977).

3.3.3 Learning in Gestalt and techniques for classroom application

At this time, the co-founder of Gestalt therapy, Paul Goodman, encouraged educators to offer practical resistance to conventional forms of public education. He thus became a protagonist of anti-pedagogy and an activist of the Free School movement along with Illich (1970), Dennison (1969), Reimer (1970), Graubard (1972) and

Holt (1969; 1976), who also demanded a radical de-schooling of society. Proponents of Confluent Education, however, also using Gestalt therapy as a base, were directing their efforts towards changing schools and colleges from the inside. Clearly reformist in character compared to the radical position taken by Goodman and the free school activists, Confluent Education nevertheless believed that humanizing learning in the classroom would necessarily go hand in hand with humanizing the institutions.

Supported by the Gestalt therapy, Confluent Education holds that people possess a fundamental need for learning, which directs itself towards self-exploration and personal growth. Just as the human organism will spontaneously reach out for food when it is hungry to sustain itself, so the need for learning will be spontaneous and intrinsically motivated:

> Appetite seems either to be stimulated by something in the environment or to rise spontaneously from the organism. But of course the environment would not excite, it would not be a stimulus, unless the organism were set to respond; and further, it can often be shown that it was a dimly aware appetite that put one in the way of the stimulus at the appropriate time. The response reaches out to the stimulus.
>
> (Perls et al. 1951, p. 404)

However, this natural interest to reach out and learn requires conditions which allow it to unfold, or which remove hindrances or blockages and thus promote its unfolding. A learning environment conducive to growth includes an atmosphere of trust, forms of interaction between partners, learning situations which stimulate encounters, and above all, learning arrangements which allow for creative ways of exploration by making contact with both the world inside the learner and the world outside.

According to Gestalt therapy and pedagogy, people find themselves as learners in a physical environment, in a social, cultural context and in relation to each other. The relationship to the environment is ambivalent because, on the one hand, as learners they are dependent on it and on the interchange with it. On the other hand, by exploring it, they seek to reshape it according to their changing needs. Manipulating and mastering one's environment can come about as a result of routine actions which can be learnt (known as *adjustment*) or as a result of new and creative solutions (known as *change*). To maintain and structure this complex relationship with the environment requires, according to Gestalt therapy, the ability of the individual to make 'contact'. Whether this contact comes about from a subjective need (for example, a specific interest in finding something out) or from a particular stimulus in the environment (for example, the images in a poem), it always constitutes a subjectively significant event. The latter encapsulates a moment and a process at the same time, i.e. an interaction between the subject with his collective life and social experiences and a part of the environment, which is itself determined by the structure and importance of its context. The interaction which takes place within this contact is at the same time both an encounter and a drawing up of limits and constitutes, therefore, identity (Perls et al. 1951, p. 229).

In Gestalt 'awareness' is the tool which allows the individual organism to be in contact. It has been compared with a kind of psychological searchlight which can be pointed within limits, as a person chooses:

> A person can usually 'be aware of' whatever he considers himself to be (that which is inside the ego boundary), although he most likely cannot do this all at once; thus the play of the searchlight. He will experience great difficulty being aware of parts of himself which he does not consider 'him' (that which is outside the ego boundary), those parts which for some reason he has disowned. Much of Gestalt therapy works precisely with this problem, by attempting, through the focusing of awareness (the therapist 'stating the obvious and making implicit explicit'), to break open ego boundaries and encapsulated elements in order to reintegrate disowned elements and to clear out or assimilate introjected or rigidified elements. Awareness is a capacity which is used as tool in this task.
>
> (Yeomans 1975, p. 146)

A lack of awareness is directly linked to a lack of access to oneself and one's potential for growth (both of which are seen as an essential component for learning). The most important task of the therapist/ teacher is to expand this awareness in the here and now of the therapeutic session or the classroom. The role of the teacher is to help the learner to direct his attention inwardly towards physical sensations, emotions, wishes, fantasies, accessible memories, experiences and dreams, and outwardly to the environment. In doing so, learners will expand their awareness and assume responsibility for what they are and what they are capable of doing. Thus, by advocating the enhancement of learners' awareness, Confluent Education, drawing on Perls' double concept of responsibility, pursues a two-fold goal. It aims at teaching the ability to react to the intellectual challenges of topic and text as well as the ability to participate in explorations of emotional contexts. The latter, of course, requires from learners an inward and an outward openness. According to Perls, it is always the whole person who is a participant in this process of involvement in contact with himself, with others and with themes using his perception, feelings, thoughts and actions. Learning is, therefore, understood as a learning experience which contains its own dynamic and could be seen as possessing its own psycho-motoric force and emotional excitement (Perls et al. 1951, p. 128).

The answers which the learners offer in the process of contact (their responses) provide the key to their individuality. This individuality grows via the communicative exchange involving renewed self-perception and perception of others. In this way, the responses provide essential material for the learning process. The central categories of Confluent Education, namely awareness and responsibility, emphasize what is special and what is unique in each learner. In this view of learning, learners cannot be reduced to the level of an abstraction often referred to in educational theory and teaching methodology as the 'average learner'. We can illustrate diagramatically the concept of Confluent Education drawing on Gloria Castillo's ideas (1974) in the following way: (see fig. 3.1)

If Confluent Education can be said to have gone to war against the deadening effect of an over-intellectualized school system – one important publication of Confluent Education, a collection of essays, carried the title *The Live Classroom* (Brown 1975) – it is also criticizing the alienation of people from their own bodies accelerated by education in schools. As Völker (1980, p. 221) says this alienation is 'a long process which begins in infancy and reaches its climax during the years at school'. It seems to be the hidden curriculum that progressive maturity and education is accompanied with commensurately dwindling attention to the feelings and the body. Just how clear the relevance of the criticism is can be seen by the progressive lifelessness of learners in schools particularly in the upper levels, as they move towards their final exam. The more academic and serious the learning, the more energy needs to be concentrated 'from the neck up'. For Confluent Education the excitement of the learning experience resides in the dynamic balance of all parts, spheres and capacities of the human body: thinking, feeling, acting and creating.

In order to achieve the aims of such holistic learning Confluent Education makes use of the large arsenal of techniques which the various disciplines of humanistic psychology, and particularly Gestalt Therapy, provided in the USA during the 1960s and 1970s. There was a veritable boom in growth and awareness techniques. A flood of new books were published, offering awareness-raising techniques in the following areas:

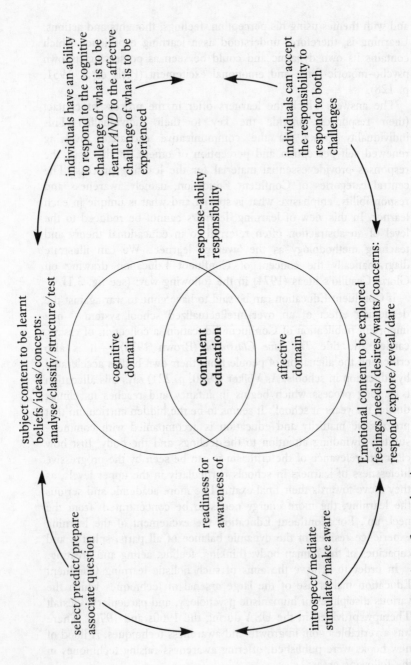

Figure 3.1 Patterns in confluent education

(1) sensitivity training;
(2) the perception and activation of emotions;
(3) body training (relaxation, breathing, movement);
(4) psychodramatic expression of feelings (drama);
(5) making contact and for empathy training;
(6) the training of communication skills;
(7) the stimulation of imagination, projection and creativity.[1]

Both Brown (1971) and Castillo (1974) and many other representatives of Confluent Education have introduced these essentially therapeutic techniques into educational contexts. In many cases, it was a straightforward transfer. As one or two authors have self-critically pointed out, the sets of techniques they were offering were in danger of creating the feelings associated with a recipe book or a laboratory manual, if taken out of their working context and if separated from their underlying educational philosophy (Brown 1971, p. 27). But this is exactly what happened. These educators were thus unintentionally setting in motion a tendency to reduce their pedagogy to mere group techniques (Heintel 1978, p. 119). Greater momentum was given to this tendency by an almost naive enthusiasm and belief in the feasibility of holistic education as the 'right' method: 'We have a sense of what prevents growth and what wastes energy in the personality; we have a technology for facilitating growth, for increasing the amount of energy available to the person, and for healing splits, conflicts or blocks within the personality.' (Yeomans 1975b, p. 151).

3.3.4 Conclusion

Apart from having provided a wide range of classroom strategies and techniques, Confluent Education had an impact on educational thought in general and foreign language teaching in particular in two important ways. With its primary emphasis on the integration of the affective and the cognitive domain, it has reiterated notions of holistic and experiential learning, which are rooted in the pedagogical reform movements of the 1920s (cf. below, chapter 5 and Goodman 1986; Bohnsack 1984; Prengel 1983; Fauser et al. 1983). With its orientation towards expressiveness and creativity, it has recaptured what for many learners had ceased to be a part of learning beyond the first few years in school, namely practical and body-involving forms of action.

As a person-centred concept, Confluent Education attempts to take the individuality of each learner seriously and sets out to create a learning environment which is conducive to the individual's potential for self-exploration and self-expression. Learner responses are seen as necessary and relevant contributions to a jointly constructed process. In addition, educators are challenged to turn the sequences of learning into a meaningful experience for the learners in the here and now of the classroom, rather than justifying their efforts with deferred gratifications.

However, as we will see in the following discussion of critical criteria for tasks, Confluent Education has a number of serious shortcomings. The naive belief in the general feasibility of confluent techniques is bought at the cost of ignoring fundamental institutional and social constraints which derive from the evaluative nature of school learning. Furthermore, little or no attention is given to the issues of initiative and control, or to learner participation in classroom management. In spite of the subjectivism of Confluent Education the notion of responsibility is not extended to the organization of learning itself. Confluent Education remains fundamentally interventionist. The techniques remain tools in the hands of the teachers who can easily turn them into manipulative instruments of human technology.

3.4 Critical criteria

We now wish to turn our attention to individual tasks taken from humanistic approaches and related resource books. Our purpose is to examine their relevance for communicative language teaching. To do this we will look, among others, at the work of Galyean (1975; 1976; 1977; 1979), Moskowitz (1978), Christison and Bassano (1981; 1987a, 1987b), Frank and Rinvolucri (1983), and Puchta and Schratz (1984). We will propose seven criteria to be applied when using exercise types taken from this background. Although these criteria are treated separately and sequentially, the reader will note that they overlap in many ways.

The early adaptations of growth-promoting and self-enhancing techniques which mushroomed from therapeutic and non-therapeutic group experiments represented little more than modified language exercises (Galyean 1975). In spite of claims to the contrary, the new approaches provided exercises for the practice of particular grammatical, lexical or functional parts of the language. They were attempts to imbue stale language practice, itself derived from audio-lingualism and totally dominating the majority of language classrooms in the US with new, i.e. personal, life. Since the content for these exercises was supposed to come from the experience of the learners who were thereby, at least potentially, given the opportunity to express personal meaning, they could be said to contain a communicative element. In many cases, however, the drill and practice phases were part of more complex action scenarios which combined various skills of a linguistic, interactive and reflexive kind and could, therefore, be called communicative tasks in the real sense. It was claimed that such tasks, supposedly focused on issues that were relevant and meaningful to students, would help develop learners' communicative competence. To enhance language acquisition would, therefore, require the incorporation of such a 'student-centred component' into traditional language programmes (Taylor 1983).

3.4.1 Criterion 1: Context and topicality

The theory of confluent education takes into account the thematic dimension in holistic learning processes. However, in its derivative forms in modern language methodology, the importance of topic relevance as a governing principle for student-centred learning sequences is widely ignored. True to their Gestalt therapeutic tradition, the proponents of humanistic approaches criticize the 'aboutism' of a rationalistic pedagogy which entrenches itself behind facts to be learned, linguistic structures and learning aims which have to be realized whether they have any relevance to learners' lives or not. In place of the schematic manipulation of language items, they substituted the personalization of content through interpersonal processes in classroom settings. Language learning through using living experiences was intended to replace the lifeless exercises and clichéd textbook characters. However, several important questions remain unanswered:

– What pedagogical and methodological decisions lie behind the choice of areas of sensory awareness and self-discovery to be stimulated and/or explored?
– What is the systematic relationship between these experiences and themes and aspects of the target culture which have equally to be explored and researched?
– What is the role of the L2 culture? (Note that the notion of culture is completely excluded in most of the resource books.)

Unless we can find answers to these questions, we are opening the door to a dubious arbitrariness of self-experience. The following example will make this clear. In exercise 52 'Hair! Hair!' (Moskowitz 1978, p. 118), Moskowitz's students activate and exchange experiences and memories which make them aware how strongly their self-image is connected with the style of their hair and the reactions of other people to it. At the same time, the linguistic aim is to provide practice in written and oral form for the past tense and descriptive adjectives. However, neither grammatical nor lexical parts of the language provide a justification for exploring these personal experiences and idiosyncrasies.

A decision to embark on such a task as 'Hair! Hair!' would at best be justified within a context identified by theme and content where particular linguistic aspects were subordinate. The task might be used, for example, as support in interpreting the short story 'Bernice Bobs Her Hair' by F. Scott Fitzgerald, where it would function either as a pre-reading activity to open the field of awareness, or it could intensify learner responses to the story and thus help personalize the joint efforts of creating meaning after the story has been read by the class.

It is only when they are related to a theme that most of the communicative tasks, especially those derived from humanistic psychology, are really justified. Without a connection to content areas and representations of the target culture, the stimulation of self-discovery and self-disclosure in the language classroom will remain arbitrary and could further aggravate learner alienation, and thus be counterproductive to its initial intent. Just how arbitrary this becomes is evident when the justification for activating experience is based on discrete linguistic items and their systematic progression, as can be seen in Galyean's and Rinvolucri's work. Only in very few cases are such tasks suitable for teaching discrete language items. If they are, however, integrated into thematically related contexts they could provide a framework within which learner-contributed content, be it in oral or written form, could become available to the whole class. We will return to the issue of language later in this chapter (3.4.6).

3.4.2 Criterion 2: Awareness

If communicative tasks are related to texts and themes, and integrated in the learning process, they can 'open doors and windows' (Oaklander 1978) to previously unused areas of communicative action on which a multiplicity of new activities of exploration, contact, expression and learning will arise. The concept of awareness is seen as crucial in widening learners' understanding of self, the group, and the external world. The role of the communicative task is to facilitate this awareness. Even if it is not as obvious as with the tasks derived from humanistic psychology, all the other alternative approaches explicitly or implicitly make the assumption that an increased awareness of the learner's potential and an expansion of this awareness into hitherto untapped areas will be conducive to language acquisition.

However, the precise extension of this concept has become blurred in the process of adapting it from related fields (e.g. from psychology) into language-teaching methodology. The second criterion therefore requires teachers to clarify three major aspects of awareness when selecting tasks from resource books.

(1) *The object of awareness*: What should the learners become aware of? Should they focus their awareness on *subject content* such as beliefs, ideas, concepts, events and fields of knowledge with the aim of analysing, classifying, structuring or testing it? Or should they be concerned with *emotional content* such as feelings, needs, desires, memories and dreams, with the aim of activating, exploring and revealing it? Or will their awareness be directed to *linguistic content* with the aim of raising the learners' discoursal, semantic and grammatical consciousness (Rutherford 1987; Stevick 1980). Furthermore, the question is whether learners should become aware of the *nature of learning*, their own *learning experiences* or of issues of interpersonality and *group dynamics* as essential factors for successful learning.

(2) *The mode of awareness*: Through which perceptual faculties does the learner reach this awareness? Is its object more likely to be brought into focus through *mental operations* such as associating, predicting, selecting or questioning, or is it contacted through ways of direct *sensory perception* such as touching, listening, smelling, tasting, seeing, and body expression (e.g. pantomimes), or do the tasks ask for *an introspective and meditative mode* of becoming aware? Or are all three processes involved contemporaneously?

(3) *The techniques to raise this awareness*: How does the teacher stimulate and frame the process of becoming aware? What techniques must she be able to master to stimulate projection, introspection, association, to initiate meditation, relaxation and sensory perception? Furthermore, which work formats are best suited for these kinds of activities and which ones would be counterproductive to the goal of developing the learner's ability to

respond to the cognitive challenge of what is to be learnt and to the affective challenge of what is to be experienced?

During the task 'My Ideal School' (Moskowitz 1978, pp. 181f), for example, learners are requested to embark on a teacher-guided fantasy journey to draw out and stimulate wishes and fantasies. They should experience the ideal school day from the time of awakening in the morning until they return home at in the evening. The complete sequence of the task involves relaxation activities prior to the guided fantasy, which is conducted with closed eyes and is followed by a phase of group sharing. Finally, the activity cycle leads to a writing assignment requiring learners to describe their ideal school. In doing so they are expected to practise using 'the future or the conditional tenses'.

Applying the first criterion to this task would lead to the question: What is the contextual justification for the exploration of this particular topic? Is the latter just an arbitrary gimmick for the practice of some grammatical structures like 'the future', or does it relate to some larger syllabus unit, which, for example, would deal with intercultural aspects of school life? In such a context, the task and its outcome (the learner texts from the written assignment) might have the function of a pre-organizer to the exploration of new data on the topic (pictures of classrooms, poems by students from the target culture, report cards, year books, statistics, etc.).

Applying the second criterion would define subject and emotional content as the main object of awareness, which would require learners' value systems with regard to schooling to be brought to the surface through the activity. Since the mode of becoming aware would primarily be introspective and involve behaviour which could be experienced as threatening, the task's procedure could cause problems with certain groups of learners (see criteria 3 and 5).

The bulk of tasks, deriving from the 'growth movements' of the 1970s, are concerned with becoming aware of emotional content, which, according to their proponents, has been suppressed in schools. By opening doors to fantasies and by sharing the experience it is suggested that enough relevant content is generated for learners to engage in meaningful discourse in the target language.

3.4.3 Criterion 3: Prior knowledge and prerequisites for learning

This criterion raises the question of previous exposure to communicative tasks by both teacher and learner, in particular those which derive from non-language teaching disciplines. It also considers the prerequisites which any class must possess in order to participate in such activities. In the example just quoted (My Ideal School) it would be necessary to find out whether the teacher was able to judge the extent of the guided introspection phase and to lead the class accordingly. With regard to learners, one needs to decide whether they are ready and able to participate in introspection, journeys of fantasy or projective procedures. This task, as many other communicative ones, requires a high degree of social mobility within the classroom (for example changing partners and pairwork several times). Often tasks ask for individual expression and risk-taking (such as acting something out or using mime) and they might contain unencountered – and therefore anxiety-creating – forms of behaviour (such as closing one's eyes).

It is exactly this criterion – which states the need to take into account the prior experiences of all participants in the learning process – which Puchta and Schratz seem to ignore in several of their examples of *Active Learning* (Puchta and Schratz 1984, Vol. 2). The activity sequence 'Pressure' (pp. 50ff) is possibly the clearest example of this. In order to activate experiences of pressure to provide a personal backdrop to a text-decoding exercise (the text in question was a newspaper article on the mass hysteria of girls at a pop concert) twenty learners in a seventh-grade secondary school class (about thirteen years of age) are asked to step inside a rope laid out on the ground which the teacher then ties around them. He asks them to close their eyes and waits until they are all quiet: 'During the silence the circle formed by the rope is made smaller. The teacher pulls the rope tighter so that the distance between the learners becomes smaller and smaller until finally under the pressure of the rope they are pushed against each other backwards and forwards' (Puchta and Schratz 1984, p. 53). The authors offer no discussion or comment on what learners may require in terms of preparation to do such a task, nor do they reflect on the problems of activating experience in this way. There is not only an implicit suggestion that any teacher could undertake this activity with any group but the authors also seem to presuppose a general psychic stability of their learners because they ignore possible anxieties which might result from such an experience.

In the following phases of this activity, Puchta and Schratz seek to attain a certain reflective distance. However, it is difficult to avoid the conclusion that passing over the anxiety/trauma dimension (this will be addressed by criterion 5) and the issue of the pre-experiences of the class, turns this form of experience activation into a dangerous psycho-technique which at best satisfies the manipulative needs of teachers than the real learning requirements of learners. In addition, there is the danger of possible counter-productive reactions which may emerge when teachers attempt to conduct classes with quasi-therapeutic pretensions.

The third criterion also addresses the issue of learners' expectations and beliefs as to how learning should be organized. Since any group of learners will come into the classroom conditioned by previous educational experiences (Knowles 1970; Wenden 1986a, 1986b), they will react towards unfamiliar forms of learning on the basis of what they bring to the classroom (Kleppin and Königs 1987). Different learning habits and beliefs need to be taken into account especially when students from diverse cultural backgrounds and learning traditions have come together. Under such conditions it might pose a threat to some learners, and thus stifle their initiative, if the teacher asks them to close their eyes, because in their cultural discourse it would be strange to do so, or, indeed face-threatening. None of the resource books for communicative tasks touches upon this crucial issue.

3.4.4 Criterion 4: Self-determination and selective authenticity

First and foremost, communicative tasks are under the control and initiative of the teacher who selects them, sets the aims of the activity, stages them, and moderates their effects and outcomes. As far as the learners are concerned they are, by definition, interventions upon personal approaches to content and personal concepts of what language learning is or should be like (cf. Breen 1987). Being impositions from the outside, communicative tasks nevertheless require, through the way they have been set up or the way that they unfold, the willingness on the part of the learner to engage in a communicative exchange which often includes self-disclosure through sharing.

In her reference to psychologists such as Jourard, Luft and Ingham, Moskowitz (1978, p. 17) has, of all the representatives of humanistic approaches, formulated most aptly their shared view of *authentic self-disclosure* (Moskowitz 1978, p. 18; 1982) which is considered characteristic of the process of communication. The model she refers to is seen as a communication window through which information is given and received. It contains four areas of information which determine the communication process. They are typically illustrated in the literature by four large squares. The first square contains the public domain, that is information which is available to all participants (*public, knowledge/public arena*). The second domain contains that information which is known to everyone apart from the person who is involved in the communication (*blind spot*). The third domain embraces things which the subject of the communication keeps hidden from the others (*hidden area*). And lastly, the fourth domain includes information which is still undisclosed to all the participants (*unknown*) as well as the information stored in the *unconscious* of the group and the individual (cf. also Johnson 1972). According to Moskowitz (1982, p. 23), it is an essential function of *humanistic communication activities* to extend the public domain by constantly narrowing the three other domains through a process of self-disclosure and feedback. This in turn will stimulate a constantly developing need to participate in the adventure of self-discovery and the discovery of others.

There are two reasons why it is difficult to share the euphoria which Moskowitz and others feel when they put forward this concept. Firstly, she suggests that this model is generally applicable under conditions of organized learning in schools; secondly, the quasi-therapeutic role through which the teacher seeks to lead the learners to the salvation of self-experience is at least questionable from the perspective of an educational philosophy which is based on principles of self-determination and learner participation (cf. Brumfit 1982). Since there is no critical consideration offered on the important role of leadership during these tasks, the danger increases that learners become pawns within a pedagogical game. The concept of a participating leader or of a learner who determines his own work is incompatible with the nature of such exercises.

If the learner becomes the object of the lesson by means of tasks led by the teacher without his consent this can only accentuate existing feelings of manipulation. New forms of alienation may be the result if learners are required to talk about themselves by representatives of an institution which holds the power to issue certificates of achievement and to influence their prospects for the future. This is even more the case since classes neither have the power to choose their teachers, their classmates, their work, nor when they should start and finish. Proponents of humanistic approaches emphasize, of course, the freedom of learners to participate or not in such tasks, to remain silent or to talk (Moskowitz 1978, p. 29). However, when one considers the conditions in any institution, this offer of participating or not participating could be seen as a pedagogical trap, a double-bind, and could narrow even further the already limited scope for self-determination.

The fourth criterion further directs teachers' attention to the necessary distinction between *task-as-workplan* and *task-in-process*. As Breen (1987a) points out, any language learning task and any communicative activity will be reinterpreted by learners in their own terms. In superimposing individual/group purposes on a given task, in drawing on prior knowledge of content and learning experiences, and in mobilizing procedural capacities, learners change and thus redesign a given task while undertaking it. However, the structure of a task, as well as the conditions under which it is undertaken in the classroom, will determine the amount of space and freedom for such reinterpretations. The question is: how much space does the task structure and the staging of it in the learning situation allow for the involvement of prior knowledge and learner decisions as the basis for solving a problem, voicing feelings, or sharing experiences?

The fourth criterion, therefore, concerns itself with the proportion of determination – manipulation – from the outside which the teacher believes she can justify. It concerns itself with those real areas of co-determination which are at the disposal of learners within tasks, extended activity sequences and above all in the choice of areas of experiences which are to be explored. In which ways can learners take the initiative in exploring, communicating and processing content – especially of emotions – and thus as participants take over leader functions? Many teaching experiments lend justified support to the view that learners initially look for much more indirect ways of self-communication, identifying with characters from literary texts, acting out play sequences or in various forms of masque-monologues (Seletzky 1984; Bredella and Legutke 1985a).

Finally the fourth criterion focuses on the aspect of the authenticity of learner utterances. Moskowitz's notion of *authentic self-disclosure* reflects a problematic relationship to the institutional constraints of school and an intangible mixture of therapy and pedagogy. In contrast, we would like to propose Cohn's concept of *selective authenticity* (Cohn 1979, p. 27) as an aim and not a condition of pedagogic endeavours. The fourth criterion poses the question whether learners engaging in a particular activity are free to involve themselves in communicative processes through selective authenticity, to distance themselves from them and to determine their own forms of contribution and content. This presupposes among other conditions a positive working climate and, above all, procedures of evaluation which are clear and identifiable to the learners.

Let us clarify what we have said so far with an example which Rinvolucri quotes to elucidate the function and nature of awareness activities for the teaching of particular language structures. In the exercise 'Where Do I Fit?' (Rinvolucri 1982, p. 50), the learners are asked to choose half a dozen groupings to which they see themselves belonging or have at one time belonged to. These could be large and impersonal groupings or small and very intimate ones. The learners are asked then to draw a shape for each of the collectives on a piece of paper and to mark with a cross their emotional relationship within and to the group. In the next step the learners are asked to explain the outlines to their partner or neighbour.

After completing this activity, groups of learners at various levels (German high-school pupils from the eleventh, twelfth and thirteenth grades: sixteen to eighteen years old, methodology student teachers, and teachers in in-service training) gave the following feedback and evaluation:

(1) None of the groups saw the exercise as an opportunity to practise grammatical structures, as Rinvolucri (ibid.) suggests. Rather they all needed to know the thematic context (criterion 1). Possible contexts offered were: 'Getting to know each other' at the beginning of a course, 'Individual and society', 'group – group relations – peer group', etc.

(2) Participants agreed with Rinvolucri that the exercise opened up an interesting and unusual perspective on their own personality and as a result could be quite motivating (criterion 5, see below).

(3) The participants also accepted Rinvolucri's Iceberg Thesis which says :

> Awareness exercises are icebergs in which what is said is the visible tip of the vast number of things very rapidly thought and felt. In this way awareness exercises are much nearer full, effective communication between human beings than many of the rather shallow 'information gap' exercises that seem fairly central to certain types of 'communicative' language teaching.
>
> (Ibid., p. 51)

However, referring to the issues of self-determination and selective authenticity, some participants repeatedly emphasized the point that when they drew their shapes they experienced in part strong emotions, and time and again quite surprising outlines emerged on the paper. Subconscious or semi-conscious contexts were uncovered in this way. In many cases, particularly with non-adult learners, this procedure has been accompanied variously by painful emotions because it exposed desires of group belonging or positions of being placed on the outside of the group. The inner dynamic of the exercise forced learners into momentary undesired public exposure.

(4) It was argued that the space granted to the individuals for determining events themselves is enlarged only by an insignificant amount if at the beginning of the exercise it is explained to them. With regard to the iceberg thesis, it is not always possible to determine or steer the dynamic of an exercise which forces participants into self-discovery. Apart from the dynamics of the task, the situation in which it was undertaken (for example: peer pressure in the classroom, uncertainty whether participation in the task was part of general grading by the teacher), and the perception of how learners should become engaged in it, exerted considerable pressure on a number of participants. They felt forced to work through it even if they experienced a strong resistance towards disclosing aspects of their personality.

The problem with many of these tasks emerges not just through the painful feelings which are the residue for some learners because there is neither time nor opportunity at school to process or attend to them. The fourth criterion therefore asks how near to the learners the teacher herself wishes to be, in order to take a critical look at the feelings and experiences set in motion by her tasks.

3.4.5 Criterion 5: Motivation – resistance

Closely connected with the above is the criterion of motivation and resistance. There is at the root of most communicative tasks the Gestalt therapeutic assumption of a general willingness of learners to communicate. This is attributed to the motivational power of learning about oneself. As a result these tasks seem to imply a learner who can be guided by the teacher into the unknown areas of self-discovery. It can, beyond any doubt, be argued that many of the tasks possess a high degree of communicative potential because they open up new ways of self-experience for the learner and this has a significant effect on the motivation of the individual learner or the whole class. We would say that proponents of humanistic approaches, and – *cum grano salis* – authors of resource books, tend to overlook, however, the possibility of learner resistance to such activities. Learners will invest effort in any communicative task, if they expect benefit from it.

> This benefit will continually vary between a sense of real progress in the language to the maintenance of self-esteem in an evaluative milieu such as a classroom. If a task confronts a learner with psychological and social uncertainty or disequilibrium, that learner will endeavor to reduce the uncertainty and restore personal equilibrium by whatever means possible.
>
> (Breen 1987a, p. 39)

One such means is resistance. We should not understand this as resistance to learning, rather, it needs to be seen as fulfilling a justified and necessary protective function against intrusions by the teacher and fellow learners into intimate and private domains. Moreover, resistance may be an expression of insecurity and anxiety, particularly in classes under conditions of mandatory schooling which are formed on an involuntary basis and thus determined by unavoidable, institutional rivalries and competition. Resistance can be the legitimate attempt to counteract the threat of personal destabilization.

Moskowitz only implicitly addresses the concept of resistance when she proposes the use of lower risk activities at the beginning. Low-risk topics would be *Something I am glad happened* or *What I like about myself* (Moskowitz 1978, p. 27), whereas high-risk activities would focus on *Something I wish had never happened* or *What I dislike about myself* (ibid.). As a way of overcoming resistance, she proposes that one should concentrate exclusively on positive aspects of learning about oneself (ibid., p. 25). Quite apart from the fact that the notion 'positive' would be understood subjectively in all manner of ways, this proposal is in sharp contradiction to her concept of authentic self-disclosure. This is because, if we are to take it seriously, it would necessarily include aggressive, anxiety-ridden and even injurious responses, as Frank and Rinvolucri (1983, p. 51) quite rightly point out.

For these reasons Moskowitz's task 'How strong I am' (Moskowitz 1978, p. 87), classified as a low-risk activity in which learners describe their own strengths, give feedback to each other and receive feedback on their comments, caused considerable unease among several groups of learners in the upper classes at German high schools although the students were used to working together in an atmosphere of trust. Their rejection stemmed from three areas:

(1) They were embarrassed and felt ashamed when they were asked to praise themselves in public.

(2) Several members of the class were afraid to appear as over-enthusiastic pupils or looking as if they were currying favour with the teacher.

(3) Many learners were afraid that those in the group with whom they had an uneasy or negative relationship would make sarcastic remarks.

What Moskowitz classifies as a 'low-risk activity', was felt, in fact, to be quite risky by most groups of learners in a German high school and university context. The overall effect of the activity was not only demotivating, it created considerable resistance against similar kinds of 'psycho-tasks'.

Likewise, Rinvolucri avoids the problem of resistance by trusting instead in the ability of learners to indulge in self-censorship: 'Censorship can, does and must operate in this kind of exercise. If self-censorship did not operate naturally, such exercises would be dynamite' (Rinvolucri 1982, p. 55). By neglecting the problem of resistance and placing one's trust instead in the motivational quality of these tasks, the tendency of the teacher to make the learner the object of a form of pseudo-therapy is once more underlined. There is a bias in this attitude towards coercion to communicate as the following statement makes clear: 'What we are after is building a climate of trust where it is safe to share. The many personal benefits that can result from using affective exercises are possible only if sharing takes place. This means that students must [sic!] share themselves: their feelings, experiences, interests, memories, day-dreams, fantasies' (Moskowitz 1978, p. 27).

Whenever teachers work with communicative tasks which activate experience and stimulate self-discovery they have to expect resistance as a legitimate and justifiable form of behaviour from the learner. It should not be forgotten, children as well as adults are resistant and defensive for good and healthy reasons. 'They must do what they can to take care of themselves, to remain protected against intrusion' (Oaklander 1978, p. 198) and destabilization. Resistance, however, cannot always be anticipated. One reliable way of finding out is for the teachers to check out themselves whether they are prepared to do what they are asking of their learners: would they disclose to others their ideas for the future, act out a pantomime, meditate with their eyes closed, engage in a conversation using a fantasy language with a partner, talk about their feelings as a child, etc.? Finally they should ask themselves if they are prepared and capable of not acting repressively, should resistance occur. Are they able to help learners take on the risk of going into unknown, but potentially highly motivating areas? The fifth criterion, therefore, underscores the need for the teacher to recognize any potential resistance and to be aware of ways of coping with it.

3.4.6 Criterion 6: Language – learner needs and discoursal outcomes

Here we are concerned with what functional language and means of expression a learner must have in order to participate productively in a communicative task. It certainly is a matter of some surprise that most of the resource books offering communicative tasks for language learning avoid the issue of language altogether or address it in a very unsatisfactory manner. Those which do take it into consideration refer almost exclusively to grammatical targets ('to practise the past tense') or to very general word-field areas ('to practise the vocabulary of adjectives'). In some cases vague indications of skill areas are given ('practise writing'). For this reason, teachers will need to look at them very carefully, if only to consider (after sequencing them according to notional categories as mentioned in criterion 1) language function and vocabulary. They will need to be clear about the learners' level of competence and their language needs.

Of course, it is part and parcel of openly-framed, learner-centred tasks that it is not possible to predict their discoursal outcomes and thus define the exact language needs of those who are undertaking them. In fact, there often is a disparity between what task designers/teachers intend or hope learners should achieve, and what learners actually derive from a particular task (Wright 1987b). This fundamental discrepancy not only derives from the fact that any task-as-workplan will be reinterpreted by learners on the basis of their prior knowledge and learning experiences, and thus be changed into a task-in-process (Breen 1987a). In a communicative task, learners will also mobilize their views of the world, their personal values and own experience content. This, in turn, might create new and unforeseen needs for text input, language functions and vocabulary.

However, the essential unpredictability of both learner needs and discoursal outcomes does not relieve the teacher from addressing the language issue when selecting or designing communicative tasks. If the teacher omits to do this it could lead to considerable frustration and demotivation when learners try, and subsequently fail, to communicate after intensive personal investment and group activity. What can also happen is that instead of using the target language they all slip constantly into their native language. On the positive side, countless tests have shown that learners who have reached the limits of their ability to communicate in the foreign language are ready and willing to absorb new language whenever they have something worth communicating and know how and where to find help to bridge the language gap (Kramsch 1984). This is because they experience reassurance and satisfaction when they undertake achievable investigative work (Seletzky 1989).

Whereas language needs are quite unpredictable in some areas, they can be defined more clearly in others, namely for purposes of task management and completion. Any task, when undertaken in pair or group formations, requires metacommunicative activities, by means of which learners negotiate their interpretation of its content, objectives, expected outcomes and procedures. Furthermore, such discourse can include learner contributions to task evaluation prior to its execution and after its completion. None of the resource books seem to be aware of this potential for genuine and communicative language-learning activities.

The above leads to the following questions, on which the sixth criterion focuses:

(1) To what extent can learner contributions to content areas inherent in tasks-as-workplan be predicted, and what notional and functional language needs might arise for the successful realization of such contributions?

(2) Can learners satisfy these needs on the basis of what they already know? Do they require additional input or even training prior to undertaking the tasks?

(3) Do learners have access to information and content materials to accommodate newly arisen content and language needs?

(4) Have learners acquired the necessary self-access skills to resort to these materials successfully without the help of the teacher, or do they require additional teacher guidance?

(5) Have learners acquired functional language to manage the task, negotiate its objectives and evaluate its outcome? Or should they be encouraged to rely on their mother tongues for such metacommunicative activities? (Functional areas of language would include giving information/explanation and asking for it, articulating resistance, asserting oneself, disagreeing with group members, etc.)

(6) Do learners have access to information materials or model texts where they could find help?

In addition to information materials and text models, the teacher herself functions as an important source of help. Most of the authors who write in this area (e.g. Moskowitz 1978, p. 29; Frank and Rinvolucri 1983, p. 9) refer quite appropriately to this essential role of the teacher, i.e. a person who is flexible and a source of expertise in the target language. However, in view of the complex nature of communicative tasks, learners may need more than the teacher's linguistic competence. Rather, they need to learn how to structure and pursue their own learning within the parameters of particular tasks. Teacher guidance and learner autonomy are two inseparable components of a task-based language classroom.

As far as the issue of language is concerned, there remains an additional problem with resource books. None of them offers useful indications of levels of proficiency and language progression at which the activities would be appropriate. The guidance given to teachers (e.g.: *all levels, intermediate, advanced*) is not only vague, it is quite often misleading. Because the bulk of tasks, especially those deriving from US contexts, were developed with adults in college language programmes and adult language schools in mind, the term *elementary* often cannot refer to beginning classes in schools. If content dimensions presuppose a knowledge of the world, which, for example, fifth-graders in school do not possess, tasks, which might be called elementary in linguistic terms, will qualify as fairly advanced in terms of content, values and concepts.

3.4.7 Criterion 7: Process relevance

Whereas the previous criterion seeks to make teachers aware of the tension between learners' linguistic needs and the predictability of discoursal outcomes generated by a task, we are here concerned with the role and impact of a particular task in terms of process continuity and learning development. This last criterion, therefore, relates communicative tasks to larger sequences of teaching and learning. Any task-as-workplan, even if it will be redesigned by learners' interpretations, will, because of its interventionist nature, influence the ensuing steps in the learning process.

Since the function of different task types in terms of their relevance for the whole teaching/learning process will be dealt with extensively in the following chapter, a few remarks shall suffice here. In chapter 4 we will argue that, although some tasks or types of tasks may have potentially limited application, others may have quite a range of possible functions within the learning process. For example, a *value clarification task* can open up a learning sequence, by mobilizing learner schemata, which will be used as a starting point for further investigation. At a later stage in the process, the same task could be used again, this time to assess the group's progress and determine what would require further investigation. This task could be used for a third time to conclude the learning sequence. At this stage the outcomes of its first and second application will be compared with its final results. Here, the task would have a retrospective and reflexive function. It is a tool of summative self-assessment and feedback.

Some of the basic questions to the teacher subsumed under the seventh criterion are:

(1) What do I expect this particular task to do and achieve for the individual learner, the group/s, and the teacher in process terms? How does it connect to what happened before it? How does it link to following activities?

(2) Is the process capacity of the task selected or offered in keeping with my understanding of what should happen during this task, and what should result from it? Or would it be more feasible to change the task or select a different one?

(3) Is the function of the task for example a prospective one? Is it to initiate a new learning sequence in which all the learners do the same, or will the group continue working multidirectionally?

(4) Is its process goal retrospective and reflexive in order to stimulate further research and learning? Should learners undertaking this task be challenged to summarize their experience in terms of knowledge gained, of how they exploited the group's potential in solving a problem, and use these insights as stepping stones into new, and expanded learning worlds?

(5) Or does the task define, frame or even redirect learner awareness and and activities by sensitizing them to deal with something new?

We will return to these questions in chapter 4.

3.5 The two premises: clarity and trust

Underlying the seven criteria for the selection and evaluation of communicative tasks in the language classroom are two premises: the premises of clarity and a learning climate of trust. As premises governing teachers' choices, decisions and implementation efforts, they precede the learning process. At the same time, however, they depend entirely on the dynamics of the learning process for their practical realizations. In this respect, they are indispensable goals which have to be constantly re-established and worked for in any communicative classroom.

Engaging learners in communicative encounters, especially if their aim is to explore emotional content and experiences, can become too bound up in itself unless this activity also reaches an evaluation stage. Trying to understand what has happened while undertaking a particular task, why it was suggested by the teacher, and contributing actively to the evaluation of learning arrangements, sequences, resources and input materials by means of reflection and meta-communicative discourse – all these are considered indispensable forms of learner activities in CLT.

Three main reasons are put forward in support of this view. The first is *educational* in orientation because it links the growing capacity to communicate with others in a foreign language to a growth in self-confidence and self-determination. The language classroom, in this respect, is contributory to the development of a democratic society (Piepho 1974; 1979; Breen and Candlin 1980; Dietrich 1979b; Oskarsson 1984). The second reason is related to *experience and learning*, and finds backing from extensive research, which shows that the reflection on both knowledge and learning leads to heightened 'cognitive sensibility' which in turn will have a significant impact on new cycles of experiential learning. Working through or processing knowledge and experience from the distance of a reflective position can then be referred back to everyday situations and knowledge about the world, which includes the world of learning (Kohonen 1987; 1989; Prokop 1990). The third reason, finally, is supported by insights into *language acquisition* under the specific conditions of a classroom situation. Here the argument emphasizes the culture of the classroom as a jointly constructed world (Breen 1985a). The very process of its construction renders an authentic communicative situation, which when used systematically will enlarge the field for communicative encounters in the classroom, and thus help language acquisition (cf. above 2.2, below 7.3 and Martin 1985; Kramsch 1984).

Most of the resource books leave at best the reasoning for undertaking a particular task and the way it is implemented to the teachers, who are implicitly empowered with a bag of magic devices for a humanistic classroom they can control. Where, on the other hand, the need for some reflective distance is seen – as in Moskowitz (1978) – learner activities are rather limited. She suggests that the purpose of a humanistic task should be explained to learners at the outset, and continues:

> At the close of an exercise, students are asked what they learned from the activity and/or feelings or reactions they would like to share about the activity with the total class. This is called processing the activity; it is a very important phase in the learning and should not be overlooked. In this phase, students share insights they've gained about themselves and about the group or class and any feelings they've experienced. You can then summarize the purpose and the learnings for the class.
>
> (Moskowitz 1978, p. 33)

There are, however, no suggestions as to how the potentially difficult processing of the activity is to be conducted in the L2, unless we are to imply that learners resort to their mother tongue. They need to have acquired means of expression for example in order to make evaluations in the target language. This raises the question once again of what they need to know and what level of proficiency they must have reached before embarking on an activity.

Moskowitz also limits the reflective phase to the knowledge brought to light by the activity and the experience which has been activated by it, leaving unconsidered the relationship of these experiences to the objects of the teaching, such as texts dealing with the culture or aspects of communication, language and learning. In order to maintain the dynamic balance of all four components of interaction one needs to ensure that the introductory explanations and the work of the reflective phase make the purposes of a task transparent, as well as help to evaluate its potential/real outcomes with regard to the four components: to the *I*, *we*, the *theme* and the *interactive process* through which the social world of the classroom is jointly constructed.

While only a few of the authors emphasize the relevance of clarity, all of them attach importance to the social-affective learning climate which must be 'positive, caring, supportive, and growth-promoting' (Canfield and Wells 1976, p. xv). Moskowitz characterizes it as 'A climate of acceptance ... warm, supportive, accepting and non-threatening' (Moskowitz 1978, p. 24) and Frank and Rinvolucri (1983, p. 9) state: 'Real communication can only take place in a relaxed atmosphere of mutual trust and confidence.'

However, it is consistent with their primarily interventionist and teacher-centred view of learning, that the creation and maintenance of the learning climate is not seen to result from cooperative effort and discussion. Only Canfield and Wells (1976, p. 5) want to include the learner as a partner in the planning process and as a responsible co-producer of his learning environment:

> We must strive for a natural, human, democratic relationship. This means involving students from the beginning in creating the environment. They must help in decision-making about the physical setting (the arrangement of the room, care for equipment, bulletin boards, etc.). Students must also be involved in planning the academic environment. This includes decisions about contents, sequence of activities, even methods of study. This must take place within the limits defined by school district policies, of course, but these too must be openly acknowledged and confronted.

The other authors also recognize the contribution of learners to the social affective climate but they place it in a subordinate position to the leadership function of the teacher. Once more, learners are in danger of becoming pawns in the teacher's strategy to improve the learning climate without their having an opportunity to make this task their own. The lack of clarity, therefore, corresponds to a lack of opportunities for co-determination directed towards the creation of space for learning about oneself. Choosing for oneself to become involved, without being persuaded or manipulated to do so, in activities where the outcome is uncertain requires learners to be clear as to how these learning procedures will unfold. Only when they *are*, can they be expected to place their trust in the teacher whenever she introduces guided tasks for self-disclosure through talking about one's dreams, hopes, fantasies or feelings. The security which is supposed to arise from a positive social-affective climate, granting each learner a quite personal 'life space' in which neither the teacher nor fellow learners may intrude, will remain questionable unless this security has come out of collective negotiation and co-determination. Part of this joint endeavour will also involve the collective agreement on rules of behaviour such as the ones Cohn has outlined. She sees them as supportive rules (*Hilfsregeln*), which need to be redesigned by and for each new group.

- Only represent yourself through your statements; use 'I' and not 'we' or 'one'.
- Be sparing in the use of generalizations.
- Only one at a time.
- Be authentic and selective in your contributions. Become aware of what you think, feel and believe. Think it over, before you decide to speak or act.
- Avoid false questions. Instead make direct statements.
- Avoid interpreting other people's motives. Instead, record your reactions to what you experience through this person.

(Cohn 1975, p. 124)

Moskowitz (1978, pp. 31–2), on the other hand, has teachers introduce three basic rules:

- Everyone gets listened to. We will listen to everyone in our group as each speaks.
- No put-downs. . . . We will not tease or laugh at anyone who shares.
- Passing. If you have reason for not wanting to respond to a particular question or to share an experience for a certain exercise, when it's your turn you can pass. Everyone will respect your right to do this and no one will ask you why.

If the climate is created here as the result of a cooperative effort this does not in any way mean that the teacher's role is diminished. She still retains, among others, the responsibility to initiate and frame the communication process.

The social-affective climate arises as a result of the individual behaviour of all those participants in the learning process, and is an expression of their relationships. Even in a school context these could take on characteristics of partnership, caring and cooperative responsibility. It must not be overlooked, however, that such qualities not least depend on the clarity among participants about the fundamental asymmetry of roles, which distinguish any evaluative and institutional learning milieu. Even from a 'partner-like' position as 'counsellor' or 'adviser', teachers in state schools retain the responsibility and power of grading, which represents the societal need for achievement ratification and creditation for future careers. Just 'forgetting the typical teacher role', as Frank and Rinvolucri (1983, p. 9) suggest, does certainly not lead to a real improvement of the learning climate. Rather, it could produce pitfalls in relationships and generate a new form of alienation: the alienation of learners from their teacher.

In company with a long tradition of research into motivation in modern-language teaching (Solmecke 1976; 1983), we need to point out that sensitive teachers have always recognized the importance and significance of tensions, anxieties and other emotions in second-language acquisition. They have either intuitively or consciously tried to create situations which allow learners to move from the security of their mother tongue to the disquieting experience of partial aphasia and restricted communication in the target language. The influence of communicative language-teaching methodology, and the various alternative methods which emphasize affective and interactive dimensions, have made themselves felt, however. Discussion of these issues in the literature indicate increased attention on the socioaffective component (Taylor 1983; Solmecke 1983; Rivers 1983; Puchta and Schratz 1984).

By taking into account the two fundamental premises of clarity and trust and by applying the criteria which we have spelled out, communicative tasks, especially those generated by humanistic approaches, could have a major influence in the communicative classroom. They could have the effect of activating learners in several ways by increasing their receptivity, releasing a willingness towards self-investment and communication, and promoting response-ability and responsibility. As such they could function as communicative tasks in a genuine sense. In the following chapter we will therefore take a closer look at a variety of these tasks in action. However, tasks alone do not guarantee the realization of a communicative classroom. The need is – as we will argue in chapter 5 – the larger framework of projects in which they can enfold their inherent potential for learning through communication.

Note

1. The following is only a representative selection of such techniques most of which have already gone through some adaptation from therapy to educational settings: Stevens 1971 *Awareness. Exploring, Experimenting, Experiencing;* Lewis et al. 1970 *Growth games. How to Tune Yourself, Your Family, Your Friends;* Canfield 1976 *100 Ways to Enhance Self-Concept in the Classroom;* Remocker 1977 *Action Speaks Louder. A Handbook of Non-Verbal Group Techniques;* Johnson 1972 *Reaching out. Interpersonal Effectiveness and Self-Actualization;* Schrank 1972 *Teaching Human Beings.*

   The following books show the transition from therapeutic work to education quite clearly: Hendricks et al. 1975 *The Centering Book. Awareness Activities for Children, Parents, and Teachers;* 1975 *The Second Centering Book. More Awareness Activities for Children, Parents, and Teachers.* The chapter headlines to the collection of activities indicate the programme (*Relaxing the Mind, Expanding Perception, Relaxing the Body, Working with Dreams, Teaching with Fantasy,* etc.).

   Polomares and Ball 1977, 1980 have developed a complete curriculum for affective and interpersonal learning, which attempts to systematize hundreds of these activities. *Innerchange* is the most well-known programme of this kind (Ball 1977).

   A specific sub-group of humanistic techniques became known under the heading of *Value Clarification Activities,* which aim at personalizing learners' views towards cognitive content to be learnt. Howe and Howe 1975 *Personalizing Education. Value Clarification and Beyond;* Casteel and Stahl 1975 *Value Clarification in the Classroom. A Primer.*

   Quite a number of these collections of activities were translated into major European languages or were heavily exploited for new resource books in various national languages. In West Germany for example,

Stevens and Lewis' selections of activities appeared in the early 1970s. In 1981 Vopel presented four volumes of *Interaktionsspiele für Jugendliche* (Interaction Games for Young People) and a *Handbuch für Trainer*, which are massive compilations of the Anglo-American sources with a few original contributions.

4 Building bricks:
communicative learning tasks

4.1 Task-based language learning and exercise typologies

We now turn our attention to tasks themselves. Any teacher nowadays interested in broadening her repertoire of communicative tasks has a wide range of publications to choose from. There has been a proliferation of supplementary books offering games, problem-solving or information-gap activities, role-plays, simulations or scenarios to meet the demand for a vehicle for communication in the classroom (Moskowitz 1978; Frank et al. 1982; Maley and Duff 1982; Klippel 1984; Christison and Bassano 1987a, 1987b; Di Pietro 1987; Pattison 1987). Although these resource books seem to meet an apparent demand from language teachers we would doubt in company with Solmecke (1984) whether they have really led to changes in the classroom learning process itself. Our suspicion is that these tasks are predominantly used as 'fillers' without connection or relevance to a theme or the 'really serious' part of the curriculum. This suspicion finds support not only from the very nature of these publications as a form of recipe book, but also more importantly from an apparent and interesting dichotomy. The growth in resource books for communicative activities over the last ten years has not been paralleled by any kind of conclusive or encompassing debate on task-based learning. The discussion which demonstrates that tasks 'serve as compelling and appropriate means for realizing certain characteristic principles of communicative language teaching and learning' (Candlin 1987) has only just begun (Candlin and Murphy 1987); Kramsch 1984; Puchta and Schratz 1984; Legutke 1988a) and has so far largely remained programmatic (Candlin 1987) and issue-raising (Breen 1987a). Nunan (1989), however, has broadened the debate by providing an overview of how the term 'task' may be applied to existing course materials. His analysis looks at communicative tasks from the perspective of grading, sequencing and designing, together with the wider considerations for teachers of syllabus design and teacher/learner roles. In doing so he suggests a more central role for communicative tasks, whereby they could be the starting point for a teacher's workplan, and that the syllabus specification, which would be the conventional starting point for the task choice, could act as a checklist. 'The course designer/material writer's task is thus to carry out a delicate juggling act between the various curriculum components, including sets of syllabus specifications, task and activity types, texts and input data' (Nunan 1989, p. 19). One of the crucial issues in this discussion is that the outcomes of tasks are not easy to predict and too frequently give rise to dissatisfaction on the part of teacher and learner (Breen 1987a). There are many possible reasons for these shortcomings. Our discussion above (see chapter 3), for example, underscores the importance for teachers to apply a clear set of criteria when selecting tasks, to be mindful that many tasks have outcomes which relate to areas outside language teaching, and to make tasks relevant to the underlying theme of the learning. Breen also makes the crucial point that the learner's 'agenda' and his perception of a task can be markedly different to the teacher's. He further notes that tasks are, 'by definition, an intervention upon personal approaches to learning and personal concepts of what language learning is like'. The teacher needs, therefore, to take into account 'the affective involvement' of learners when selecting, adapting or designing tasks for the classroom. Breen summarizes the role of the teacher as task designer as follows:

> . . . the task designer has to enter into a 'dialogue' with language learners
> for whom the tasks are being planned. Such a dialogue cannot take the
> form of some diffuse negotiation about what learners think they like, but
> will be a careful *cycle* of initial awareness-raising tasks concerning the
> learners' own purposes in learning the language, learners' background
> knowledge, their own preferred ways of working, their views on the 'best'
> uses to which the classroom can be put, and their interests, motivations
> and attitudes in relation to learning the language. This cycle could be
> maintained through the direct involvement of learners in the *evaluation* of
> tasks.
>
> (Breen 1987a, p. 43)

The course of action which Breen outlines here not only raises the issue of how learners and teachers change traditional perceptions of their roles (Nunan 1989a, pp. 79–95), but, and more immediately, of where materials to support and mediate this new dialogue can be found. For if teachers are going to enter into a process of negotiation with learners, they will need to be able to draw on and adapt the available stock of tasks or devise new ones in order to facilitate awareness-raising, learner-interactive skill development, information exchange, comprehension and exploration of content, and task/

learning process evaluation. Our purpose in this chapter is, therefore, to present a typology of tasks which will provide the teacher with a framework for decision-making and selection and offer guidelines for task deployment.

The typology is heuristic because its scope is not meant to be exhaustive or comprehensive. Moreover, it offers working categories which are open to continued development, practical experimentation and the critical reflection of the user. The examples we have used are taken from classroom practice, and where we have made compromises in the level of detail provided, we have done so in order to focus on useful and practical generalizations. The typology also relates directly to the model of interactive potential in the classroom described earlier. It proposes a way of systematizing various ways of exploiting this potential. In so doing, it does not seek to replace any existing exercise typologies of the communicative classroom (see e.g. Candlin 1981; Neuner et al. 1981; Sexton and Williams 1984), but complement what they have to offer.

Any exercise typology is an organizational construct, an attempt to create clarity and order. It is, as Candlin (1987) says a 'managerial convenience', a way of helping us to understand the complexities of learning processes and to make them available for the classroom. The danger is, of course, that, when tasks are categorized, complex phenomena are sometimes forced into boxes into which they do not fit. There are areas of overlap of function and design. This is to some extent inevitable, but it underlines the point nevertheless that it is both sensible and necessary to combine different types of tasks. Another difficulty which arises when allocating tasks within a typology is that tasks of the same type fulfil different functions. Here the responsibility lies with the teacher in matching her knowledge of what the tasks are capable of with the needs of the learners.

The labels we have given to the task categories relate to both *what* they do, e.g. awareness-raising, and *how* they function, e.g. role-playing. Here again the rigour of description throws up problems of overlap of function which prevent systematizing under one heading or the other. Likewise attempts to systematize tasks according to phases in lessons are also unsuccessful, as are those which try to categorize tasks according to the skills upon which they are supposed to focus. This is because they integrate a multitude of skills of a linguistic and social nature by dint of their communicative character. We would also suggest that organizing tasks according to lexical, functional, or grammatical categories is equally unhelpful. We are not proposing that such formal aspects of the language do not play an essential role in these tasks, but they are secondary and ordered according to their *content*. They become significant because of their *communicative* character, serving as they do in this sense another purpose than that of formal language training.

It is important also to point out, that the order in which the tasks appear does not imply any necessary increase in complexity. Neither does it imply a grading in the length of time they take, nor in the degree of difficulty they present. Just as complex learning processes cannot be represented in a linear fashion, neither can the activities which reveal them.

A number of the examples we have chosen to illustrate the typology have been taken from Humanistic Approaches, Confluent Education and from Gestalt therapy. Their particular form and function, however, is a result of a critical process of adaptation arising out of a conscious eclecticism on our part (Scovel 1983). Ideas from these sources were taken up and modified according to the criteria and premises of classroom practice. In some cases it is no longer possible to identify their origin, not least because we have found, like others, that we have been able to devise our own activities and exercises, the more we have adapted and amended standard formats. For this reason we only acknowledge sources which we have taken over directly. We also need to add that the typology goes beyond the experience-activating exercises of the Humanistic Approaches, by integrating in part activities taken from didactic games which have a language-teaching orientation. Whatever the origin of the activity we have tried to show how it relates to the overall programme of teaching and how it or teachers' own derivative versions can be exploited and integrated into a superordinate learning scheme. It is not our intention to contribute to the list of available supplementary material.

The tasks are in the following sequence:

(1) trust-building and relaxation;
(2) awareness and sensitivity training;
(3) information-sharing activities;
(4) thinking strategies and problem-solving;
(5) imagination-gap, fantasy and creative expression;
(6) role-playing and creative dramatics;
(7) interaction and interpersonality;
(8) values clarification and discussion;
(9) process evaluation.

4.2 Communicative learning tasks

4.2.1 Trust-building activities and relaxation exercises (see also interaction and personality)

One of the most significant contributions of the humanist movement to classroom learning is its emphasis on the importance of a positive learning climate (see 3.5). A classroom atmosphere in which learners receive constant encouragement and support and are granted 'space' (Stevick 1980) in which to explore themes is in humanist terms a precondition for effective learning. In such an environment language learners in particular can develop the ability to take risks and experiment with the target language. There are several factors which can contribute to the creation of a positive learning climate. They include the forms of learning undertaken, the amount of 'space' granted to the learner, the choice and techniques of exploitation of materials and the nature of interpersonal relationships within the classroom. For task-based classrooms the latter is of particular importance. The self-confidence of the individual learner and trust both in other learners and the teacher is essential because classroom procedures demand of the learner flexibility, cooperation, a willingness to learn in different group formations and the ability to accept increasing responsibility for his/her own learning. Building the groundswell of trust to work in this way depends on various complex factors, e.g. the attitude and behaviour of the teacher, the character of the group, etc. It is beyond the capacity of any one task to achieve this end. It is the case, as this chapter will show, that trust and cooperation are products of the cumulative effect of a series of communicative tasks. Nevertheless, tasks can be deployed to focus specifically on the aim of trust-building and it is particularly important that such tasks are utilized at the outset of a course so that patterns of interpersonal behaviour are established very quickly. Two factors common to these tasks are:

– the free exchange of personal information;
– the involvement of all the participants including the teacher.

Initial course tasks, commonly known as 'openers' or 'ice-breakers', are typically employed in the communicative classroom to begin the process of trust-building:

Example 1: 'Find someone who'

Step 1: The learners are asked to move the furniture to clear a space in which the group can stand and circulate.

Step 2: They are given a work-sheet containing a series of personally-oriented questions:

FIND SOMEONE WHO:

chews chewing gum: _____

has been to France: _____

can recite the alphabet in under 10 seconds: _____

has got more than three brothers or sisters: _____

can tell a joke in English: _____

has flown in a helicopter: _____

believes in ghosts: _____

goes jogging: _____

Step 3: The group circulates to allow everyone to ask questions and find out about the people in the group.

Step 4: According to the level of the class, learners exchange information about names or relate the most interesting and amusing stories they had collected during the activity.

This activity is typically used during the very first meeting of a new group to introduce learners to one another. It functions by inviting participants to divulge interesting but non-threatening information about themselves in a stimulating way. It is successful because all the participants are equally affected and involved, including the teacher. It also demonstrates to the group the wide range of backgrounds and experience available as a resource for their future work together.

Example 2: The profile task

A task which serves the same purpose as the 'Find someone who' example but which offers greater scope is the profile task.

Step 1: Learners are invited to clear the furniture to allow the group to circulate around the room.

Step 2: Each participant is given a sheet of paper with different

questions on it which they put to each of the other members of the
group. The type of questions used are:

– Which famous person would you like to be?
– What do you normally eat for breakfast?
– How do you relax?
– Where did you spend your last summer holiday?
– What would be your dream car?
– What star sign were you born under?

Step 3: After they have collected answers from all the other members
of the group, the teacher gives each learner a sheet containing all the
questions. They already have the answer to the one question which
they asked. They now have to circulate again and ask the others for
the answers to the remaining questions for the person whose name is
at the top of the sheet.

Step 4: When they have completed the second round of questioning,
they have in their possession a list of information about another
member of the group. Their task now is to write a profile of the
person based on the information ready for the next lesson (see fig. 4.1).

Step 5: At the beginning of the next lesson they are invited to display
their 'profile' texts on the class noticeboard and to circulate and read
the 'life story' of the group.

It is in the data collection phase of this task that the ice-breaking
element of example 1 is replicated. However, the second phase of
the task introduces the dimension of trust-building, since each
member is invited to be creative and to interpret information about
someone they have only just met. The intervention and participation
of the teacher is important here because at this stage groups rely on
the teacher to determine the tone of the piece of writing. A useful
additional aid during the execution of this task is a camera to take
snapshots of the group, which are then pinned up next to the profile
text.

Example 3: 'Autobiography'

The following example was designed and used with intermediate
learners in a high-school situation, (see also Canfield and Wells
1976; pp. 27, 33) in connection with the theme 'Growing Up'. (The
main text for this course was Salinger's *The Catcher in the Rye*. Since
it is of value to show the relationship of tasks to the learning process
as a whole, this example is one of several taken from the same series

N from Japan !

Because she loves her pillow, she wakes up
very late. Her appetite is massive even
in the morning, so she needs to have boilded
rice, miso soup, grilled fish, eggs... .

When she's grown up, she wants to be a singer,
actress or comedian. I don't know why. This
sounds like she hasn't grown up yet, well actually
she has, but I don't know how old she is exactly.
I heard she's older than I by one year. I'm 21.
So if you good at math, you can work it out.

If you think that you're short - tempered, I suggest
you should not have a fight against her, because
she thinks she is, as well. You'd better not try it !

In her opinion, Switzerland, W. Germany and
England are similar to her country 'Japan'.
She loves these countries. She's been there several
times. Therefore she wants to live there in new
future with a strong man who takes care of her
like "Super man", it possible.

Figure 4.1 A profile of N by a fellow student

of classes.) The task is not an ice-breaker in the sense that examples
1 and 2 are, since it is an extended task with many facets. However it
demonstrates how trust-building commences with some form of ice-
breaking procedure before moving on to foster the development of
new insights for the participants involved into their interpersonal
behaviour.

Background: All teachers are familiar with the inhibited way in which
learners tend to behave at the beginning of a course. As part of the
process of dismantling these inhibitions a homework task was set at

the end of the first lesson. The learners were asked to write down their *personal life-lines* on a piece of A4 paper placed horizontally, i.e. to note down in more or less chronological order as many key points or important moments in their life, as in for example:

born	*learned to walk*	*sister born*	*moved to a new house*
1971	1973	1974	1983

The teacher pointed out that a useful way of starting was to collect as much information as possible in an unstructured way. Learners were able to use photograph albums, diaries, etc. to recall key events. The focus of the task here was to try and regenerate the feelings and emotions which they associated with those events. It was not necessary to show one's personal life line either to the teacher or to the other learners. However, the teacher insisted that they all complete the task because it constituted for each individual a personalized introduction to the theme. At the same time each participant would be able to establish to what extent he was able to relate and reproduce events of particular personal importance in the target language. In order to carry out the task learners were told that they could utilize dictionaries, previous textbooks, vocabulary lists, etc. for any language data they needed.

Autobiography – a case study

Step 1: Rearranging. At the beginning of the lesson the teacher explained that communicating required an arrangement of the room which promoted communication, in other words flexible groupings and seating arrangements. Therefore a circular arrangement was chosen for the first full lesson (*circle session*). At the end of the lesson the group reflected upon the function and appropriacy of the circular form. (When learners are asked to sit in a circle there is a not unfamiliar tendency to react very unenthusiastically. They have normally 'found' their fixed seating arrangement for the course and getting up to move tables and chairs around again makes them feel insecure. Opposition is often audible from the noise they make moving desks around and the circle is more 'egg'-shaped than round, with one or two learners still not part of the new formation. Without the protection of the desks learners can become even more insecure and their tension becomes very noticeable.)

Step 2: Autobiographical sharing (circle session). After the formation of the circle the teacher asked the learners to check that they knew everyone's names. A few exchanged names and the atmosphere was eased a little. One of the group, Werner, who joined the circle very reluctantly, refused to speak English and asked one of the girls her name in German. Werner was clearly demonstrating some form of conflict. He was representative of the others in expressing his protest against doing things differently to what he was used to. At the same time it was a form of test for the teacher. The teacher brought the conflict out into the open without naming Werner directly. She explained that she understood how difficult it was to express personal needs in another language when it was just as easy to use one's own. However, that was one of the central aims of a language lesson, i.e. to learn to use language for one's own purposes. To play a game in English and to negotiate everything in English was like skiing. After summoning up the courage to push off down the slope, it could only get better and more enjoyable. All of them had had at least six and a half years English tuition and should have had enough courage to take the first step forward. One of the class, Christoph, spoke up in defence of the group. He explained that it was true that they had spent a long time learning English but they had only spoken it to the teacher and not amongst themselves. To do that would have been odd to say the least. The teacher was sympathetic to this argument, but nevertheless invited them to experiment with English for the whole of the double lesson and to exchange experiences afterwards in a review phase.

The learners were asked to recall their 'personal life-line' and to pace it out in their thoughts. The intention was that they should try to express the individual moments in a kind of inner monologue and at the same time try to put some shape and form to them. Afterwards each one had a minute to share with the others some details from his/her biography.

Someone was chosen to keep track of the time and to toss a coin to decide who was to start. Should anyone not want use up his/her minute, he/she could pass their turn on to the next person. At the end of a minute anyone wishing to finish the sentence he/she had started was able to do so. In the first few biographies facts seemed to dominate, e.g. sisters, brothers, new flat, own room, new motor-bike, etc. The English was awkward and there were mistakes with tenses, irregular verbs, and uncertainty with word order. However, the responses were indicative of the personal investment of learners. Sybille, for example, started like the others, but after about thirty seconds hesitated and searched for words, blushed and ran her hands through her hair. She looked down and announced before her minute was up, 'I didn't want to say it but I must say it. My grandfather died two years ago. I was very sad.' As she turned to Andreas, she was clearly relieved that he could take over from her. Yet everyone was affected for a moment by what she had said and Andreas could not bring himself to say what he had prepared. Only when Sybille encouraged him was he able to tell of a walk at night with his father on the cliffs in Brittany.

The last in the circle was Mark, a US citizen with a German background, who had only been in Germany for six months. He talked very quickly with a broad American accent. What he had to say was directed at the teacher and hardly any of his classmates were able to follow him. There was unease in the group, their faces reflecting their anxiety that he could set standards in the target language which were out of their reach. The teacher was pleased that he was joining the group because the whole class would be able to benefit from his competence in the language and his knowledge of the culture. In the ensuing weeks his particular task was to make certain that the other group members could understand him without his feeling that he had to make any concessions in the way he expressed himself. The teacher asked Mark to repeat what he had said but this time to check by means of eye contact that the others can follow him. He cooperated immediately, but found it difficult to make himself clear; he became muddled and had to start again several times. The rest of the group not only understood him a lot better but they noticed that, despite his ability in the language he found it just as difficult to communicate. The effect that this had on them was one of clear relief.

Step 3: Small group sharing. The next task consisted of sub-groups of four learners (wherever possible those who did not know each other) feeding back to each other what they had remembered from the biographies of the others and trying to find any common elements. Susanne asked if she might use her *personal life-line* for the group work. The others followed suit. Susanne had three pages of text with her *life-line* decorated with photos and sketches. All three pages had a border of carefully drawn flowers. She had spent hours doing it and now wished to show off what she had done. Several had produced similar work. At this point, the teacher deliberately attached herself to a group of three boys which included Werner. They had known each other since the beginning of their high-school days and within their clique had fixed roles and agreed behaviour patterns. Far from taking the opportunity in this phase to get to know each other better, they had withdrawn into the security of their group. It became clear that they were only talking English because her presence was forcing them to do so. What they had to say was mainly about the artificiality of the situation. Meanwhile the whole classroom was filled with the hubbub of the other groups, all of whom were talking in English. The noise was infectious and liberating at the same time so that even the reluctant three began to relax as they recounted the story of their friendship.

Step 4: Common experiences (circle session). Before returning to the circle each group was asked to select three common elements from their autobiographies which they could present to the others. Two groups performed very amusing presentations and everyone joined in the laughter. For that moment at least, English seemed to be accepted as a means of communication.

Step 5: Processing the activity. After five minutes the group gathered again in a circle. The teacher asked the learners to review the activity sequence and to comment on it, using the questions prepared by the teacher on an OHP. (This step in the procedure is referred to later in 4.2.9: process evaluation activities.)

They had clearly enjoyed *Autobiography*. The homework was seen as sensible language and thematic preparation for presentations about themselves in the target language which was something they had not done before. Although most of them felt distinctly uneasy at the beginning they felt that the change in the seating arrangement was a positive move. The majority also were in favour of the way in which the teacher had insisted on using the target language. Here as well, they emphasized the unusualness and novelty of the situation. They were quite obviously able to use the target language even in the reflection phase. The teacher decided not to comment on the correctness of language performance on this occasion but to complete a check-list of mistakes later from memory during a quiet work phase.

Step 6: Writing a short autobiography. The group reverted to the previous seating arrangement and each learner began writing a section of his/her autobiography. They were able to choose between an overview or a detailed account of a few events. They were to finish the task for homework and what they wrote became the first piece of work in their project book which could be further elaborated upon with pictures or drawings. They were asked to use a grammar book and to check their use of tenses before they wrote it up in their project books.

The above account is only a short synopsis of what was a complex interactive event arising out of the autobiography task. As an example of an exercise type, it demonstrates that success is crucially dependent on how it is set up and on how the teacher manages her interventions.

Summary

(1) The tasks allowed participants to experience themselves as individuals and the group in a new light by providing them with opportunities to talk about themselves. This experience would involve *inter alia* some decision-making with regard to the social relationships within the classroom, such as confidence and trust in the other participants.

(2) The aim of the 'Autobiography' task was, in particular, to create trust. It achieved this by facilitating the exchange of information, sharpening perceptions and by encouraging participants to listen to each other. Because the structure of the exercise and its targets were made clear and because the relationship to the theme had been created, the participants could determine for themselves the degree of information they wanted to impart and also predict the consequences of what they were doing. In this way the learners had the opportunity of distancing themselves whenever they wanted to.

(3) The tasks required an open classroom format and a flexible physical arrangement. They serve therefore to introduce learners to the notion of a new classroom convention which sanctions freedom of movement to allow task participants to communicate more easily.

(4) The teacher in all three tasks participated in the process as a 'participating manager' without coming into conflict with her role as a teacher. The involvement of the teacher in this way helps to create an acceptance of a new role for the teacher, namely as a participant.

(5) The advantages offered by such tasks are, however, dependent on the behaviour of the teacher. Specific skills are required to be able manage a learner-centred environment which provides space for learners, and demands of the teacher the awareness to know when to intervene.

(6) Since these tasks encourage learners to make frequent, extended

contributions in the target language, they also provide the teacher with the opportunity to make diagnostic evaluations of learner performance.

(7) Tasks of this type are also known as restructuring activities (Christison and Bassano 1981, p. xvi, 1–3) because they help to restructure the learning situation by promoting changes in learner behaviour and a qualitative change in the learning climate. In this sense they are forms of learner training for the communicative classroom. (For further exercises of this type see Christison and Bassano 1980, pp. 2–9; Canfield and Wells 1976, pp. 17–87.)

Relaxation exercises

Relaxation exercises contribute to the learning climate in the classroom by relaxing both learners and teacher physically and mentally. As classroom events they are exclusively teacher-led and as such are exercises which are of limited scope compared to the tasks described above. They function by tuning learners in, making them ready, awake and receptive to activities, by focusing their awareness. Simple exercises as outlined below are not only valuable at didactically critical points in the learning process. They are employed to maximum advantage at the beginning of a lesson as in the following contexts:

– listening concentration exercises	before a listening input;
– relaxed breathing exercises	before an imagination-gap activity;
– guided silence	before listening to a poem/after phases of intense activity;
– body relaxation	at the beginning of the lesson; prior to phases of activity; prior to a difficult grammar exercise.

The following example is a well-known body-relaxation exercise, taken from the standard repertoire of autogenic training.

Example 1: Talking to the body
Learners are asked to take up the most comfortable position they can find on their chairs and to make quite deliberate contact with the ground when they put their feet down. Checking against criterion 3 (see above) the teacher may ask the learners to close their eyes or not, then proceeds thus:

Now we are going to go through various parts of the body, telling each part to relax. You will be able to feel how that part of your body begins to relax. Now let your attention go to your feet [pause]. Tell your feet to relax [pause]. Tell your hands to relax [pause]. Tell your legs to relax [pause] ... Tell your face to relax [pause]. Tell your mind to relax [pause]. Just tell your whole body to relax. – Now I will count from ten to one, and as I do so, you will feel yourself becoming more awake and alert. Ten, nine, eight, seven, feel your body beginning to stir ... six, five, four, let your mind wake up ... three, two, one, wake up feeling rested and alert.

(Further exercises of this type can be found in Hendricks and Wills et al. 1975; Spaventa et al. 1980; Vopel 1981; Maley and Duff 1982).

Summary
(1) These exercises have an important function in helping learners switch from other activities, e.g. typically moving from other lessons into a language class, to a new focus.
(2) They help to develop powers of concentration.
(3) They contribute together with other activities (see below) to the importance of body awareness and relaxation in learners.
(4) Not every teacher will feel able to embark on pre-learning exercises with learners who are unused to them from other learning contexts. Such teachers will benefit from training and practice in these techniques.

4.2.2 Awareness and sensibility training

This category encompasses activities which increase the self-awareness of the learner by focusing on the role of the senses within language learning. They also illustrate the importance and the value of the individual's experience as potential input in the language lesson. As Oaklander (1978) points out, they open 'doors and windows' to new worlds by providing a new perspective on familiar things and making learners conscious of things which they might have forgotten. As far as classroom implementation is concerned they could be used as discrete activities in themselves or as part of more complex teaching sequences. They have much in common with other activities such as *imagination gap* and *creative expression activities* as well as *interaction and interpersonality* activities, in conjunction with which they can also be employed.

Sensual awareness
We include in this section any task which uses in a conscious way one or more of the senses as a medium of perception. The following examples are taken from classes with different types of learners.

Example 1: Listening with one's hands

This exercise was used with a high-school beginners' class aged between ten and twelve years who were working on the theme of 'Our Classroom'.

Step 1: Words. The class had been working on the vocabulary for all the items they needed for their day-to-day work in class. With the help of the text-book, a dictionary and the teacher, a list was drawn up and organized into a wordfield on the board. Pronunciation was practised and the words memorized as far as possible.

Step two: Talking things. The learners had access to the wordfield on the blackboard or on the OHP. Partner teams were formed. One of the partners closed his eyes and was led by the other. The learner entrusted with the role of leading had to make particularly sure that his 'blind' partner did not come into contact with anyone or anything. The 'blind' person was allowed to feel the shape of particular objects. The purpose of this activity was to 'see' the objects in the classroom with one's hands. The person who was being led identified and pronounced the names of the objects which his partner showed to him. After they had come in contact with five or six objects the team stopped. The person with his eyes shut whispered to his partner the words which he had 'heard': 'I heard: apple, sponge, window, chair, flower', etc. His 'sighted' partner then confirmed or corrected his responses as appropriate.

Step 3: The teams exchange roles. This exercise requires a high degree of trust among the participants.

The following sequence 'Seeing with one's ears, from soundtrack to film' preceded work on the film *The Graduate*. The information content of the film was decoded initially aurally. The learners then turned what they had heard into pictures and text.

Example 2: Seeing with one's ears
Step 1: Relaxation exercise from type one.

Step 2: Sound focusing directed by the teacher. In this exercise it is useful for participants to close their eyes if they had had previous preparation for doing so. The teacher tells the students: 'Listen to the sounds you can hear outside the room. – pause – Listen to the sounds you can hear outside the building. – pause – Listen to the sounds you can hear far away from here. – pause – Now, come back to this room. Listen to the sounds you can hear in the room. – pause – Become aware of the chair you are sitting on, slowly, open your eyes . . .'

Step 3: Sharing. Learners working in pairs exchanged what they had heard.

Step 4: From sound to film. Wherever possible, learners closed their eyes. The teacher outlined the following situation: 'You are in the cinema, there is no picture, only sound. I am going to make a series of sounds. What is happening in the film? What kind of film is it?' The teacher then made a series of noises to suggest the scene, e.g. banging a book on the desk, drumming with his fingers, biting into an apple, etc.

Step 5: Developing ideas for a film scene. Learners sketched out the scene individually for about five minutes and compared their work with partners. Some examples were discussed in an open forum with the class.

Step 6: From sound-track to film sequence. Learners at this point listened to two minutes of the sound-track of the film they were going to work with (*The Graduate*). They then noted down what they had heard on a grid in preparation for writing a film script. There were columns in the grid for the following points: field sizes/camera; angles/picture/dialogue/music/sound effects. Working in groups of four they discussed what pictures were appropriate to what they had heard.

Step 7: Viewing. Only at this stage did the learners see the complete sequence of sound and picture. They were now able to compare the images which they had created from the sound-track with the film itself. From this first sequence they then made inferences about the film as a whole: the type of film, plot, characters, position of the scene in the film as a whole, etc.

The next example 'Reading through sensory awareness: experiencing Shakespearean London' indicates possible ways of introducing an increased sensory awareness into work with texts. Here learners were encouraged to 'read' a text with their other senses. One can talk here also of listening with one's eyes or smelling with one's eyes. The reduction of sensory awareness in the reading process is fleetingly addressed and then picked up again when looking at the whole picture in a final group activity.

Example 3: Reading through sensory awareness: experiencing Shakespearean London

This was used with a post-intermediate group of high-school learners working on the theme 'Understanding English Drama – Shakespeare'.

Work began with a brainstorming phase to gather learners' reactions to a copperplate engraving of Shakespearean London. Next the learners were given a passage from the novel by Erica Jong, *Fanny* (1980, pp. 162–5) for homework. At the beginning of the second section of the novel, Fanny Hackabout Jones, still an innocent young girl from the country, becomes acquainted for the first time with the city of London. It is an experience which she registers primarily through her senses. The task for the learners was to react to the description in the novel as follows:

---

(1) Read this passage with your nose. Make notes of all the smells the heroine experiences during her first encounter with London.

(2) Read this passage with your ears. Make notes of all the sounds Fanny hears on her first encounter with London.

(3) While reading try and see London through Fanny's eyes. Take notes of what she sees.

(4) While reading try and identify with Fanny during her first encounter with London. Take notes of how Fanny feels.

In the following lesson sub-groups created a comprehensive picture of Fanny's experience of London using the evidence from their various reading tasks. At the same time they checked back with the picture shown on the copper engraving.

We also include in this category exercises which can deepen processes of understanding or negotiation of meaning with the help of body expression and body awareness. In this sense an essential means of communication and of mediating experience is the pantomime. Here are two examples:

Example 4(a): Body awareness
This activity was carried out with a post-intermediate class at high school working on 'Growing Up' and using as their base text the novel, *The Catcher in the Rye* by J. Salinger.

In the second chapter of the novel (Salinger 1958, pp. 11–19) Holden Caulfield describes his visit to old Spencer, his former history teacher, to say goodbye to him. Holden's ambivalent attitude in this situation is conveyed by the discrepancy between what he does and what he thinks and feels, which becomes significant for an overall interpretation of the novel. It is this ambivalence which is to be explored when the learners receive the following reading task:

> Try and become aware of Holden's body movements, gestures and facial expressions in this chapter. Imitate them while you are reading and examine what they are saying to you. Imagine that you are acting the part of Holden in a silent movie.

The next class work began with a mimed reconstruction of the chapter in short sections. Members of the class presented short mimes and, following the comments of the others, made adjustments and added words to the mime.

Example 4(b): Body awareness: square versus circle

Used with an advanced class of high-school learners working on the theme 'The First American. Understanding the Indian experience.'

The group were given extracts from the life story of the Oglala Sioux warrior and medicine man, Black Elk: *Black Elk Speaks* (Neihardt 1972), written by John G. Neihardt in the 1930s. In one of the extracts the old Indian warrior explains:

> I came to live here where I am now between Wounded Knee Creek and Grass Creek. Others came too, and we made these little grey houses of logs that you can see and they are square. It is a bad way to live, for there can be no power in the square.
>   You'll have noticed that everything an Indian does is in a circle, and that is because the power of the world always works in circles . . . .
> (Neihardt 1972, p. 164)

The group had difficulty in understanding what Black Elk meant, so they were asked to complete the following tasks:

Step 1: With their desks pushed to one side and their chairs forming a circle, the group sat quietly to see what it felt like to sit in a circle.

Step 2: The teacher then asked the learners to exchange thoughts and feelings. Here are some of their comments:

> There is no beginning and no end/nobody has a superior position/I could see everybody/togetherness/I felt warm/energy flow/we had the same central point/. . . .

Step 3: Then they changed the seating arrangement to form a square to see in turn what it felt like to sit in a square.

Step 4: Their comments were revealing:

> I couldn't see anybody/some are further away than others/I felt that

people at the corners were in control of the situation/the energy doesn't flow/it felt more like school/it reminded me of all the squares in school, everything is in squares here. In nature there aren't squares . . . .

Step 5: They looked at the text again, this time reading it quietly against the background of this new experience. When the reading was over, a lively conversation took place on the cyclical world picture of the Indians and on Black Elk's statement on the powerlessness of the square. They concluded by making a criticism of the school's architecture based on the dominance of squares in the classroom (blackboard, sponge, pictures, light switches, bottles of orange juice, roof panels and the wall sections).

For further exercises see Oaklander 1978, pp. 127ff; Maley and Duff 1982.

Activating experience

The task types of the first sub-group direct attention outwards, i.e. on objects, people or texts of various types. It is rather like inviting learners to switch on their radar and become aware of all there is to be discovered. In this second sub-category, however, *awareness activities* direct the attention of the learner inwards. Here it is more a question of looking and listening inwards to discover the richness of their own experiences. Tasks of this type serve to reactivate experiences from the lives of the learners and introduce them into the classroom. It is important to note at this point that this needs to be done with the criteria in mind we have referred to above. It is worth emphasizing that the purpose of these techniques is learning and not therapy (see 3.4).

The following example 'Utilizing personal memory banks: first day at school' shows how activating experience as an individual and group process is integrated into the exploration of an experience of another culture. At the same time it can act as an important element in the process of comprehension, moving from what is known and to what is new. It also illustrates that it is possible to achieve learner-centred, task-based work when working with poetry. The sequence is based on the hypothesis: 'the best way to learn how to read poetry is to learn how to write it'.

Example 1: Utilizing personal memory banks on first day at school (post-intermediate/12th grade German high school; theme: Poetry Workshop)

The learners had already had experience of a variety of creative and interactive approaches to poetry as developed in Legutke (1985),

Lach-Newinsky and Seletzky (1986), Maley and Moulding (1985). The particular sequence quoted below focused on writing a poem on the theme of *childhood*.

Step 1: Relaxation activities (as in type 1).

Step 2: Evoking individual memories. The teacher projected an overhead transparency onto the screen which he uncovered in stages. After each new stimulus the learners had time to filter out from their memories the images which were being evoked. It was very important that nobody talked during this phase and that their attention was directed inwardly after each stimulus sentence.

OHP: first day at school

- Try and remember your first day at school.
- Take your time and let the memories emerge. Explore them.
- Remember the morning before you went to school.
- Did you go alone?
- What did you wear?
- How did you feel?
- Do you remember the school building?
- Your classroom?
- Your classmates?
- Your first teacher?
- etc.

(One could make this a richer experience by announcing the theme in the lesson beforehand so that the learners could bring along pictures from their first day at school and also ask their parents what they can remember from their first day at school. Photographs can be very supportive in the pairwork phase that follows.)

Step 3: Notemaking. Next the learners wrote down what they remembered in note form, e.g. key words, parts of sentences, images and associations.

Step 4: Sharing experiences. At this point pairs of teams shared their experiences with each other. (This phase is particularly useful because it helps learners to clarify their recollections.) After this discussion the notes were expanded.

Step 5: Public sharing. Each member of the group offered two particular memories as working material to the group. They were written on the board or on an overhead projector transparency.

Step 6: Listening/imagining. The recollections were read out loud; the group listened to the rhythm of the words and the sentences and the fragments of sentences and tried to see what the words suggested: e.g. laughter/blue dress/dark corridor/Mum/I am hungry/no pictures on the wall/ . . .

Step 7: Poetry writing. Using the personal notes or the photographs and what was written on the board as raw material each learner then wrote an individual text (prose, poetical prose or poetry) on the theme 'first day at school'.

Step 8: Presentation. It was made clear to all the learners before they began to write that nobody would be pressed to publish his text. Various possibilities of presenting text were now conceivable. Those who wanted to publish their text handed it in. They were shuffled, distributed and read out. If the group is able to work without this anonymous and more secure form of working then they could be asked to present on a more voluntary basis. Experience has shown that where the social atmosphere in the classroom is positive participants readily exchange personal experiences. Another possibility is to pin up the poems on the classroom wall. They can then be read and commented on at any time. It is important to note that the teacher is also a participant in the activity and should also contribute a poem if possible. In this particular group the class had about thirty minutes to write the texts in their draft form; here are three examples:

(a) *First Day at School*
    it is hard to go back in time
    when you never tried that before
    but suddenly the pictures
    flash into my mind
    i remember the building
    which seemed to be so big
    twelve years ago –
    there were so many doors –
    which one was the one
    that led to my classroom?
    but then i remember
    and i see the small coat-hooks again

exactly the right height
there it was dark
then, entering the room
through the large dark door
light is reaching my eyes
coming from the small garden
i can see through the windows.
finally i've made it.
finally i am a person
like my brothers
and not a baby anymore.

(b)   A
                 KID
              EXCITED
            SCHULTÜTE
           NICETEACHER
            CLASSROOM
              PICTURE
                DRESS
                 NEW
                  A

(c) I was wearing a big new school bag on my back
    which I was very proud of
    holding my mother's hand
    I went into the classroom
    on every desk was a sheet of paper
    with a name on it
    we had to look for our own
    and sit down there
    one by one
    our parents left
    some of the pupils started to cry
    I didn't

Step 9: Text reception/analysis. After making contact with their own experiences, the teacher's and those of the others in the group in the form of poetic text, the learners finally listened to a tape recording of the poet, Roger McGough, reading his own poem 'First Day at School'. They were now able to study the text and examine the poetic devices used by McGough to express the experience of the first day at school. They could also determine to what extent the experiences

First Day at School

A millionbillionwillion miles from home
Waiting for the bell to go. (To go where?)
Why are they all so big, other children?
So noisy? So much at home they must have been born in uniform
Lived all their lives in playgrounds
Spent the years inventing games that don't let me in.
Games that are rough, that swallow you up.

And the railings.
All around, the railings.
Are they to keep out wolves and monsters?
Things that carry off and eat children?
Things you don't take sweets from?
Perhaps they're to stop us getting out
Running away from the lessins. Lessin.
What does a lessin look like?
Sounds small and slimey.
They keep them in glassrooms.
Whole rooms made out of glass. Imagine.

I wish I could remember my name.
Mummy said it would come in useful.
Like wellies. When there's puddles.
Yellowwellies. I wish she was here.
I think my name is sewn on somewhere.
Perhaps the teacher will read it for me.
Tea-cher. The one who makes the tea.

(Roger McGough)

Figure 4.2 The target language text for analysis and discussion

of the narrator in the poem differed from their own experiences as expressed in their texts.

Step 10: Project work. The learners, working in groups of three or four, selected a poem on the theme of childhood from various anthologies and collections of texts. After investigating possible choices and analysing the poem of their choice, the group presented their findings to the class. The presentation included a review of the role of their own experiences and a reading of the poem.

Summary

These activities help learners to understand important facets of learning in general and language learning in particular:

(1) They make learners aware that the senses are an interrelated system for decoding the world and can be exploited in an interrelated way to decode language (Corder 1973).

(2) They demonstrate that learning is whole-person-orientated, namely that it has both a physical and an intellectual dimension.

(3) One activity focuses solely on the crucial importance of the physical environment and its effect on the learning climate. It invites learners to be co-responsible for this affective dimension of their learning.

(4) They develop an awareness within learners that the experience which they as individuals bring to the class can be seen as potential input into the class. When learners make contributions to the work of the class in this way they become 'stakeholders' in the progress and outcome of the learning.

(5) They provide opportunities for small-scale independent work and decision-making which prepares the ground for future project work.

(6) Where the activity requires participants to share personal or private information, a minimum level of trust within the group is needed. In carrying out the activity, however, the group can help to foster mutual trust and to create an understanding of cooperative behaviour.

4.2.3 *Information-sharing activities*

The concept which has given rise to a range of activities closely identified with the communicative classroom is the 'information gap'. When one conversation partner, for example, has knowledge relevant to the situation they are discussing , which is unknown by the other partner, an 'information gap' is said to exist. The need to acquire the information triggers communication between the two which bridges the 'information gap'. There is now no lack of readily available materials which exploit the information gap principle (see e.g. Candlin 1981; Klippel 1984; Lewis 1981; Littlewood 1981; Matthews and Read, 1981; Pattison 1987; Sexton and Williams 1984) and many main-course-book authors make widespread use of the technique, thus underlining Morrow's view (1981) that it is fundamental to the communicative approach. What is of real value in this essentially simple classroom procedure is that it promotes a form of communication that takes place independently of the teacher. Such classroom behaviour is in sharp contrast to teacher-led dialogues where a great deal of time is spent in drilling language for no effective communicative purpose. For example, a teacher may point to a window and ask learners whether it was a door or a chair with the sole purpose of eliciting the response, 'No, it's a window . . .' As we shall see later (chapter 5), the ability to work independently and effectively in the communicative classroom relies very much on how far learners are able to share relevant information and negotiate procedures and outcomes. Information-sharing activities help learners to appreciate that they can use the target language to communicate without the direct intervention of the teacher. They help prepare learners for learning environments such as the project classroom, in which large-scale tasks are undertaken often with consequences for the world outside the classroom. In such situations the information gap bridged by one learner for another may be part of a much larger task. It could involve a grammar explanation in order to improve a text being prepared for publication, or advice on how to manipulate the word-processing programme on the class computer.

The examples that follow are merely illustrative of the various manifestations of the technique, reflecting its communicative potential and its flexibility of application.

Example 1: Using pictures (adult and high-school learners of English at intermediate level)

(1) The class is subdivided into pairs and one person in the pair is given an unusual, abstract drawing (see Figure 4.3) which he has to describe to his partner so that the latter can draw it unseen. The 'drawer' can ask clarification questions but the 'describer' may not help by pointing to the 'drawer's' work and commenting on its likeness or otherwise to the original drawing.

(2) When the participants agree that the drawing is finished, the versions from the other members of the class are displayed and learners exchange comments on the various representations produced.

(3) The teacher elicits from the class the areas of difficulty in the task and feeds in key vocabulary items, 'diagonal line, wavy line, etc.', suggestions for possible communication strategies, e.g. 'it looks like . . .; it's shaped like . . .'; and essential language of location, e.g. 'at the bottom of the page . . .; in the top corner, etc.'.

(4) The two learners exchange roles and are given a different picture to work with.

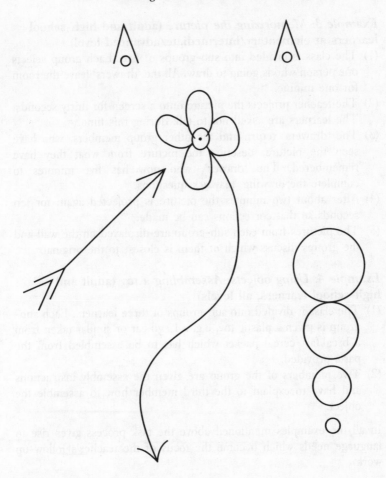

Figure 4.3 An example of a 'crazy' picture

Example 2: Spot the difference (adult and high-school learners at elementary/intermediate/advanced level

(1) Learners working in pairs are given a picture each which is identical apart from a number of small alterations.
(2) Without showing each other the pictures they must describe them to each other in such a way that they can identify all the differences.

Example 3: Memorizing the picture (adult and high-school learners at elementary/intermediate/advanced level)

(1) The class is divided into sub-groups of five. Each group selects one person who is going to draw. All the 'drawers' leave the room for one minute.

(2) The teacher projects the picture onto a screen for thirty seconds. The learners are asked not to talk during this time.

(3) The 'drawers' return and the other group members, who have seen the picture, describe the picture from what they have remembered. The 'drawer', who now has five minutes to complete the drawing, may ask questions.

(4) After about two minutes the picture is projected again for ten seconds so that corrections can be made.

(5) The pictures from each sub-group are displayed on the wall and the groups discuss which of them is closest to the original.

Example 4: Using objects: Assembling a toy (adult and high-school learners, all levels)

(1) The class is divided into sub-groups of three learners. Each sub-group is given a plastic toy, e.g. a Lego car or similar taken from a breakfast cereal packet which has to be assembled from the parts provided.

(2) Two members of the group are given the assembly instructions and have to explain to the third member how to assemble the object.

In all the examples mentioned above the task process gives rise to language needs which become the focus of the teacher's follow-up work.

Example 5: Using the jigsaw technique
Following the work of Geddes and Sturtridge (1979), activities which rely on the 'jigsaw technique' have become widespread in the communicative classroom. The technique has been adapted for use in a variety of contexts fulfilling a variety of purposes such as problem-solving or bridging an imagination gap (see below) as well as exploiting an information gap.

Jigsaw listening/reading
(1) The class is divided into three groups each of whom is given a listening/reading text relating to a theme common to all three texts. In order to find a solution to a problem, e.g. choosing a job

for a particular person, planning a meal, or dealing with a business problem, information from all three listening/reading texts is required.

(2) When the group members have discussed and understood the information on their text, the class is regrouped in groups of three to include one member each from one of the previous groups.

(3) Each person in the sub-group of three has information which the other two do not have. They now share their information and try to solve the problem.

Example 6: Reassembling a text

(1) The class is divided into sub-groups of four and each sub-group is given a text which has been photocopied and cut into several pieces according to the number of paragraphs in the text.

(2) Each individual in the sub-group reads a piece of the text and shares the information with the others. From this collective pool of information, they try to sequence the paragraphs and thus reassemble the text.

Example 7: Assembling a poem

(1) The class is divided into sub-groups of three or four each of whom is given a short poem which has been photocopied and cut up line by line or word for word.

(2) Individuals share their pieces and try to create a poem (which may or may not resemble the original). In so doing, they not only share information but perceptions and feelings so that their product becomes a negotiated reshaping using the raw material of the original.

(3) They are asked to remember their reasons for choosing to locate particular words together.

(4) The finished poems are then displayed on the classroom wall and the productions of each of the sub-groups is read and discussed by the class as a whole.

This activity has many similarities with activities below which we call imagination gap activities, since what the participants share can only very loosely be described as 'information'.

Summary

(1) Information-sharing activities are a way of introducing teacher-independent tasks to learners unused to learner-centred learning.

They help to define a new norm in which convening and sharing information, and negotiating aims takes place in larger contexts, e.g. project-oriented work. In this sense they function as a training activity for the communicative classroom.

(2) In the narrow sense of language practice they provide the learner with space within which to practise and experiment with the language at his disposal without any external pressure on accuracy. They also allow the learner to focus on specific areas of functional language use which reoccur in more complex negotiation processes.

(3) Learners working together where the aim is to convey accurate information are encouraged to use and extend their range of positive 'communication strategies' which they employ as means of overcoming any shortcomings in language competence.

(4) Information-sharing also includes the dimension of negotiation of meaning as a significant component in the comprehension process. Learners experience this as a by-product of the activity.

(5) Learners have an opportunity to identify language performance deficiences themselves, thereby developing the need and motivation to overcome them.

4.2.4 Thinking strategies and problem-solving

We have already noted that an important defining characteristic of an *information-sharing* activity is the stimulus it provides to learners to practise sharing information and negotiating its meaning. The sharing of information is necessary because the participants are each in possession of different pieces. In a *problem-solving* activity participants are similarly invited to negotiate a solution, but they are normally all exposed to the same input data. In everyday classroom situations when using texts which have been cut into pieces, or a series of pictures to tell a story, there is only a minor technical difference between an information-sharing activity and a problem-solving activity. It is merely a question of how the teacher decides to frame the activity. However, the activities which we refer to in this section share the characteristic that the information, although available to everyone in the group, is sometimes obscure, often presented in the form of a riddle or a puzzle, needing deductive and inferential skills on the part of the learners. It is important to distinguish them from language games in the classroom for which there are now many valuable collections (Wright et al. 1979; Hadfield 1984; 1987). It is more than a question of degree. The latter concentrate on providing practice for particular language items, often in the form of an extended drill, while the information in the former is more complex and the solution only approachable through extensive negotiation. They often require additionally a multi-skilled response on the part of the learner.

There are now many flexible and stimulating collections of problem-solving activities which promote thinking strategies (see Klippel 1984, p. 96–114; Frank et al. 1982; Pattison 1987; p. 195–238; Porter-Ladousse 1983). Much is owed here to the work of de Bono (1973) who first drew attention to the value of teaching creative thinking. The examples below have been used in the teaching of English as a foreign language to adults at different points in the learning process.

Example 1: The design team (adult EFL learners, intermediate level)

This activity centres around a main task which is further divided into a series of sub-tasks. The information is not obscure or difficult but the task is neither simple to execute nor open to any one discernible solution.

Step 1: The class was divided into sub-groups which were each given the following scenario:

- You are the members of the marketing department of a company which produces a famous brand of cornflakes.

- Your boss is very worried about competition from other companies in the same market sector and is determined to increase sales.

- She believes that the best way to boost sales is to give the product an additional attraction.

- She can't change the product itself so she decides to change the packaging.

- YOUR TASK is to design an object for the back of the packet which the buyer can cut out and 'use' at home.

Step 2: The groups were then given the following sub-tasks to be completed within the time limit of the lesson:

- Decide on the object.
- Make a note of the reasons for the choice of the object.
- Design the object on a piece of A4 paper.
- Produce a test model for the 'boss' to inspect.
- Incorporate the object into the design for the back of the cornflakes packet.
- Write up instructions for assembly.
- Invent a name for the product.
- Write a text for the packet to describe the object.
- Write a short text to describe the contents of the packet.

Step 3: Using card and drawing materials the groups carried out the task.

Step 4: After the 'products' were completed, they were displayed in the classroom and the designs were defended in open forum as the various teams questioned and criticized each other.

This activity was introduced after the class had been exposed to initial activities which had made them familiar with learning and working in sub-groups independent of the teacher. They were no longer strangers to one another, but they had not yet learned to cooperate in sub-groups for a common purpose. The activity was introduced therefore to provide an opportunity to develop an awareness of a positive group dynamic. It also provided the participants with an extended opportunity to negotiate procedures and a variety of outcomes. The successful completion of the task also relied on the realization that roles needed to be identified and allocated. (For further and more varied examples of this type see 'Insight into Industry', CRAC 1986.)

Example 2: Boats in the harbour (adult EFL learners, intermediate; high school advanced)

Here the given information does not necessarily present difficulties of textual comprehension. However, the question which the activity poses requires deductive reasoning and also compels learners to negotiate how they are going to set about the task.

Step 1: The learners working in groups of three or four were presented with the following scenario:

- While visiting Avonmouth harbour one day you see five boats.
- All the boats have names relating to sea creatures.
- All the boats are owned by companies from different countries.
- Each boat has a different marking on its funnel.
- The captains of the boats all speak a different mother tongue.

Step 2: At this point groups brain-stormed the possible connections between the information given and what they could be asked to do with it.

Step 3: They were then given the following support data and then the target question:

- The company which owns the boat in the middle is German.
- The first boat on the left has a yellow stripe on its funnel.
- The *Mermaid* is next to the boat with the yellow-striped funnel.
- The *Sealion* is just to the right of the *Dolphin* which is flying the French flag.
- The captain of the French-owned boat speaks only Norwegian.
- The *Sealion* is flying the Icelandic flag.
- The boat with a blue star on its funnel is Belgian-owned.

WHICH IS THE SCOTTISH-OWNED BOAT?

Klippel (1984) describes several activities based on the same principle, namely, where the characteristics in a given set of data are permutated so that learners are forced to examine the data in order to deduce the answer. These activities require refined negotiating skills on the part of the learners. They should therefore not be used at the beginning of a learning programme before participants have become familiar with one another and have had practice in working together in groups on more straightforward tasks. The value of these tasks is that they not only train thinking in the foreign language but they emphasize experientially for learners the need to clarify the procedure of the task before they can hope to solve it. If there is a drawback with this type of activity it is that it may disadvantage learners from cultural backgrounds which do not prioritize this kind of creative thinking. A more accessible example of group creative thinking is provided by the next activity.

Example 3: *The geometric puzzle* (adult, non-adult learners, EFL/non-EFL, intermediate to advanced)

The crux of this activity devised by Roberts (personal communication) and widely used with adult EFL learners and in in-service teacher training is not to solve a problem from given data but to design a puzzle based on a suggested outline.

Step 1: The class was divided into sub-groups of three or four learners who were provided with a triangular piece of white card measuring approximately 40 cm on its longest side, an envelope, a pair of scissors, some writing paper, a ruler and a pencil. They were told that they were going to make a puzzle and write a set of instructions explaining how to do it. The guidelines for the puzzle were as follows:

- Take your piece of card and draw five straight pencil lines on it.
- Draw an outline of the card with the lines on it on the piece of paper.
- Cut the card into six pieces.
- Mark each of the cards with a symbol (use any symbols but do not use Arabic or Roman numerals, or letters from the Roman alphabet) so that they can be distinguished from one another.
- Now write a list of instructions which show how the six pieces of card should be put together in order to form the original shape of the card before it was cut up.
- Place the pieces and the instructions in the envelope and pass them on to another group to see if they can solve the problem.

Step 2: Having completed their own puzzle participants received another puzzle and the accompanying instructions from another group and attempted to solve it.

Step 3: The puzzles were passed around the class until every group had had an opportunity to try out the other puzzles.

Step 4: The final phase was a plenary discussion to compare experiences. This raised questions on the varying levels of difficulty, interest and satisfaction in the puzzles.

This is an integrated skills activity which places particular emphasis on cooperative negotiation in that participants have to both create and solve a problem. In the creative phase there is more than one level of negotiation involved. They have to agree on how to interpret the guidelines, the shape of their puzzle, the choice of symbols, and how to formulate the instructions. In doing so sub-groups become committed to their own versions and are intrigued to compare them with the others. The value of this activity lies very much in its layered communicative potential not only in the execution of the task, but in the way that it naturally leads the group into comparisons and therefore into an evaluation of the task and the language it generates.

Summary
(1) The content of problem-solving activities engages learners' interest and challenges them to negotiate not only the meaning of the given data but how to approach it.
(2) They invite learners to invest part of their experience and knowledge into the work of the group in a creative and cooperative way.
(3) Where different solutions are possible the activities stimulate feedback discussions characterized by the personal commitment of the learners to their arguments.
(4) They follow on naturally from information-sharing activities and build on the negotiating skills which they introduce.
(5) Many of these activities require of learners a language level which enables them to compare, agree, suggest, summarize, etc. They are not suited therefore to beginner or elementary learners.
(6) Since they may also rely on deductive reasoning they are not best suited to the beginning of a language programme where the participants are new to each other. Learners unsure of themselves and of the others in the group tend to withhold their participation until their confidence matches their language competence.
(7) Problem-solving is not prioritized equally in all cultures. It may be that some participants in multilingual classes could feel disadvantaged by the extra demands on creativity and thought which these activities demand.

4.2.5 Imagination-gap, fantasy and creative expression

We have referred above to the role of *information-gap activities* in the communicative classroom whereby learners combine the different pieces of information they possess as individuals to form an overall picture. In the case of a murder mystery, for example, learners may be given various pieces of information. By exchanging what they know the pieces of information are forged together to solve the problem. *Imagination-gap activities* on the other hand function by using the *same* input for every learner whatever it may be: a word, a picture, a series of pictures, a film sequence or a part of a literary text. Stimulus materials can be used with or without a context. In the case of the latter, learners respond by producing a variety of free associations, in contrast to the more structured response within a context. The driving force behind an *imagination-gap* activity is the variety of learner perceptions of and reactions to the task stimulus.

We wish to distinguish between three types of activity which rely on using this learner input to bridge an imagination gap:

(1) an imagination-gap activity;
(2) a projection and identification activity;
(3) a guided fantasy activity.

(1) Imagination-gap

Example 1: Brain-storming ideas

The simplest and most familiar form of this type of activity is the brain-storming exercise carried out within a 'snowball' procedure and combined with a value-clarification task (see below). The 'snowball' starts with an individual task, e.g. the learner may be asked to write down what associations spring to mind from a particular film or book title, picture, photos or symbols, etc. The activity now snowballs with pairs of learners discussing their ideas and creating new associations. The pairs combine to form small groups which undertake an evaluation exercise ranking the ideas produced.

A variation of this approach has been suggested by Bredella (1984a) in his work with the short stories. When studying the story, 'Manhood', by John Wain, learners were given the title and asked to collect pictures which conveyed their idea of manhood. Later in class, working in pairs and small groups, they shared and explained their various responses. The activity served to create expectations in readiness for the ensuing reading task.

Example 2: Sentences without context

This is another form of imagination-gap activity which brings together the different perceptions which learners have. Learners are given a sentence and asked to contextualize it. They begin first of all by trying to determine the context of situation, e.g.:

---

sentence 1: 'It's rather hot today isn't it?'

Who says this? When? How old are the people? What time is it?

sentence 2: 'Jane and George spent the afternoon on the beach.'

Who are Jane and George? How old are they? Why were they on the beach? What did they do there? What was the weather like? How did they get to the beach? When did they arrive? When did they leave? What did they do in the evening? Who says this sentence? etc. . . .

The work of contextualization starts with a group brain-storming activity with the results written up on an overhead transparency or classroom board. Classroom experience reveals the remarkable variety of how learners perceive even simple situations such as these. Jane and George have been seen not only as young members of the dominant youth culture but all ages from young children to senior citizens. Learners have also 'seen' them as the pet dogs of unnamed humans on the beach. Around these central figures have been woven a range of biographical possibilities from relatively anonymous figures to the high adventure of espionage, crime, romantic fiction, etc. The development of story-lines such as these is carried out in sub-groups who give it a textual form such as a story, a newspaper report, a scene from a play or a scene to be mimed, etc.

Sentences could be selected from an existing context such as a short story, before the class has read it. The associations which learners produce are their predictions of what may happen in the story and can function as a comprehension guide during the reading phase. If, however, the context and speaker are known (e.g. the sentence could be taken from a chapter of a novel which the group had read), the guesses of the class (Who could have said that? What possibly could have happened? etc.) stimulate further discussion of how plausible their guesses are, leading to a reconsideration of the original text. This type of imagination gap activity provides an opportunity for creative work as an alternative to textbook exercises (Tomlinson 1986). Textbooks themselves can be the source of the kind of decontextualized sentences suited to this treatment. The procedure can be applied equally to films and listening texts. Learners can begin comprehension work on a film by generating expectations and predictions before viewing it. They may be given work involving the title or shown a short sequence which they can attempt to contextualize.

Example 3: Pictures in imagination gap

Comprehension tasks using pictures are particularly suited to imagination-gap work. As Maley and Duff (1982) have pointed out, pictures provide many opportunities for learners to negotiate and make sense of ambiguous situations. A picture of Arnold Schwarzenegger, for example, the famous body-builder and actor showing off his upper body muscles is the starting point of a longer text-decoding sequence in *Confidence* (Bredella et al. 1984, pp. 91–100). The task for the learner is given as follows:

Have a close look at the picture and try to get an impression of the person depicted.

Imagine you are listening to the person depicted in the picture. You are listening to him talking about himself. What topics might he touch upon? How does he express himself? He starts with 'Call me Arnold', go on and write down what he is telling you.

Ideas are developed as a pair exercise and presented to the class. The presentation phase produces a list of themes which are collected on the board. Finally the learners are given a transcript of an interview with the person to read so that they can compare this version of the character with their own.

Example 4: Sequences of pictures

Working with pictures is a common phenomenon in classes conducted with a communicative orientation. Individual learners or groups are given pictures with the aim of telling a story and putting them into some kind of sequence. This is a relatively easy task for teachers to create for themselves since picture sequences can be taken out of magazines. Just how many possible interpretations and combinations learners are capable of producing becomes evident when every sub-group is given the same pictures. However, one can use random pictures, i.e. not taken from any given sequence, as long as they can be linked together in some way or another. Here the challenge facing the learners is to create their own sequence.

Oakley (personal communication 1983) has pointed out that the more diverse the pictures, the more productive is the work of the learners. In an exercise developed by him called 'Biographies', learners are given a collection of magazine pictures, often bizarre in character, with various themes running through them, some have water as a leitmotif, others music or musical instruments, or scenes of disasters. Each set contains pictures of infants, parents, young people, parents, old people, various exotic settings and occupations. Learners are told that the pictures depict the life story of a particular person. It is their task to construct the biography of the person, inventing a name and using the pictures as illustrations of the events. Having decided on their story and the sequence of the pictures, the second task is to write the story in caption form below each of the pictures, which are stuck onto a large piece of card for display on the classroom wall. The different sub-groups are now able to read each others' work.

Example 5: Imagination gap and areas of indeterminacy

Recent work in the didactics of literature has re-emphasized the role of the learner as a 'reader' of literature (Hunfeld 1982; Bredella 1985a). What is meant here by the term 'reader' is that the reader of any text is someone who interacts with the text to create for him/herself an interpretation and a meaning. On its own the text is a neutral object without any meaning or interpretation until this is created by the 'reader'. In this view a 'reader' is not just a passive recipient of someone else's interpretation but an active participant in a meaning-creating process. Along with other readers of the text the 'reader' forms a community of 'readers' who may represent a range of views or possibly a general consensus on what the text means for them.

The implications of this view for language teachers who wish to focus attention on the benefits of working with original texts in the literature of the target language are interesting. The challenge is now to find ways of enabling the learner to engage with the text and develop his own interpretation. It becomes a question not so much of producing exercises to accompany texts, but of developing activities which elicit responses from learners who proceed to codify them in a text form. Recent proposals (see also Bredella 1984a; 1985; Collie and Slater) make the point clearly that learners who have experienced trying to write creatively are better able to read and interact with original texts. In other words, learners learn to read literature by trying to write it themselves.

There are many tasks which provide learners with a structure within which they can be creative. Many of them work by directing the imagination of the learner towards developing expectations before working with the text, others invite the learner to take a fresh, creative look at the central parts of the original text. There are clear indications here on how much the teaching of literature has drawn from insights taken from views of comprehension processes developed by linguistics, applied linguistics and cognitive psychology. What the contribution of humanistic psychology has shown, is that the process of comprehension includes the imaginative and projective ability of the learner and his pre-knowledge and attitudes (Zinker 1977, p. 13). The exercise types listed below encourage the reader to express reactions arising out of the comprehension process, to articulate implicit and explicit meanings in the text and to clarify them by communicating them to others. They are components of the collective process of creating meaning.

Here are several possible exercises of dealing with literature in this way:

- writing further sections to short stories, building up open endings;
- verbalizing the feelings of characters;
- writing inner monologues;
- allowing characters to be active in different situations;
- picking up ideas which have been only suggested at or hinted in the text and making them concrete;
- acting out the scene of a novel or transforming the scene of a novel into a series of pictures;
- designing a front cover for a novel ... (Bredella 1984a, 1985; Collie and Slater; Tomlinson 1986)

From text to film

This is an area which is rich in communicative potential for learners, particularly if it is concerned with the transformation of literary texts into film texts, i.e. feature films. Even if a film version of the literary work which learners could discuss and reshape is not available, there is still value in transforming one text type into another since it requires a renewed interpretation of the original text. The following example taken from *Confidence* (Bredella et al. 1984, p. 86) indicates how a 'text to film' sequence could be exploited when used as an accompaniment to a reading of Richard Wright's 'Almos' a Man' (see page 111).

This approach has been used in schools, in classes for adults and in teacher training. What occurs when learners make a film together in small groups is that their own visual experiences, gathered from the many hours of watching films and television are activated and brought to the surface. This does not imply that learners are now capable of making a professional film. However they tend to have sophisticated notions of the shape their product

Step 1: Before you watch the film, think about the difficulties of using a short story to make a film. What must be changed? Which scenes must be added or omitted? etc.

Imagine that you have been asked to make a film of the short story. How would your film begin? How would it end? Work in groups of three or four students.

If you worked as the director of the film 'Almos' a Man', you would have to choose the actors you wanted to work with. Select your cast. Bring along pictures of potential characters, if possible.

Step 2: Even if you have not got the film, it is worth studying the following excerpt from the screen-play:

Stage the scene. Use video equipment and/or cassette recorders to monitor your performance if possible.

Write additional scenes for the screen-play.

should take. These notions are based on the models provided by the professional practices of network television.

(2) Projection and identification

What is meant here by the concept of projection is *creative projection*, as it is understood in Gestalt therapy (Zinker 1977, p. 15). That is, it is the process in which a person projects himself into someone or something else (whether it be a living thing or an inanimate object) and expresses himself through the other person or thing. Gestalt therapy uses projection techniques in order to integrate previously unintegrated parts of the personality. However, teachers make use of such techniques principally for purposes of self-awareness. When dealing with comprehension and production processes in language teaching, projective forms of behaviour are suitable both for theme-centred self-experience and for a personalized exploration of themes. Their value is to provide the learner with an unexpected access to himself and to the theme by allowing him to articulate knowledge, values and feelings. When it comes to the language used in projective exercises it is often the case that language registers have to be used which are frequently neglected in modern language teaching.

Example 6: Be the window, be the man (post-intermediate, German high school; topic: Northern Ireland)

Here learners investigated through a variety of texts the division of

Northern Ireland and the escalation of violence, particularly in the 1960s and the early 1970s. They were acquainted with various attempts to explain the situation and had formed their own hypotheses. Their work on *The Derry Confrontation* of October 1968 was concluded with a check test. They were given a picture which portrayed an old man who had picked some flowers growing in the ruins of a street devastated by bomb attacks. The old man and the wild flowers were the only signs of life in the street. The task was to:

---

(1) Study the picture very carefully. Take your time and try to get an impression of the atmosphere which the picture conveys.

(2) Try and imagine you are the old man. Speak as if you were the old man. What does he have to say? What does he want to say? How does he feel?

(3) Try and imagine that you are one of the broken windows or barricaded doors. Make the window/door talk: 'I was a kitchen window . . .'

Example 7: I was there/I'm a pair of glasses (post-intermediate, German high school; theme: War and Peace)

The class was given the short story by Ernest Hemingway 'The Old Man at the Bridge' to read. They were asked to read the story for homework. The analysis of the story in the lesson which followed was initiated by the following task set by the teacher:

Take a couple of minutes to read through the short story again. Imagine that you were present at the bridge. You were there as a film reporter. What would you have seen, what you have filmed? How long did you spend at the Bridge?

Their differing reactions to the theme gave rise to different points on which to concentrate for filming. To achieve a better understanding of the old man the following projection exercise was suggested as an experiment: the learners were to try to tell the story of the old man from the perspective of his glasses. An example of a learner's response is from Andrea V. who begins her text:

I'm a pair of glasses. I'm 39 now and very dirty, because the carts and trucks have caused clouds of dust. I belong to this old man who used to clean me ever so often that I hated him sometimes for it. I have never been so dusty in my life for such a long time. I can hardly see, has he given up? Why doesn't he clean me? Maybe he thinks of his goats. He really loves his goats and the cat, I can still smell the goats. I can see the milk in the bucket, that was yesterday evening . . .

(Legutke 1988a, p. 133)

Example 8: What if . . ./If I were . . . (advanced class, German high school; theme: Poetry Workshop)
Work from this particular course has already been mentioned above (see also Canfield and Wells 1976; Moskowitz 1978). During the first part of their course the learners looked at the theme of identity and studied poems related to it. The poems were taken mainly from the book *Working with Poetry* (Lach-Newinsky and Seletzky 1986) which includes such authors as Sandburg, Wanieck and Plath. Both exercises 'What if . . .' and 'If I were . . .' are designed as stimuli for the learners to pursue the question 'Who do you think you are?' (the title of a poem by Sandburg) in an unusual way using the projection technique as prop. 'What if . . .' begins with the following instruction:

Do you ever think of things like . . . What if my motor-bike could talk? What do you think your motor-bike or your bicycle would say about you? Imagine you are an object on this list. Make notes about what it would say about you:

> toothbrush
> doll
> hamster
> coat
> stereo set
> chair
> mirror
> pen
> comb
> shoes
> desk
> etc. . . .

After making some notes on their ideas the learners share their thoughts with their partners or with their group. A variation of the exercise would be to have learners talk about themselves as if they were their own father, or mother, or brother, or sister, or teacher, or friend, who was talking. An essential prerequisite to this exercise is a learning climate of trust (criterion 3).

'*If I were. . .*' functions in a similar way using projections and the learners' imagination, i.e. learners project themselves into various things and give expression to their particular characteristics and qualities:

> *Question*: If you were a colour, what colour would you be? My answer would be: if I were a colour I would be blue because it is as bright as the Greek sea and full of surprises.

The learners are now given a list of stimulus questions on an overhead projector transparency from which they can choose. It is very important at first not to pursue the question of why particular choices are made but simply to allow spontaneous ideas to unfold and to write them down. It is better to leave the issue of *why?* to the second stage since learners normally need further language work on adjectives. After both individual phases of projection and justification a third step, that of exchanging ideas, could be added. What arises out of this activity could also be used as input for the creation of a self-portrait. The following list derives from Moskowitz *(1978, p. 69)*:

If I were   a season of the year
            a day of the week
            a country
            a musical instrument
            a piece of fruit
            a number
            a TV show
            a feeling
            a flower
            a building
            a sweet

Which would you be?

Why?

---

(3) Guided fantasy

Guided fantasies are, as the name suggests, fantasies stimulated under the guidance of another person and are not to be confused with daydreams which arise spontaneously. Creating fantasies is part of the repertoire of psychotherapy within *humanistic psychology*. The methods derive from the work of Perls on the effect of the imagination as a means to bring about structural changes in the personality (Perls et al. 1951; and cf. chapter 3.2).

During a guided fantasy the therapist offers the patient a

framework for his imagination which can be filled with images. There is, however, an important difference between the work of the therapist and the work of the teacher in the classroom. The therapist will direct his attentions towards mobilizing unconscious fantasies to locate suppressed fantasies and fears. There can be no justification for a teacher to carry out work of this nature since it not only requires specialist skills as a therapist, but also lies outside the frame of reference of the teacher's role. However, what can be considered legitimate for the teacher would be to activate the fantasies of learners in the area of the conscious imagination and of daydreams. It is this form of imaginative activity which has received attention within *humanistic approaches* movement in language teaching and is also prevalent in Gestalt pedagogy. We are not suggesting, however, that what is stored in the subconscious is not transported by means of these activities into the area of the conscious nor that they cannot be meaningful (Moskowitz 1978, p. 178). It is simply that until recently the ability of learners to become involved in creative activities, i.e. finding unusual solutions to problems, creating imaginative or surreal worlds and being able to verbalize their actions has received little attention in educational circles and language teaching in particular. In this sense *humanistic approaches* and Gestalt pedagogy have enriched the educational discussion by informing and guiding practice in the classroom. Nevertheless, whenever techniques and practices are transferred from the background of therapy into the classroom, it is important that the inherent conceptual and practical differences between the needs of therapy and the needs of education are recognized. It is therefore necessary to examine exercises extracted from the world of guided fantasy critically with an eye to possible adaptation. In doing so, we maintain, teachers need to take into consideration the relationship to the theme of their work (criterion 1), the preconditions for experiential learning for the group and for the teacher (criterion 3) and how far the aims and the process in the classroom are clear to all participants. The extent to which one can work with guided fantasy and the intensity of the experience depends on a range of variables:

> the degree to which the learners can relax;
> the degree to which the teacher can relax;
> the kind of guidance provided by the teacher;
> how the task was carried out (with eyes open, with eyes shut, in a darkened room);
> the previous experiences of the learners with guided fantasy exercises;
> disturbances within the class;

disturbances from outside;
trust of the learners for the teacher;
clarity of the content and the method of procedure.

In our experience with guided fantasy work learners have produced successsful oral work and a range of stimulating written texts, for example student texts in example 9 below.

Example 9: Junk shop

This activity was one of several used in a poetry-writing option course for adult learners of English. The aim of the course was to maximize learners' enjoyment of reading poetry by first allowing them the opportunity to try writing their own poetry. This encourages empathy and an understanding of the creative process and an appreciation of original texts. After the creative phase participants in this activity went on to read and explore the mood and images in the lyric 'Soldier's Things' by Tom Waits (Thomas 1989).

Step 1: Introduction. The class was arranged in a circle and the words *Junk Shop* and *Antique Shop* were introduced, and class reactions and associations were elicited.

Step 2: Guided fantasy. The learners were asked to imagine a junk shop or antique shop they had visited personally:

Stimulus tasks/questions:	What can you see?
	Explore the shop.
	What kind of objects can you identify?
	What is on the walls?
	Are there any boxes with small items in them?
	What does the shop smell like?

A few minutes were allowed for learners to explore and regenerate their memories.

Step 3: Elicitation. Now their responses were elicited in the form of a brain-storming activity and gathered on the board.

During this phase the students were encouraged to make extended contributions by means of questions which stimulated them to probe their thoughts. Often what one student said was built upon by another so that a great deal of fragmented detail was displayed on the board.

Step 4: Processing the data. Sub-groups of three students were formed and then asked to select up to six items from the board and together to brain-storm the life histories of the objects and to make notes. At this point they were asked to rearrange their notes in a poetic form, i.e. to try and shape a poem from the material they had assembled. They were able to add or subtract words in order to develop their ideas. In order to make sense of this stage of the task they had to rely on their pre-knowledge and experience of poetry. However, they were not bound by any rules that the poem should be rhymed or unrhymed, in a fixed or varying form. They were given the general guideline that poetry is suggestive rather than explanatory, and often enigmatic because it attempts to convey experiences in a compact and provocative form. They were allowed to complete their work outside the class.

Step 5: Exhibition. The learners made large displays of their work and displayed the finished poems on the classroom wall. They were asked to identify as many poems which were different in form and content as possible.

Step 6: Preliminary feedback. Individual students were asked to read out any poem which they found interesting and enjoyable.

Step 7: Opinion Exchange. Feelings and viewpoints were explored by means of stimulus tasks/questions:

What kind of mood did you create?

Identify the atmosphere in the poems on the wall.

etc.

Step 8: Looking at 'Soldier's Things'. The Tom Waits lyric was distributed and read by the students. Questions of mood and how it should be read were discussed. The learners also made comparisons between the Waits text and their own work, concluding that each of them had an equally valid response to the theme and that the variety of the response in the class to the stimulus idea was evidence of the richness of their different perceptions.

Step 9: Adaptation. The learners now discussed how to set their own lyrics to music and what kind of music would be appropriate.

Proposals were drawn up in sub-groups and presented to the class.
Their suggestions were then compared to the Waits song version and
their reactions to his music and its appropriacy discussed. A group of
learners volunteered to set their work to music and present it to the
class in the next lesson.

Soldier's Things
Davenports and kettle drums
and swallow tail coats
table cloths and patent leather shoes
bathing suits and bowling balls
and clarinets and rings
and all this radio really
needs is a fuse
a tinker, a tailor
a soldier's things
his rifle, his boots full of rocks
and this one is for bravery
and this one is for me
and everything's a dollar
in this box

Cuff links and hub caps
trophies and paperbacks
it's good transportation
but the brakes aren't so hot
neck tie and boxing gloves
this jackknife's rusted
you can pound that dent out
on the hood
a tinker, a tailor
a soldier's things
his rifle, his boots full of rocks
oh and this one is for bravery
and this one is for me
and everything's a dollar
in this box.

(Tom Waits)

Two student texts
bits 'n' pieces

in the obscure light
lying there
the old map of a sailor
pieces of cork
chains and a mysterious suitcase
all covered with dust
old rusty swords

used in numerous battles
peaceful lying there.

old plastic beads
passing through the ancient coffee grinder
filtered through faded quilts
aromatic as moldy records
settled in a rusty coffee pot
beside the ceramic cookie jar

Summary

(1) All the activities in this group demonstrate a feature of great value in the communicative classroom. They create conditions for learners to produce a variety of responses to tasks and in doing so, they allow learners to express their individuality through their opinions and feelings concerning task, content and procedure.

(2) These activities have no 'correct' or 'incorrect' answers. Neither do they require a set of responses to meet any perceived expectations of the teacher. As a result learners are faced with the need to exchange views, argue their opinions, negotiate compromises and arrive at a consensus, wherever appropriate.

(3) A particular advantage of these activities is that learners are encouraged to take risks and experiment when they speak and write.

(4) What they produce, i.e. learner texts, moreover, have a role in the development of the activity. As artifacts in the learning process they are not corrected and discarded. Instead, as items displayed and exhibited in the classroom, they become contributions to the process which are discussed and analysed by the class. In this way the texts produced by the learner are given a status rarely accorded to them in language lessons. (This is an issue which we will discuss in detail in chapter 5, see 5.4.2).

(5) The learner as a creative user of the target language is a new role for him/her in the language classroom. As a participant he is able to determine much of his input into the work of the group. These activities encourage in this way a different form of learner behaviour with regard to their own classroom roles and that of the teacher. They can be used as a form of learner training for the communicative classroom by providing space for learners to act independently.

(6) These activities can be used to initiate work in a given area or as follow-up work. They can also be adapted for use at most levels of learner attainment.

(7) Imagination-gap work is powerful in motivation terms since it deals with the affective domain. It provides a means of expressing feelings and opinions within an overall structure which also allows the learner a maximum of freedom for decision-making.

(8) It must be emphasized that imagination-gap activities require conditions of trust within a learner-centred classroom atmosphere. They work effectively when preceded by activities which foster trust and a positive group dynamic in the class.

(9) Much of the work of these activities involves working with literature. This is often a neglected area in the language classroom because there have been few creative activities in current use which access literature in an interactive, democratic way to learners. They provide a means of approaching the richest corpus of text which the target language possesses. (For further reading on projection and fantasy see: Oaklander 1978; Yeomans 1975a; Perls et al. 1951; de Mille 1974; Zinker 1977. For further activities and teaching suggestions see: Moskowitz 1978, p. 178ff; Spaventa et al. 1980; Hendricks 1975; 1977; de Mille 1973; Collie and Slater 1987; Pulverness 1989.)

4.2.6 Role-playing and creative dramatics

Role-play is now such a common feature in the language classroom that it has become a standard activity for the post presentation, free language practice phase of a language lesson. There are many variations in the way it is used. They range from the survival language of shopping and ordering meals in a restaurant to problem-oriented themes relating to the lives of young people (conflict at home, friendship, relationships, rivalries, etc.) all of which produce motivating and productive situations for speaking. The former example of role-play is clearly limited in its scope for spontaneous development beyond the prescribed scenario, whereas the open-ended nature of the latter provides opportunities to investigate issues. Di Pietro (1987) and many other authors take role-play beyond the level of classroom games by combining role-plays of a socially educative orientation (cooperation and solidarity, role-distance and tolerance of ambiguity, the ability to negotiate, take action and empathize, etc.) with more content specific role-plays containing both a language and subject orientation. Whatever the level of didacticism, such role-plays are of value to the communicative classroom as experiments in exploring problems and finding solutions in the target language. Nevertheless, it is worth noting in passing that not all such communicative situations need be serious or problem-oriented. As Maley and Duff (1982) point out, 'absurd' situations can also produce the motivated use of language as a result of trying to solve comical and unusual problems.

In this section we wish to focus, however, on a technique which allows the teacher to extend the scope of the familiar, problem-oriented role-play. Called the 'empty chair' technique, it derives from Gestalt therapy (Zinker 1977, p. 122) and encourages learners to draw on personal experiences related to a particular theme. It functions by allowing the participants to act out these experiences which then serve to increase their understanding of the theme in hand. It is most effectively used in conjunction with an imagination-gap activity and is either implemented in an *intra*-personal or an *inter*-personal way.

(1) Intra-personal role-play

This group contains role-play activities in which the roles (normally there are only two) are carried out by the same person by means of the technique of the 'empty chair'. In Gestalt therapy this technique helps the client or patient to explore inner polarities, ambivalences and conflicts with representatives of the environment (parents, boss, teacher, etc.) with the aim of achieving a new level of awareness of the problem in hand. The patient commences the dialogue with a part of himself (an introject) whom he confronts as his conversation partner in the empty chair. As he changes from chair to chair he also changes his role (cf. Oaklander 1977; Zinker 1977).

Such conversations can be particularly valuable in the classroom when working with texts and themes. They can be used to seek out solutions for conflicts or to find ways of verbalizing opinions and viewpoints by acting them out. Unlike a therapy session it would, of course, only lead to direct exploration of inner conflicts in the rarest of instances. Conversational partners 'on the chair' are usually projected characters out of fictional texts, figures from pictures or historical personages. The role-play can be a spontaneous acting out or it could relate to written work already done or it could be written down after the spontaneous dramatization. In the latter case it is often adapted and changed. One person role-plays of this type can be split up into two groups:

(a) writing a dialogue or dramatizing intra-personal polarities and conflicts with oneself, tensions or pressures or tensions from external pressures and unacceptable desires. Here the aim is to bring the tensions out into the open and to find solutions, for example:

the leisure persona versus the school persona
the child versus adolescent
head versus heart

(b) creating a dialogue or dramatizing the encounter of the learner with projected figures, fictional characters from texts.

The learner as himself – character from a literary text, figures from a picture
e.g. Salinger's *The Catcher in the Rye*:
Learner meets Holden, Jane, etc.
Northern Ireland
Learner meets old man in Roden Street (see above).

Fictional character to fictional character
* Richard Wright's 'Almos' a Man'
Dave talks to the dead mule after he has shot it
* Salinger's *The Catcher in the Rye*
Holden meets D.B., Holden meets Allie, Holden meets the headmaster, Holden meets his father.

Part of fictional character versus part of fictional character
* Shakespeare's *Macbeth*
Mac versus Beth (see below)
* D.H. Lawrence's *Lady Chatterley's Lover*
Constance as a wife versus Constance as a lover.

Example 1: A dialogue with a deal mule (University seminar, English methodology class; theme: the American short story on film)

In Richard Wright's short story 'Almos' a Man', Dave, a seventeen-year-old black youth, seeks social recognition on the one hand and on the other his manhood through the possession of a pistol. Initially he is refused the revolver because he is too young but later succeeds in acquiring one through cunning and patience. However, practising with the weapon leads to a catastrophe because he accidently shoots the mule which he uses to work the fields of his white master. The farmer forces him to work off the debt incurred over the next two years. He is unwilling to face this penalty and one night runs away. He unearths the pistol which he had buried after the accident and jumps on a passing train.

The students' initial interpretation of the catastrophe wrought by the shot was framed exclusively in terms of an accident, a stupid mistake, or an expression of immaturity. At this point they ruled out any attempt to interpret from a social psychological perspective. They were able to see a film version of the short story and the scene which follows the accidental shooting was played again. At the point where Dave is bent crying despairingly over the body of the dead animal, the film was stopped and a task given to the students based on the freeze-frame picture of the scene. This took the form of a role-play with the instruction 'Could you try and act out a dialogue between Dave and the dead mule'. Student Monica A undertook a dramatization using the 'empty chair' technique, alternating between the role of Dave and the mule (see below):

Mule You've shot me, you damn fool!

Dave I know! I'm so sad. I don't understand.

Mule Why did you do it? I've always done my work for you. Every morning I was ready. I've never complained about the plough, the hot weather. I've always listened to you.

Dave I know, I'm so sad.

Mule I was your only friend. I did everything you wanted me to do, what are you going to do now? They are going to laugh at you.

Dave I don't know . . . .

Mule You've destroyed yourself. How are you going to plough the fields without me? They are going to punish you.

Dave (After a long pause) No. Now I've shot you, I'll run away. I've always wanted to run away one day. I'll leave this place where I've had to work like a mule.

Monica's role-play fascinated the other participants in the class because she herself was so absorbed in her projection. It also led the way to an analysis previously unforeseen, namely, that the killing of the animal could be interpreted as an unconscious act of rebellion and liberation: Dave shot the mule in himself to create the opportunity to relinquish his serfdom.

(2) Inter-personal role-play

We understand by this term text and theme-related role-plays which explore and analyse inter-personal polarities and conflicts with particular reference to characters in fictional texts. An advantage which they bring to the communicative classroom is that they facilitate the creation of learner dialogues in which such inter-personal relationships are enacted. First of all, we need to distinguish between *partner and group role-plays*. Groups of learners can, of course, as example 1 will show, take on the part of one of these partners. However, group role-plays normally refer to complex sequences which have more than two roles and imply various group activities involving preparation, execution and detailing of the scene, and drawing up sharp and clear role-profiles in order to work on texts. This would be followed by the role-play itself which would require three groups, the actors, audience and a group, to evaluate the performance. What these role-plays offer as a way of exploiting the interaction potential in a class is, as Seletzky points out, the opportunity to get away from the type of classroom discourse which is only concerned with talking about problems, in itself a special type of language, and to practise a livelier, richer form of communication. They appeal to the desire to play and have fun that learners bring to a class, making possible a richer interaction with the theme. Preparing such role-plays of this type, in itself as important as the presentation, requires of learners considerable research. The following examples illustrate how they function:

Example 2: Encitement to murder (German high school, grade 12; understanding English drama – William Shakespeare)

The aim of this unit, a dramatized role-play developed from Shakespeare's *Macbeth* (Act 1, scene 7), is to identify from the interaction between Macbeth and Lady Macbeth, the key factors which determined the decision to murder Duncan. A most productive starting point was the vividness of the language in the original text. (The preceding lessons had dealt with Lady Macbeth's fears and her conflict with her own femininity.) The focus of the class was a study of Lady Macbeth's methods of persuasion and Macbeth's struggle with himself. It is in the conflict between the desire for power and his conscience, that Lady Macbeth becomes a decisive catalyst. The stages of the work in terms of teacher aims were as follows:

- learners should be able to work out the genesis of the decision to carry out the murder from the structure of the relationships in the play
- learners should be able to identify key points in this process
- learners should be able to identify the poles of conflict for Macbeth and analyse them
- they should be able to make a list and evaluate the persuasion strategies of Lady Macbeth
- they should be able to identify the key images and explain their dramatic function
- they should be able to explain the question of responsibility for the murder

Learner preparation for this task included:
- intensive oral and written work on Lady Macbeth's invocation of

the powers of darkness
- familiarization with the dramatic function of the imagery of darkness (I, V, pp. 36) and comparison with the imagery of light and life as shown in other parts of the text (for example, I, vi)
- intensive reading of the relevant part of the text for homework I, vii) and recording in written form their reactions to the scene.

Step 1: The lesson began with the tape-recording of scene I, 7 from the play to refresh the learners' minds of what they had been reading. It functioned also as an additional prop to comprehension, since the class found Shakespeare easier to understand when spoken.

Step 2: Next the group shared their reactions from the reading and their notes and wrote down the modes of conflict in a grid prepared on the blackboard. Macbeth's name was split up into Mac and Beth preparing the way for the role-play which was to continue:

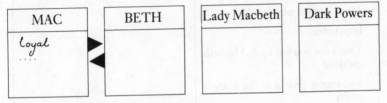

Figure 4.4 Collecting learner reactions to the characters

Step 3: The preparation in small sub-groups prior to the role-play required the class participants to evaluate the potential for conflict in the situation, that is to say each group tried to identify with it. Using texts, a structure on the board and prepared prompt cards the group composed a role which it was to act out later as one protagonist or as several within the role-play.
The learners were faced with several tasks:

At the level of text analysis: using the prompt cards (see fig. 4.5), they had to gather together relevant information, which would show how they had understood the scene.

At the level of organizing information: they had to organize the information according to key points in the discourse namely the argumentative strategies used: here they could call on the help of STARTERS which were marked on the prompt cards.

At the level of expression: the task facing the learners was to articulate

PROMPT-CARD MAC:

You are 'MAC', a vital part of Macbeth, strongly convinced that murdering DUNCAN is out of the question, as a matter of fact, such a deed runs contrary to your set of values. Of course, you can support your conviction with good arguments, however, you need to defend them against 'BETH'.

Starters	Arguments
Listen . . .	
Can't you listen . . .?	
Well, I thought about it once more . . .	
Don't you agree . . .?	
Nobody would understand . . .	
There's no doubt that . . .	
Impossible!	
That's not you but Lady Macbeth speaking . . .	
You simply give in to the Lady if you're . . .	

PROMPT-CARD BETH:

You are 'BETH', a vital part of Macbeth and are burning to murder DUNCAN. You would gain so much if you did it. The earlier the better! However, you need to assert yourself against 'MAC'.

Starters	Arguments
Forget about . . .	
Why do you have second thoughts?	
It's so simple . . .	
Don't you think . . .	
It's my last chance . . .	
If I don't do it Banquo will do it . . .	
Imagine . . .	

Try to imagine . . .

She told me it would work and she knows . . .

I am settled . . .

You . . . !!!

PROMPT-CARD LADY MACBETH

You are terribly disappointed and angry about your husband because he has just told you 'We will proceed no further in this business' (I, vii, 31). For the time being you are at a loss and turn to the powers of darkness for guidance and advice. You need to communicate your husband's attitude and your anxieties.

Starters	Arguments
I need your advice . . .	
What can I do if he . . .?	
He seems to be torn between . . .	
He keeps talking about . . .	
How would you talk to him . . .?	
But I am his wife . . .	
I am a woman and . . .	
Couldn't it be dangerous . . .	
What are his weak points?	
What would you recommend?	
That's a good idea, but . . .	

Figure 4.5 Learner-devised roles

PROMPT-CARD POWERS OF DARKNESS

You represent the dark powers and know exactly what strategies Lady Macbeth must employ in order to let the dark sides in Macbeth take the lead. Since you know both Macbeth's weak points and the Lady's powers, you can arouse the latter. You have absolute faith in the validity and persuasive power of your arguments.

Starters	Arguments
Don't give up so quickly . . .	
You are more powerful than that . . .	
Just . . .	
Don't be a fool! He's a man, just tell him . . .	
That's true, but . . .	
Don't give up halfway . . .	
He won't carry on saying 'no' if you . . .	
Be more . . .	
Don't forget . . .	

Figure 4.5 cont.

the arguments that they had identified from the text: this involved transforming Shakespearean language into colloquial English.

Alongside these tasks, the role-play also made possible the opportunity to express personal viewpoints. By taking advantage of the opportunity presented by the role-play, learners were able to introduce their insights and find appropriate ways of expressing them.

Step 4: 'Acting out the play'. Here the principle of doubling came in useful because it guaranteed the support of the other members of the group to the protagonist, preventing that person from become isolated and at the same time offering the others the opportunity to participate. At this point weaker learners felt confident enough to participate.

Step 5: 'Evaluation'. The learner texts which emerged from recording the group's presentation provided the background against which the

Shakespearean text could be seen in a new light. The learner text, thus, became an important device in the joint process of making sense of the Shakespeare text. At the same time it was the starting point for an evaluation activity. This evaluation, which also drew in learners not involved in the role-play, was an important final element in the interpretation phase. It was preceded by individual work after which the class met in a plenary discussion to express their views on the question of responsibility for the murder of Duncan.

Complex role-plays such as those compiled by Seletzky (1984), Lach-Newinsky and Seletzky (1986) or Bredella and Legutke (1985b) make use of fixed role descriptions and outlines of functions for the roles. They sometimes fix time limits on the length of the action, or stipulate precisely how the scenario is to develop. In these cases they are inseparable from *simulations*, an activity which provides the most differentiated scenarios for communicative action in the modern language classroom. However, we do not propose here to take up the issue surrounding the methodology of simulations. (See Jones K. 1982.)

Summary
(1) Both intra-personal and inter-personal role-plays personalize the theme and object of the role-play, i.e. they enable the participant to generate empathy. They achieve this by providing him/her with an opportunity to experience an involvement with the theme through a personal dramatization, which in turn opens up ways of understanding (cf. class discussions which take place at a 'meta' level in relation to the theme).
(2) They allow learners to separate out strands of an argument or ways of perceiving a problem or aspects of character and personality.
(3) When used in relation to fictional texts they prioritize dramatic involvement as a means of processing, understanding and interpreting the text.
(4) It allows learners to be creative in their own right when faced with literature, thereby widening their scope for independent action in thematic areas in the language classroom conventionally regarded as teacher-centred.
(5) Both forms of role-play provide individual learners with opportunities to create and communicate their own oral and written texts.

4.2.7 Interaction and interpersonality

It could be said that all the exercise types that we have dealt with so far are interactive in character because they all involve the sharing of information and the negotiation of meaning. What we are referring to here, however, are activities in which the focus is directed explicitly on the interaction between the participants as themselves. The significant difference between these exercises and role-play is that here the learner acts in his own right without the role as protection. As Stankewitz (1977, p. 24) points out, the psychological argument for the use of role-play is that the role guarantees opportunities of speaking without ever threatening to expose the reality of the speaker, because the speaker is distanced from the real situation. When the speaker takes on a role he is in a sense protected from consequences for himself in the real world. It is as if he were wearing a mask or a disguise. He may adopt modes of behaviour which he would reject for himself under normal circumstances and explore aspects of himself which he may have up to then resisted or not yet given vent to. Above all he may distance himself at any time from the role. It is exactly in this duality of character 'both figure and actor are neither completely identical nor can they be completely separated' (Stankewitz 1977, p. 26) that the educational justification for using role-play can be found.

However, in interaction and interpersonality tasks, learners have to learn to make do without such protection. It is, therefore, essential that teachers give due consideration to criteria 3, 4 and 5 when selecting such tasks. Clearly instructions and procedural rules limit the scope for action and provide a certain amount of protection. Where the rules of a game limit the participants' freedom of action, their intellectual and emotional energy can be directed towards a particular focus. Such simplified situations make it possible for learners to experience 'structures and structural contexts more effectively than in a reality over which they would not be able to find an overview'. The uptake in learning would consist of expanding the possibilities for self-perception and the perception of others, predominantly by the giving and receiving of feed-back, which is itself dependent on the willingness and openness of the participants. The pedagogic justification for such tasks can be readily demonstrated in that they encourage a high level of involvement of all skills, i.e. subject, linguistic and communicative skills.

The exercises we describe in this section have been adapted for modern language teaching from group dynamic training, communication and behavioural training and humanistic psychology (see above 3.2). These disciplines all seek to enable participants to achieve some form of self-experience in encounters with other learners. Such encounters occur in the act of giving and receiving feed-back, informing and asking for personal information, particularly of feelings and emotions, i.e. the perceiving and sharing of layers of the personality which lie below the surface and which are brought to light by the interaction.

Earlier, when dealing with task selection criteria, we referred on several occasions to tasks which we believe to belong in this section. The following examples illustrate what was referred to earlier (see 3.2, 3.3, 3.4, and also Seletzky and Thomas 1982). Variations on this type of task occur in a variety of handbooks as well (Remocker and Storch 1979, p. 50ff; Moskowitz 1978, p. 158; Canfield and Wells 1976, p. 55).

Example: Self-portrait (Intermediate grade 11 to post-intermediate grade 12, German high school; theme: growing up; theme: Poetry Workshop, sequence identity)

Step 1: Homework. Making an individual collage. The teacher brings a pile of English and American magazines into the class and a piece of A3 paper for each learner. One or two magazines are given out to everyone to be cut up with the following instruction for homework:

> for next lesson, please make a poster that illustrates your personality and lifestyle by selecting appropriate pictures from these magazines. You can also take pictures from other magazines. Try to include pictures that show some of the following things about yourself: attitudes, interests, likes, dislikes, ambitions, feelings, etc. Be selective, because it is impossible to elicit every aspect of yourself. Please do not show your collage to any member of this class and DO NOT SIGN IT. But don't forget to bring it along for the next lesson.

The teacher also joins in and compiles a collage which is brought along to the next lesson.

Step 2: Procedure (beginning of the next lesson). The exercise is explained by the teacher and the purpose of the sequence outlined.

Step 3: Making the collage speak. The collages are placed face down on a table and mixed up. The learners and the teacher each choose one (not their own) which they try to describe to the class. This can be in the form of a description or a verbalization in the first person, as if the speaker were talking about himself (I am . . ., I . . .).

- Write down what the collage tells you.
- Was it done by a boy or a girl? What makes you think so?
- What kind of a person is he/she? What makes you think so? etc.
- You could either write about the collage or make the collage talk to you. In the latter case your text will start with 'I . . .'. When you are finished, please sign your text.

The collages are hung on the wall together with the text in such a way that the classroom takes on the air of an exhibition.

Step 4: Self collage gallery. The learners now view the gallery in their classroom and look at their collage self-portrait and read the texts written about them. Then groups of learners discuss in pairs (the composer of the collage and the interpreter) the visual self-portrait and the explanatory text.

Did he/she understand who I am?
What did he/she understand?
What did he/she not understand?
What was left out?
Appropriate/inappropriate?

Step 5: Circle session. The learners sit in a circle with their collages and interpretations. They are free now to state their opinions on the way their collages have been interpreted by other people, i.e. their satisfaction, unease, agreement or rejection, and, if appropriate, annoyance. Whatever was new or surprising can receive particular attention.

Instead of moving from steps 3 to 5, a series of alternatives are also conceivable: for example the collages can be pinned up and numbered immediately after they have been mixed up. Each learner can walk around and make notes on each individual collage. The collages can then be taken down by the learners who had compiled them. Next, the class forms sub-groups of five or six. Within the groups the self-portraits can be commented upon, clarified and questions can be posed. The circle sessions which round the unit off could have the function of reflecting upon the learning cycle as a whole and the experiences that have been gained through it.

The considerable communicative potential in the various areas of language use (description, pair-work, conversation, discussion, inner-circle) can be maximized if learners are given language support to express what they want. A variety of functional and notional areas are covered in group discussions:

- Describing pictures.

- Drawing inferences from pictures. Qualifying shape, colours.
- Qualifying attitudes . . . .
- Notion, e.g. family, likes, dislikes, friendship, spare-time, future plans, etc.
- Expressing satisfaction, dissatisfaction, preference, liking, disliking, surprise, irritation.
- Enquiring about authors/producers intention, etc.

Brandes and Phillips (1979, p. 33) have produced another version of this particular exercise. They ask learners to devise an advert for themselves in which they describe themselves as a particularly desirable product. Christison and Bassano (1981, p. 34) have even suggested a personal advert for a newspaper 'lonely hearts' column. In both versions of this exercise the person, whose name is not given, has to be guessed by the other members of the class. However, these versions could bring the teacher into conflict with criteria 4 and 5 since the learner is rendered vulnerable. Nevertheless other thematic variations of this exercise can be taken up in themes such as 'My Dream Job', 'My Ideal Place to Live', 'My Communal Project' and 'My Ideal School'.

Summary
(1) These activities promote primarily self-awareness and help learners to articulate this self-awareness in the target language.
(2) They provide a simple and effective structure in which to broach the area of personal and group self-perceptions.
(3) The procedures of the activity encourage learners to develop a positive social attitude towards the group by providing an important change of perspective in how they view themselves, i.e. it is a way of seeing yourself as others see you.

4.2.8 Values clarification and discussion activities

The exercises which fall into this category are largely derived from the principles and the methodological groundwork of the values clarification approaches developed in the United States in the early 1970s (Simon et al. 1972; Wolfe and Howe 1973a; 1973b; Howe and Howe 1975; Casteel and Stahl 1975). This was an orientation in educational theory and practice which arose as part of the humanist movement at the beginning of the 1970s (see 3.2). Its aim was to encourage schools to help young people to develop their own sets of values which would in turn enable them to become responsible for their own actions. To this end a wide variety of exercises were created which focused on moral concepts related to personality (strengths, weaknesses, aims in life, future work, etc.) and the environment (school, leisure, local and national politics, ecology and economy, women's politics) (Castillo and Stahl 1975). These exercises are concerned with the selection and sequencing of behavioural and value role-models, the creation of lists of preferences, and the negotiation of priorities. They support processes of decision-making in learner sub-groups in areas such as the ranking of human qualities, ideas or values. All these actions involve value judgements, questions of criteria on how one formulates values, and alternative choices which require the learner to make fresh judgements. The exercises are directed precisely at the prejudices and pre-knowledge of the learners which become the springboard for further steps of clarification and differentiation.

Exercises such as these have been available to language teaching for some time (Abbs and Sexton 1978). However, recently they have become more widely and systematically used in the classroom. Several writers have made significant contributions (Bredella 1984a; 1985, with his work in the teaching of literature; Klippel 1983; Porter-Ladousse 1983).

Example 1: Values sheet: What is an American?
This was used with a methodology class of trainee teachers at Giessen University, West Germany, who were working on the subject of cross-cultural learning. They had set themselves a research task which involved local American military personnel of the NATO forces in Germany. They wanted specifically to investigate segments of the social grouping, 'English–American', and to find texts and themes for their work in class. They preceded their fieldwork with two value clarification activities (Legutke 1984). Here is a part of one of the values sheets (see fig. 4.6):

After working initially on their own, they were asked to share their responses with a partner and then in small groups, with the purpose of compiling a list of characteristics of an American which would be acceptable to every one of the participants. This was written up on an overhead transparency for reference at future points in the seminar.

Using values work sheets activates the prejudices and pre-knowledge of learners. There is no attempt to disguise, ignore or smooth over contentious areas for the sake of an apparent consensus. Rather the group is encouraged to expose through discussion those

Which of the following statements characterize   A   G   ?
Americans more appropriately than Germans
and vice versa?

1. More likely, as a soldier, to disobey orders

2. First to take a stranger into his home

3. First to start a fight because of a traffic accident

4. More likely to overheat his home

5. More likely to go to church

6. Fatter

7. More likely to bring a lawsuit if injured

8. More hostile to foreigners

9. More courteous to strangers

10. More friendly to neighbours

11. More likely to be promiscuous

12. Easier to become good friends with

13. More provincial

14. Richer

15. More likely to hold a grudge

16. More likely to betray a business associate

17. More fascinated by household gadgets and
    appliances

18. More likely to cheat on income tax

19. More likely to commit a burglary

20. More patriotic

Which of the following statements characterize   A   G   ? Americans more appropriately than Germans and vice versa?
21. More in love with his car
22. More interested in politics
23. More musically inclined
24. More interested in his country's history
25. More athletic
26. More ignorant in general
27. More efficient
28. More fascinated by the other's country
29. Travels more
30. Changes residences more
31. More subject to depression
32. Treats wife/husband more respectfully
33. Treats wife/husband more lovingly
34. Spends more time with his/her children
35. More likely to have a large dog
36. More likely to own a flag
37. More addicted to watching television
38. More likely to give money to charities
39. More likely to be happy
40. Louder

Figure 4.6 A values sheet for a cross-cultural learning task

differences of opinion that exist among them. This leads to the formulation of hypotheses and questions which will guide their research work outside the classroom. In this way learners' opinions and prejudices can be shown to be of pivotal value in the communicative classroom as they are stimuli for research projects, directed towards sections of the real world (in this case the area around Giessen) or towards representations of the real world (texts) from the country of the target language. Results of the research work and the residue from the negotiation of viewpoints can be fed back into the learning processes to make clear what progress has been made in the learning. Whenever this activity is undertaken it also emphasizes, more often than not, the need for teachers to provide an opportunity to exchange opinions and perceptions of the target culture in the classroom. As Seletzky has pointed out (1984, p. 128), learners constantly need to revise their knowledge of and attitudes towards the country of the target language.

Seletzky (1984) and Thiel (1985) have both used similar values worksheets in class projects with learners at high school level. Thiel's grade 8/9 learners investigated areas of the way of life of United States military personnel and their families in Frankfurt, while Seletzky worked with learners from the twelfth grade on the theme of 'Growing up in a small American town in the 1920s'. Seletzky notes how he succeeded in counteracting the tendency amongst learners towards uniformity of viewpoint by using values clarification procedures.

> Every learner had to announce his decision before discussing items from the questionnaire above by raising his/her hand. This very simple procedure proved to be extremely effective and advantageous. They were surprised by the interest and opposition, often from the most unexpected quarters, which their views provoked, and also reassured by the discovery that there were others who shared their views. It is important to realize that this procedure alters the value and use of the text and the input from the teacher. These now serve to clarify problems which had arisen within the group of learners themselves.
>
> (Seletzky 1984, p. 127)

Example 2: Rating scale

We have already referred in the earlier section on the 'imagination gap' to the way in which the exercise chain 'success story' from the text book *Confidence* (1984, p. 91) was set in motion. Learners were asked to react to a picture of Arnold Schwarzenegger using the following rating scale:

				0				
open								withdrawn
sensitive								insensitive
active								passive
physical								intellectual
creative								dull
self-confident								shy
trustworthy								untrustworthy
warm								cold
happy								unhappy
satisfied								dissatisfied
reticent								talkative
polite								rude
caring								selfish
humble								stuck-up

Language notes: Expressing degree

I believe	that	he is	fairly
I assume			highly
I think			extremely
It seems to me			quite
			rather
			very
	In my view		more . . . than . . .

Now work with a partner. Compare and discuss your ratings. Where do you agree and where do you disagree?

Figure 4.7 Learner values rating exercise

The following sub-tasks were carried out using the 'snowball' or 'pyramid' technique, i.e. they were first done individually then with partners or in small groups.

(1) Learners were asked to look closely at the picture and to try and get an impression of the person depicted.
(2) Using the rating scale they were asked to characterize the person depicted.
(3) They were to choose three adjectives which in their view characterized the person most accurately and three which did not fit him at all.
(4) Next they were to compare and discuss their ratings with a partner and subsequently with a group of other learners to discover where they agreed and disagreed.

The purpose of this task was to create expectations and mobilize attitudes in preparation for the analysis of the text which was to follow. These expectations were studied again after reading the text. The interesting question was to what extent their attitudes had changed and which were confirmed.

Example 3: The moral dilemma
Scenarios such as the one illustrated below (see fig. 4.8) have been used with adult mono and multilingual classes. They are particularly effective in revealing personal moral and cultural value systems and providing a range of possibilities for further work.

It will be clear from the scenario that, while there may be some measure of agreement concerning guilt and blame, there can never be any externally imposed answer or solution. It is in the nature of such tasks to admit a range of perceptions and responses which cannot be ratified against any scale depicting 'right' or 'wrong' answers. The process dimension of the task is the argument and debate which takes place and in which learners communicate their own meaning. Such tasks are successful *because* of their 'open-endedness' and their capacity to evoke the beliefs that learners hold.

Example 4: The postcard selection
This activity was developed by Carter (personal communication, 1985) for use in adult multilingual classes as the prelude to a project module on an English language course in Bath, England. Its specific purpose was to stimulate interest in the scenes depicted on the picture postcards so that the learners would be encouraged to carry

Mary's husband had been away on business for six months. Mary was not lonely – her boyfriend, Julian, made sure of that.

Suddenly, Mary realized that she was pregnant. She asked Julian what she should do. He said she should do exactly what she wanted because it was nothing to do with him.

Mary felt guilty about having an abortion because of her strict religious upbringing. When she talked to the priest about it, he told her bluntly, 'abortion is murder'.

Two weeks after her conversation with the priest, she went to her family doctor, a woman. The doctor told her that she saw no reason why she shouldn't have the child and refused to recommend a national health abortion.

Mary was short of money and borrowed some from her brother; she told him what she wanted it for.

Then she had an abortion in a private clinic; it cost her £500.

She paid back the money to her brother but he began to blackmail her. He threatened to tell her husband everything unless she gave him more money.

A neighbour told the husband all about the abortion and the boyfriend. He decided to go on living with Mary because he was afraid of the scandal if he left her.

There are seven people in the story – rank the seven people in your own order of moral preference. Be ready to justify your ranking to the rest of the group.

Figure 4.8 An example of a scenario for a moral dilemma task (Rinvolucri, M. 1981)

out external fieldwork in the environment illustrated on the cards. They showed scenes of historic Bath, an English city with important Roman remains and extensive eighteenth-century Georgian architecture.

The learners were grouped and asked to study the cards. They were required to award each card points for general appeal and photographic interest. The cards were then to be stuck on a large sheet of display card in order of merit. Below each card the learners were asked to write a small evaluative and descriptive caption.

The activity elicits at first a range of responses from the participants which draws out the level of agreement or disagreement on the merits of the pictures. However, because the task requires of participants a structured evaluation, they are forced to negotiate sets of criteria based on their own standards and values of aesthetics. Its merit for the language classroom lies not only in the way it allows values to emerge and interact but that negotiation has to take place for an acceptable group consensus to develop.

We have already referred to Klippel's work (1984) which contains a number of useful values clarification activities for language teaching. We can also mention here Bredella's values clarification tasks in connection with literary text analysis. (Bredella 1985, p. 71) He encourages learners to respond to questions such as:

What is the most important wording? aspect of
                                                image
                                            passage

Who is the most important character?

Bredella comments: 'What characterizes these questions is that they encourage the reader to address that which seems important *to him/her*. She is challenged to become aware of what attracts her attention, what she selects and how she reacts to it' (Bredella 1985a, p. 71).

Summary

(1) The tasks expose what is previously known, introducing learners' own powers of judgement into the activity serving to discover the point at which learning can take place.

(2) They highlight the role of the learner's individual opinion by providing space for learners to express differences of opinion, forcing them to revise and justify their views.

(3) They help to create expectations and enable learners to formulate questions for investigation on the basis of what learners know already. In this way they can act as stimuli for research work in or outside the classroom.

(4) They can help assess progress in learning and the change of attitude if the same tasks are repeated at different points in the learning process.

(5) They can provide a guided introduction to free discussion (Klippel 1984; Seletzky and Thomas 1982, p. 29).

(6) These tasks have the potential to motivate learners because they are encouraged to contribute their own views in an appropriate non-threatening context.

(For further reading and activities see Howe and Howe 1975; Casteel and Stahl 1975; Simon et al. 1972; Klippel 1984.)

4.2.9 Process evaluation and learner training

In this last section we look at the question of evaluating the learning process and at ways in which this can be realized by participants in the process. We follow Nunan (1988) here in making a distinction between evaluation and the related terms, assessment and testing. He points out, 'the purpose of assessment is to determine whether or not the objectives of a course of instruction have been achieved' (p. 7), whereas the purpose of evaluation is to discover reasons why the learning has been successful or otherwise. He specifies the role of evaluation in a learner-centred programme as follows:

> In traditional curriculum models, evaluation has been identified with testing and is seen as an activity which is carried out at the end of the learning process, often by someone who is not connected with the course itself. (In other words, the emphasis is on summative rather than formative evaluation.) In a learner-centred system, on the other hand, evaluation generally takes the form of an informal monitoring which is carried on alongside the teaching-learning process, principally by the participants in the process, that is, the teachers and the learners . . . .
>
> . . . during implementation (of the curriculum), elements to be evaluated may include materials, learning activities, sequencing, learning arrangements, teacher performance, and learner achievement.
>
> (Nunan 1988, p. 7)

Process-evaluation activities make it possible for learners to look at the elements in the learning process from both the affective and cognitive perspective. A balanced and productive evaluation emerges therefore when participants can articulate both their initial affective responses and their considered reflections on what has been learned and how far the procedures have been successful. What they carry forward becomes the base from which they are able to optimize their future individual and collective learning.

When a teacher introduces an evaluative activity into the classroom repertoire she also takes on a new role, in Breen's words (1987b), she becomes a researcher of her own teaching. She commences an open dialogue with her learners on the progress and outcomes of the teaching programme and receives direct feed-back on how far the planning and the execution of lesson units have been successful. For learners, the value of this type of activity is even more far-reaching. They become increasingly aware of how they, as individuals and members of a group, learn. That is, they develop an overview of their learning and are able to make productive use of their reflections (see 6.3).

However, what learners are also doing is practising being proactive with regard to their own learning, that is, they are becoming more aware of how to organize their learning programme. Moreover they gain insights into how teaching is planned and executed. As we shall see in the following chapter, it is both this emerging didactic competence and organizational ability which characterize learner behaviour in a project-oriented approach.

The practice of evaluation in the classroom needs to find answers to a wide range of questions and it is the purpose of the activity to provide the framework in which the answers can be uncovered. Some activities reveal more than others. However, as a guide, they should all enable participants to address the following questions:

(1) *The affective dimension*:
   How did you feel during the different steps of the activity?
   Did your feelings change? When did they change? Do you know why they changed?
   Which part of the activity/activities did you like? Which part/parts did you not like? Do you know why?
   Which part/s was/were important for you? Which less important, or unnecessary?
   Did the activity stimulate your interest, your willingness to speak, write, listen, etc.?
(2) *The cognitive dimension*:
   What do you think was the purpose of the various parts of the activity?
   What have you learnt? (Comment on topic, language, learning strategies, learning about yourself and learning about others.)
   Do you know how your learning took place or came about?
   What needs to be done to improve the way you learn (as an individual and as a member of a group)?
   If you were a teacher, what would you change in the activity? What would you leave out? What would you add?

The timing of an evaluation activity is important. It can be used effectively at the following points in the lesson:

- Whenever there are disturbances or disruptions in the learning process or a need to remotivate learners because they may be unclear as to the purpose or value of an activity.
- As an essential part of the tasks included in 4.2.7 since, in dealing with aspects of individual and group self-awareness such tasks constitute radical departures from the practice of the traditional classroom. They need therefore to be contextualized and addressed

by the group with regard to their purpose and effect.

— As a satisfying and rewarding way to conclude simulations, role-plays and values clarification events. Evaluating the learning experience is also a way of analysing language and the communication processes.

— After group-work phases as a way of concluding extended sequences of classwork, for example just before examinations are written, at the end of a semester, after completion of thematic units. It becomes a useful way of reflecting on aims, achievements and how things have gone.

Many valuable reviewing activities which can be used by the teacher to access the requisite feedback information are to be found in sources outside language teaching, such as in group dynamic training literature (Brocher 1967; Schwäbisch and Siems 1974), or the more directly related work of group-work learning and class processes (Wagner 1982), or in the work of pre-vocational and social education (Hunt and Hitchin 1986). The following are examples taken from classroom practice with groups of high school, adult and in-service teacher training groups.

Example 1: 'Video replay' (without video)

The learners pretend that they had made a film of the class at work in the preceding lessons. In order to check to see if the film is of any use and to establish what was in it they 'replay the video and observe the results'. After each important 'observation' (one could give learners observation tasks on an overhead projector transparency such as teacher-learner interaction, the functioning of the group, participation, etc. the learners, who are working individually, 'stop the film' and make notes for the following evaluation phase in plenary. Groups who have not done this activity would have to reconstruct the most important phase of the sequence and undertake an evaluation using questions based on this procedure as a second step. The results of these individual reflections and research are exchanged in a round-table discussion and the implications for their work together in class are discussed and brought out.

Example 2: Observation notes (group work)

In order to make the group aware of self-determined learning processes within itself various forms of observation can be used. Writing minutes of learners' observations provides a basis for discussion within the class.

Observer sheet for role-plays

Your task is to observe your class-mates performing and to evaluate their interaction. At the end you will be asked to give qualified feedback.

The following points are meant to help you:

(1) Was the performance realistic and appropriate to the situation?

(2) How were the conflicts solved?
Who gave in and why?
Did they assert to their point of view rudely?
Did they avoid hurting other people's feelings?
Who showed an awareness of the other person's situation?
Who remained true to himself? Why do you think so?
Who asserted himself most diplomatically?
Who offered compromises?

(3) Decide on the points you would like to observe.

Points to observe :   Notes :

(4) Use the following rating scale to assess the attitudes and behaviour of each actor. Don't forget: You are only asked to assess the acting/performance of the person during the role-play:

Role: Mrs Douglas	+2	+1	0	−1	−2	
self-confident						shy
honest						dishonest
polite						rude
sensitive						insensitive
fair						unfair
emotional						pragmatic
aggressive						shy
compromising						stubborn
interacting						acting
firm/decided						irresolute
	+2	+1	0	−1	−2	

Figure 4.9 An observer's worksheet for an evaluation task (Bredella, L. *et al. 1984*)

Each group is accompanied by an observer whose function is not to act as a kind of auxiliary teacher but to give advice and tips about achieving the best ways of learning within the sub-group. The observers are then in a position to produce a collective evaluation of the minutes, i.e. of notes that they have made whilst observing, and to present them to the class as a whole in the form of 'research results'.

Example 3: Observer's minutes (role-play/simulation)

Oakley (1984) in writing on the use of simulations in language work at tertiary level refers to the learning effect which can be achieved for all participants whenever an analysis and evaluation of language and interaction experiments are undertaken (p. 133). His remarks also apply to the observation of role-plays of all types. The following observer sheet is taken from *Confidence* (Bredella et al. 1984, p. 56) (see fig. 4.9).

Video clips and audio recordings can be valuable additional sources of help when using observation records to evaluate learning processes. Both forms of documentation have specific advantages and disadvantages: 'Video offers an additional visual dimension that is very selective. With an audio recording the visual characteristics are missing but it is technically much simpler and for many teachers it is the only technical aid available.' (Oakley 1984, p. 131).

Example 4: Plus/minus/interesting

This exercise taken from de Bono (1982) can be used to focus on affective, cognitive or general dimensions of previous work, i.e. members of the class can be asked by the teacher to consider any part or all the work in order for them as individuals to identify what they have perceived as positive, negative or 'interesting' (i.e. cannot be directly categorized as either positive or negative but which is worthy of fuller discussion with the rest of the group.) Learners record their thoughts on the following grid:

PLUS	MINUS

INTERESTING

When they have written their observations, the activity can either be 'snowballed' into sub-groups or opened out immediately into a plenary session. This activity not only throws up individual reactions to the teaching process which provides detailed feed-back for the teacher, but invariably demonstrates the range of perceptions within the group. Learners often articulate wide differences in acceptance or non-acceptance of the same learning process.

Example 5: Unfinished sentences

This activity taken from Hunt and Hitchin (1986) is extremely flexible and can be adapted to fit the needs of most classroom situations. Learners are invited to react to a recent learning experience by completing 'unfinished sentences' such as:

> 'The best thing about the class was . . .'
> 'The most important thing I've learned so far is . . .'
> 'Something that really helps me learn is . . .'
> 'If I could go back to the beginning of this course I would . . .'
> 'The most difficult part for me was . . .'
> 'What I enjoyed most was . . .'

The exercise can be treated orally with the answers collected on the board or an OHP, or it can be spread through the class by using the 'snowball' technique, thereby enriching the evaluation by the element of negotiation. Whichever form is used, the teacher can focus the thrust of the feed-back effectively by creating a worksheet for the sentences.

Example 6: Learner diaries

An extension of the unfinished-sentences technique has been used in diary form to provide learners with a long term reflective perspective. In this example the participants were learning English through a programme of Outdoor Education which involved rock-climbing, hill walking, canoeing (Davies 1989). They were asked to record their feelings and observations in a structured diary (see fig. 4.10). The diary entries became the basis for feed-back discussions in which their experiences were processed and worked through in the target language. The diary format is an extremely flexible one as Hunt and Hitchin (1986) point out. It need not be structured as in the example above, it can be used as a free-writing exercise for individuals who maintain it as a learning log, which is monitored on a confidential basis by the teacher. Alternatively it can be a group enterprise for a small group of learners who collect reflections and observations for a short period, maybe a week, on their experiences in the class. Individual observations are subsequently synthesized into a 'research report' and presented to the class for their comments. The format

What interesting conversations and impressions have you had today that you would like to remember?

1. Conversation in Bookshop with an old Welsh man and his wife and daughter.
2. Learning Welsh language.
3. Walking when it was raining and getting cold.

This space is for any other notes you may wish to make

Rain / Devis Kitchen /
Steps / fold in the Roads
Loom, spinning wheel / Batik Pictures / hailstones
Rocks on my Ruck sack / slippery glass / skimming
Stones / Clouds hanging in the valleys / slate bridges
ladder sliter / Weaving centre wool / shopping
Blind spot

Figure 4.10 An example of a learner log (Davies, M. 1989)

DATE 2.10.90.

What did you do today and where?

Today we visited L lembert, a town centre in which
we could buy some interesting cards and meet
lively people whom taught us how to say
Good Morning and Good Night in Welsh.
    We had an interesting walk around a small
lake until 4 o'clock. We enjoyed seeing snow,
people walking in the mountains.

A particular moment I will want to remember about today is:

Concerned during the descent with Akemi & Kyoko
Inspired by the cascading warter.
Very tired at the end of the walk.
Frozen after the shopping
Cold at the start of the walk
happy after a cup of coffee
hesitant in the morning about wether the sun
would come or not
Puzzled over which route to take for the descent
Inspiration because of the beauty of nature
The store keeper was bored in the picture shop

also lends itself to other media forms, e.g. video (see above), audio cassette and photographs.

Summary

(1) Process-evaluation activities play an essential role in the communicative classroom by guaranteeing a learner-centred perspective.

(2) They provide learners with an overview of their own learning and involvement in the planning and organization of future learning.

(3) They introduce a mechanism through which individual learners can articulate their feelings and desires, and therefore bring their own learning preferences to bear on planning.

(4) They are important as communication activities in their own right since their fundamental purpose is to promote the expression of personal meaning and the negotiation of group and individual opinion.

(5) They provide essential feed-back for the teacher on the design and execution of the curriculum.

(6) Since they constitute a radical departure from the practice of traditional curricula, they should be introduced only after classes have been previously exposed to pair-work and group-work techniques.

(7) They are the backbone of project work as we will illustrate in the following chapter.

4.3 Towards the open classroom: benefits and limits of communicative tasks

In chapter 3 we looked at the pedagogic and methodological aspects of humanistic approaches and in this chapter we have examined various types of communicative activities as component parts of a task-based, learner-centred methodology. We can now draw the discussion to a close with the following conclusions:

(1) If we disregard some of the relaxation activities from 4.2.1, which in the strictest sense cannot be categorized as communicative, we would propose that all the others in their own specific ways make it possible to extend the opportunities for interaction within the triangle of self, theme and group. They create the

preconditions for learners to communicate their own meaning.

(2) It is not a set of linguistic aims which determines the process of the action. Here language is part of the process of completing the task which provides the learner with encounters with individual co-learners and their experiences as well as themes and texts. Language therefore is not the aim of the lesson, but a means towards communication between people.

(3) The tasks are directed towards improving the receptivity and the awareness of the learner by 'opening doors to undiscovered worlds' in his/her own field of experience and in the foreign culture and language. They also foster in the learner the willingness to accept responsibility for their own contributions and inputs. However the ability to respond and to act responsibly depends upon the learning climate and the willingness of the class as a whole to involve itself in the processes we have described above. Richards and Rogers (1982, p. 164) describe these two elements as the 'response environment' and the learners' 'responsiveness'. Many of the tasks in the typology would produce such learning conditions.

(4) Because learners are given the opportunity to look for and to formulate responses which are relevant to themselves and which derive from their own experiences, the tasks can be seen as means of allowing learners to contribute their own content to the learning process in the form of learner texts.

(5) The majority of communicative tasks consists of scenarios for explorations or experiments, which Zinker (1977) defines as follows: 'the experiment is a corner stone of experiential learning. It transforms talking about into doing, stale reminiscing and theorizing into being fully here with all one's imagination, energy, and excitement' (p. 123).

The experiment activates the creative potential of learners and opens up a multiplicity of learner experiences. However, parallel to exploration and experience is, as we have seen, the reflection and evaluation of these experiences from the thematic, linguistic, group dynamic and procedural points of view. This takes place in phases of meta conversations, which either form part of the tasks or result from the tasks. A possible sequence could be:

CENTRING > EXPERIENCING > SHARING >
PRODUCING > READING > RESPONDING >
NEGOTIATING > REFLECTING

(6) Tasks which are used in connection with fictional texts can be regarded as particularly valuable phases in the comprehension process because of the way in which they utilize the pre-knowledge of the learners, their value judgements and expectations. They could equally be regarded as another type of comprehension task.

(7) It is clear from the foregoing that such tasks are not to be seen as subsidiary or subservient to texts but methodologically as important. They serve to decode target language texts and stimulate learners to produce their own: we could illustrate the relationship of communicative tasks to themes and texts as follows:

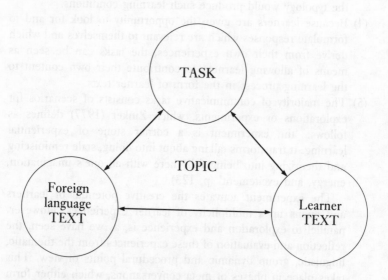

Figure 4.11 The relationship of task, texts and theme (Legutke, M. 1988a)

Task, foreign-language text and learner text should be in balance with one another within the field of the theme.

(8) Communicative tasks should set into motion investigations in the form of research projects which are experience-based, and text and theme related. How this could proceed is shown in the next chapter. They become the means for learning by research, generating the need to inform and the need to acquire language.

(9) Communicative tasks are integrated forms of learning which bring together various language, social and related skills and abilities as well as personal attitudes:

> Appropriate trust of oneself and of others openness, willingness to help, receptiveness, sensitivity, sensibility, intuition, the ability to make contact with others, the ability to play in a concentrated fashion, the ability to listen to other people, the ability to present and reproduce, combine and associate, to make implications and the ability to express oneself as a person and to situate oneself. . . .
>
> (Dufeu 1983, p. 204)

They are neither purely skill-oriented activities nor language exercises, although the extension of language competence as a part of communicative competence is as we have seen an integral part of the learning aim.

(10) The tasks are integrated, however, in the sense understood by humanistic psychology, Confluent Education and Gestalt Pedagogy. As complex events that integrate the use of skills by involving learners in encounters with texts, topics, and fellow learners, communicative activities are predominantly whole-person oriented, because they bring together the affective, cognitive and pragmatic elements in individual and group learning. They always activate several elements of the learner's personality.

(11) In Brumfit's (1984a) terms the tasks would be categorized primarily as *fluency-oriented*. This does not mean in any way that accuracy-oriented exercises are thereby undesirable in modern language teaching. There is a value in building-in special training phases to ensure the correct use of particular structures and language functions into the procedural scheme of the tasks.

(12) The tasks underline the immediacy of the classroom as a place where language can be used in a satisfying way. It is not just a question of simply getting learners to produce language which outside the classroom would be 'authentic', nor is it a question of creating or anticipating situations which learners could

possibly find themselves in in the future. The point is much more of making possible activities in the language which are in themselves in the 'here and now' of the classroom interesting, satisfying and useful.

(13) Participating in these tasks involves learners in a certain amount of risk. They are often asked to invest themselves as people in a task through the medium of their opinions or feelings where they may have to risk disagreement or conflict. In Davies' (1989) terms, individual learners achieve the point of 'peak adventure' whenever they experience the risk as having been worthwhile, i.e. the learner recognizes that significant learning has taken place. The involvement of the learner in risk-taking also has positive consequences for him with regard to his confidence and understanding of his limits and capabilities. The counterpart to peak adventure is boredom which may lead to parallel but negative consequences for the personal development of the learner.

(14) Furthermore, tasks take into account to a particularly high degree group factors within any interaction event. We include here above all sub-groups and pairs as independent social groupings, i.e. those referred to as the 'We' components. As a consequence the teacher can use many tasks or parts of tasks just as appropriately with different groupings within a class. As we have explained in this chapter these activities illustrate how communicative-language methodology can meet the challenge with which it is commonly confronted to provide a means of working in a learner-centred and interactive way in the reality of the classroom.

(15) Even with tasks to which we could attach the label 'communicative' we would be overestimating what they could achieve if at the same time we asserted that they would somehow release us from the artificiality of the language learning/teaching situation. Even with a task-based, learner-centred approach we are still faced with the responsibility of making the class aware of the 'game' which they have agreed to play and whose rules they will negotiate. We normally pretend that we only have the target language as our only available communication tool although using our native language would make working with texts and themes much easier. The task types which we have demonstrated above, however, could make this pretence more acceptable because the game itself is interesting and stimulating enough for every participant to experience some form of direct satisfaction.

It is exactly this point which is emphasized by many recent language teaching methodologists as an important and essential pre-condition for the acquisition of language (cf. Stevick's category of depth, Stevick 1976, pp. 30, 43; Dufeu 1983, p. 212; Taylor 1983; Moskowitz 1981; Prabhu 1987; Nunan 1989a).

It is all very well, however, to talk about the multitude of possibilities opened up by a task-based approach. What we must not forget is that the chance to fulfil the potential for communication in the classroom could be thrown away by poor implementation. As we have pointed out in the discussion of criteria above, this could easily happen if tasks which are designed to have an effect beyond the life of the task itself, e.g. to sensitize, raise awareness, help learners make contact with each other and to gain self-experience, etc., are conducted for their own sake and without thought or reference to the thematic context or broader educational aims (see above 3.4). It occurs also when learners are presented with these tasks without being given an opportunity to express their commitment or their agreement. It could similarly happen if teachers were to use the tasks exclusively as gimmicks to promote motivation. One could easily foresee an occasion when a teacher may, in the short term, bypass the right of learners to determine their own learning or overlook their anxieties or possible resistance. However, tasks used in this way could easily become counter-productive in the long term. Classroom practitioners who tend to see themselves as motivators of the theatrical kind run the risk of creating the very alienation with these tasks which they seek to avoid. It would be quite easy to reinforce negative tendencies such as these because all the tasks mentioned in chapter 4 are scenarios for action in the classroom set in motion and determined by the *teacher*. One cannot remove this structural feature even if the teacher in her role as participating manager involves herself and her own experiences in the learning process. The fact that these tasks contain a principally interventionist character remains untouched despite the fact that learners enjoy much greater freedom doing the group and pair-work phases contained in many of the tasks.

Any discussion of a task-based, experiential approach to modern language teaching must also include discussion on the limits and potential of learners to determine their own learning with regard to content and form. We will argue in the following chapter that the structuring of the learning, which is the responsibility of the teacher, by means of communicative tasks, can be seen as a counter-weight to learners being responsible for and leading their own learning. Task-based language teaching is concerned, namely, with creating a dynamic balance between the classroom manager who is also a participant and the participants who are also classroom managers. Learning within a project mode which is the theme of the next chapter is a form of learning which seeks to achieve such a balance.

5 Learning in projects (overview)

5.1 Background: towards a definition

The notion of a task-based and learner-centred curriculum which results from a collective planning process in a participatory classroom is not a recent one. The American pragmatists, Dewey and Kilpatrick, writing in the first half of this century, had already laid the theoretical and practical foundations of learning by and through experience. For them the educational project as 'a whole-hearted purposeful activity' (Kilpatrick 1918), taking place in a social environment upon which it has a significant impact, was seen as a new way of bringing about a more democratic society. Kilpatrick's essay 'The Project Method' (1918) spelled out the consequences of Dewey's programmatic study 'Democracy and Education' (1916). He pointed out that a learning process was required which not only prepared young people to be responsible citizens, but which mirrored in its very forms of operation an experimental society of cooperating individuals.

Dewey's and Kilpatrick's work had considerable influence on and was paralleled by the educational reform movements in Germany which explicitly referred to it in their efforts to educate children for a more democratic world after the First World War. As in Germany, Soviet educationalists took up the idea of project learning during the revolutionary and post-revolutionary period when experimentation and development of new ideas were still possible (for detailed accounts and surveys see: Suin de Boulemard 1975; Frey 1982).

More recently, during the 1960s and 1970s, project learning has been a central issue in educational debates in Europe where – in the wake of a radical critique of institutionalized schooling (Illich 1970; Graubard 1972; Reimer 1970; Winkel 1974) – it has been linked with ideas of a more 'convivial society' (Illich 1970) and the democratization of learning through the introduction of the comprehensive school (cf. GGG 1977; Bastian and Gudjohns 1986). Since that time, there has been a remarkable proliferation of project activities in various fields of education (Struck 1980; Frey 1982). At the same time, however, the term 'project' has become fashionable and increasingly blurred. Often it appears to denote simply an activity which is in some kind of opposition to whatever is considered mainstream educational practice. It has also acquired overgeneralized connotations of freedom as opposed to constraint, and, unfortunately, fun as opposed to serious and responsible work. As a result, it has been easy to marginalize the impact of Dewey's views.

In taking this historical perspective of project learning we wish to reject the view that projects are a gambit by means of which a fun element can be introduced into an otherwise lifeless and dreary classroom, in order to make the serious core of a learning programme more bearable. Furthermore, project learning cannot be reduced to a teaching method which teachers may pull out of a rag bag of available methods. Rather it needs to be understood as rooted in an educational philosophy which aims at providing the direction, and some possible routes, to a more democratic and participatory society. On the basis of the various sources of the educational reform movements – both from the 1920s and 1960s – we see the following elements as fundamental characteristics of project learning (also cf. Bastian and Gudjohns 1986, pp. 14–27):

(1) Themes and target tasks for project learning do not derive exclusively from a list of predetermined curricular items, which are based on the abstractions of academic disciplines, but from 'life'. In principle all forms and objects of life, and their interdependence – both inside and outside the classroom – are worthy of investigation by becoming a focus of a project task (Frey 1982, p. 55).

(2) However, project ideas and themes alone do not account for the educational value of project learning. Only when learners become involved with these ideas through a process of discussion, experimentation, reflection, and application of insights to new cycles of experimentation, will learning take place which deserves to be called experiential.

(3) This process manifests itself in a jointly constructed and negotiated plan of action which turns a project idea into an operational tool defining sub-topics, tasks, problem areas, predicting outcomes derived from hypotheses, etc. The plan itself undergoes constant change in the process of its realization.

(4) In this sense, project learning is investigative. Both on a micro and on a macro level, projects follow a cyclical model of experiential learning which might progress from project ideas to concrete experience, reflective observation, abstract conceptualization and new project ideas.

(5) Project learning is learner-centred, not only in the sense that it allows for learner contribution of project ideas and negotiation of topics and tasks. Because of its great variety of modes of operation in all types of settings, it also permits learners to discover their specific strengths, interests and talents.

(6) The successful completion of project tasks depends on the cooperative abilities of small groups of learners who organize their own work, monitor their learning outcomes, take responsibility and work out difficulties in group dynamics. The group members are accountable both to their team and the learning group as a whole.

(7) Whereas the traditional transmission model disregards the competence of learners to participate actively in shaping forms and outcomes of learning and to act independently of teacher control, project work assumes a basic ability for self-direction and learner autonomy in the learning process itself.

(8) Although the learning process with its experiential cycles is of great importance, the same attention is given to the notion of 'product'. Whereas, in traditional teaching, product or outcome means a change in the knowledge base and in (for the most part) cognitive skills to be tested and evaluated, project learning takes a much broader view. Products, which can appear in a great variety of representational forms, are integral parts of the process because of their *use* value. That is, they communicate learners' views of themselves and the world around them, and function as further objects of negotiation and learning. In addition, they are owned by the learners who thus identify with what they have achieved as individuals and members of a group. Last, but not least, they require a whole range of skills and actions which go beyond the cognitive domain. Products in project learning may represent the holistic and multisensory nature of learning which involves head, heart and hands.

(9) Because project work transcends the boundaries of traditional academic subject areas, it necessitates an interdisciplinary approach to learning. This has found expression in a number of team-teaching models.

(10) In contrast to mainstream classrooms, project work has largely increased the scope of action for both the teacher and the learner who take on a multiplicity of roles. The teacher may adopt those of a manager, facilitator, researcher, participant, monitor, and for the learner those of a manager, actor, writer, secretary, teacher and researcher. Consequently, the concept of

skills and abilities is open to a fresh and more comprehensive definition.

(11) Since project work takes the learners seriously as partners, who are provided with the space and the skills to contribute to the content and process of learning, it makes possible an open, process-oriented curriculum. In this respect, project work is the opposite of the linear transmission model which has shaped mainstream teaching and curriculum development in this century.

Drawing on these characteristics we can attempt a working definition of what we mean by project work. It is a theme and task-centred mode of teaching and learning which results from a joint process of negotiation between all participants. It allows for a wide scope of self-determined action for both the individual and the small group of learners within a general framework of a plan which defines goals and procedures. Project learning realizes a dynamic balance between a process and a product orientation. Finally, it is experiential and holistic because it bridges the dualism between body and mind, theory and practice, or in John Dewey's words 'experience and thinking' (Dewey 1916, p. 146ff).

5.2 Projects in foreign language learning

Since the mid-1970s a number of foreign language educators, taking, in Howatt's words, 'a strong view on CLT' (Howatt 1984, p. 287), have tried to merge the pedagogical traditions of project work with their practice as curriculum designers and classroom teachers. Although these attempts in different parts of the world have remained marginal to mainstream foreign language teaching (cf. Legutke 1989a), there is now a growing corpus of data to refer to. Data on projects in the foreign language classroom come to us in two forms:

(1) as case studies and documented accounts of classroom procedures and project experiments (for detailed survey see Schiffler 1980, pp. 127ff., Legutke 1988a, pp. 185–211; Edelhoff and Liebau 1988);

(2) as informal teacher accounts on project experiences, learner diaries and student texts produced as part of project experiences (e.g. Carter 1985b, 1985c; Hallam 1985; Turner 1987). These documents were generated in the context of the following institutions:

- The Bell Educational Trust, mainly its school in Bath, UK;
- The Hesse State Institute for In-Service Teacher Education and; Training (HILF) in Kassel, Federal Republic of Germany;
- the Office of the German Language Consultant at the Superintendent of Public Instruction in Olympia, WA, USA.

The data from this second group will be published here for the first time.

Using the characteristics of project work (see above) as criteria, we have not included data, whether formal or informal, which (a) simply claim novelty value for the term *project*, and (b) describe 'projects' solely in terms of a departure from contemporaneous mainstream teaching. Conversely, data which do not explicitly refer to project traditions and terminology could be included for consideration, because the teaching/learning procedures met most of our criteria.

5.2.1 Encounter projects

The case studies of projects which follow fall into three groups. The first group includes projects which provide learners with the opportunity to make direct contact with native speakers. They may take place in an L1 environment where learners undertake an investigation of examples or sub-systems of the L2 culture which may be available in the vicinity, e.g. military communities, religious groups, language societies, or individuals. Or, they may take place in the target culture either as an extended learning experience such as a course of language study in the foreign country; or as a brief visit as in the case of a day excursion, class trip or school exchange. In both cases, the central project phase involves face-to-face encounters with speakers of the target language, while the preparation and making sense of data collected is firmly embedded in the classroom. We shall call these projects which exploit and explore a target language environment or micro-environment *encounter projects*. Individual learners experience the target language in its primary function of communicating directly with others, needing to project and portray themselves. They react to the challenge of the environment with the need to acquire new language and extend what they have learned already in the classroom. Here are some examples of this type of project:

(1) Encounter projects in L1 environments
(1) Learners explore the communicative use of English and other

foreign languages at an international airport. The data they collect and produce serve as in-put for further learning in class: Legutke, M. 1984/85 Project Airport. Part I. *Modern English Teacher* 11/4: pp. 10–14; Part 2, *MET* 12/1: pp. 28–31.

Legutke, M. and Thiel, W. 1983 *Airport. Ein Projekt für den Englischunterricht in der Klasse 6* Hessisches Institut für Bildungsplanung und Schulentwicklung, Wiesbaden.

Humburg, L. et al. 1983 *Airport. Ein Projekt für den Englischunterricht in Klasse 6. Videofilm* PAL/VHS, Colour, 29 min. Institut für Film und Bild in Wissenschaft und Unterricht (FWU 420379.), Grünwald.

Edelhoff, C. 1983 Real Language Activities and Projects. Example 'Airport'. *Sproglæreren* (Denmark) 14/1: 16–21.

Ferragati, M. and Carminati, E. 1984: Airport: An Italian Version. *MET* 11/4: 15–17.

(2) Learners research target language communities in their L1 environment, such as Americans in Germany or Germans in America or Canada. They conduct interviews, invite representatives of the target culture into their classrooms, etc.

Bicker, N. and Swanenvleugel, J. 1985 Verslag van een Project voor Engels in een Hetergene Brugklas. *Levende Talen* (Netherlands) 399: 148–53.

Finke, C. 1985 Begegnungen mit englischsprachigen Mitbürgern. Projektorientierter Englischunterricht in der Jahrgangstufe 11. *Praxis des Neusprachlichen Unterrichts* 32: 345–53.

Fleck, M. 1988 Deutsch–Amerikanische Partnerschaft. Their life in our country. In Edelhoff, C. and Liebau, E. (eds).

Legutke, M. 1984 Americans in the Giessen/Frankfurt Area: How They Live. Anmerkungen zu einem landeskundlichen Projekt für Lehrerstudenten. In: Bredella, L (ed.).

Petronio, G. 1985 Tours of the Community as Part of the Conversation Class. *Foreign Language Annals* 18: 157–9.

Thiel, W. 1983 Eine Zugfahrt. Lernen in Projekten. Adaption des Beispiels AIRPORT für Deutsch als Fremdsprache. *Sproglæreren* (Denmark) 14/5: 18–26.

Wicke, M. and Wicke R. 1988 *German Round the Corner – the Whyte Avenue in Edmonton.* Alberta Education Publications, Edmonton.

(2) Encounter projects in L2 environments
(1) During the target task multi-lingual advanced learners of English teach for four days in junior schools in Bath. They produce extensive documentation of their teaching/learning experience
Carter, G. and Thomas, H. 1986 'Dear Brown Eyes'. Experiential learning in a project-oriented approach. *English Language Teaching Journal* **40**: 196–204.
(2) Students of a multi-lingual class design and publish a wheelchair guide for the city of Bath and provide detailed accounts of their learning experience
Fried-Booth, D. 1982 Project Work with Advanced Classes. *English Language Teaching Journal* **36**: 98–103.
Fried-Booth, D. 1986 *Project Work*. Oxford University Press, Oxford.
(3) Weekly structured field trips to sites where students need to communicate in English are part of an experimental oral communication course at a community college in New Jersey
Montgomery, C. and Eisenstein, M. 1985 Real Reality Revisited: An Experimental Communicative Course in ESL. *TESOL Quarterly* **19**: 317–33.
(4) School exchanges, class trips and cross-cultural research projects
British/French encounters
Mares, C. (ed.) 1985 *Our Europe. Environmental Awareness and Language Development through School Exchange.* (Keep Britain Tidy Group Schools Research Project) Brighton Polytechnic, Brighton.
German/French encounters
Alix, C.and Kodron, C. 1988 *Zusammenarbeiten: Gemeinsam lernen. Themenzentrierte Zusammenarbeit zwischen Schulen verschiedener Länder am Beispiel Deutschland – Frankreich.* Deutsch-Französisches Jugendwerk, Bad Honnef.
Martin, J.-P. 1987 *Paris-Torcy.* Videofilm, VHS colour, 31 min. Institut für Film und Bild (FWU 42 00701), Grünwald (see FWU 1987b).
Sendzik, J. and Rahlwes, S. 1988 Lernort Frankreich: Schüleraustausch und praktisches Lernen. In Edelhoff C. and Liebau, (eds).
German/Soviet encounters
Zeller, H. 1988 Vier Interviews in der Sowietunion. Ein Videoprojekt für aktive Landeskunde. In Edelhoff, C. and Liebau, (eds).

5.2.2 Text projects

The second group of projects also incorporates exploratory encounters but, in contrast to those mentioned above, they arise not from real world encounters outside the classroom but with texts from a variety of media, e.g. literature texts, texts from native speaker sources such as news media etc., video and audio material and even text-books. In this type of project learners come face to face not with native speakers directly but with the latter's experience and reactions to the world as revealed through text. In such 'representations', whether they are historical, contemporary or literary, learners can share attitudes and feelings and create meaning through negotiation. We shall call this project type *text project*. Texts also offer challenges which are met by the learners' need to decode them. As in the case of the environment there remains the question of accessing the object of research and exploring different solutions. Here are some examples of this type of project:

(2) Learners organize their own learning on the basis of set textbooks in public schools
    Elementary level
    Nuhn, H.-E. 1982 Schüler organisieren ihr Lernen selbst – Ein Projekt im englischen Anfangsunterricht. *Die Deutsche Schule* 74: 35–43.
    Elementary and intermediate level
    Martin, J.-P. 1985 *Zum Aufbau didaktischer Teilkompetenzen beim Schüler*. Gunter Narr, Tübingen.
    Advanced level
    Kaufmann, F. 1977 Lernen in Freiheit – im Fremdsprachenunterricht. *Praxis des Neusprachlichen Unterrichts* 24: 227–36.

Learners organize their own learning in public schools on the basis of a great variety of different texts ranging from stickers, children's books, magazines to newspapers, parents' school books to dictionaries, video films to poems, songs and even conventional textbooks
    Elementary to intermediate
    Dam, L. and Gabrielsen, G. 1988 Developing learner autonomy in a school context. A six-year experiment beginning in the learners' first year of English. In Holec, H. (ed.) *Autonomy and Self-Directed Learning. Present Fields of Application*. Council of Europe, Strasbourg.
    Dam, L. 1982 *Beginning English. An Experiment in Learning and*

Teaching. Danmarks Laererhøjskole, Copenhagen.

(3) Text projects using literary texts and feature films

- 'Little Red Ridinghood' (dramatization of the story).
  Neumann-Zöckler, H. 1980 *Märchenveränderung am Beispiel von 'Little Red Ridinghood'. Szenisches Spiel im Englischunterricht der Sekundarstufe I.* Pädagogisches Zentrum, Berlin.
- Peter Terson 'Zigger-Zagger. Mooney and his Caravans' (theatre performance as part of a regular English class).
  Heitz, S. 1985 Zigger-Zagger. Die Behandlung und Aufführung eines Dramas im Englischunterricht in einer 10. Gymnasialklasse. In: Bredella, L. and Legutke, M. (eds).
- F. Scott Fitzgerald *The Great Gatsby* (novel and film).
  Bredella, L. and Legutke, M. 1985: Ein interaktives Modell für das Verstehenlehren einer fremden Kultur am Beispiel der 'American 1920s'. In: Bredella, L. (ed.).
- F. Scott Fitzgerald 'Bernice Bobs Her Hair' (short story and film adaptation).
  Seletzky, M. 1984 Entwurf einer prozeßorientierten Methodik des Englischunterrichts in der Landeskunde (Output-Input-Model). In: Bredella, L. (ed.).
- *The Graduate* (film and novel).
  Seletzky, M. 1986 *The Graduate* as a way into the 1960s. In: Legutke, M. (ed.).
- J. D. Salinger *The Catcher in the Rye.*
  Legutke, M. 1988: Szenario für ein Textprojekt. J. D. Salinger's *The Catcher in the Rye.* In Edelhoff, C. and Liebau, E. (eds).

5.2.3 Class correspondence projects

The third group combines elements of the two former ones. Class correspondence projects involve encounters between L2 learners from different cultures and with native speakers of the target language. However, these encounters are mediated through different texts, which are produced for the specific purpose of establishing communicative exchanges between groups and individuals under conditions of organized learning. Preparation as well as text production and decoding become an integral part of daily classroom activities (cf. Dietrich 1979a).

In addition to learner texts such as letters, audioletters, videoletters, photo stories and collages, the correspondence might include L1 and L2 texts and artifacts selected with the intention of conveying what partners consider important in their own lives and culture (for

example, it might include the contents of a school wastepaper basket
or the 'clean' viz. 'dry' items of a household wastepaper bin, or a
selection of the 'junk mail' from a week's post delivery, from which
correspondence partners are invited to create for themselves a picture
of the habits and preoccupations of the other society). Because of this
textual dimension, class correspondence activities are text projects.
They function as important bridges between face-to-face encounters,
which are only possible for short periods in the life of a student, and
working with texts which will take up most of their time in the
classroom as language learning. Here are some examples of this type
of project:

(1) Cross-cultural swap shop and letter exchanges:

  Jones, B. 1984 Contacts sans voyage. In: CILT (ed.) *Using
  authentic resources in teaching French*. CILT, London.

  Voss, H. and Weber, I. 1988: Cross-Channel-Swap-Shop. Ein
  Landeskundeprojekt im Englischunterricht. In: Edelhoff, C.
  and Liebau, E. (eds).

(2) Videoletter exchanges

  Maurice, M. 1984 Un réseau vidéo correspondence (RVC). *Die
  Neueren Sprachen* 83: 352–8.

  Seidler, K. 1988 Kontakte ohne zu reisen: Video-Letter-
  Exchange. In Edelhoff, C. and Liebau, E. (eds).

5.3 Nature of a project

5.3.1 The organizing principle

Managing language learning involves teachers in making on-going
decisions concerning the sequencing and emphasis of tasks. In many
learning situations, they find themselves interpreting and executing a
pre-specified syllabus of language items, sequenced mainly according
to an assumed notion of grammatical difficulty. In project-learning
environments where language for itself is not the only object of
attention, other layers of activity such as managing the input of topic
information, organizing the social interaction of the participants, and
providing opportunities to review preceding and to plan future action
needs to be included in the planning arrangements. The organizational challenge facing teachers here is to identify the learning tasks
and to arrive at a way of putting them together in a causally
transparent sequence. It is as if the tasks are pieces of a syllabus
jigsaw which can only be completed in a particular order.

What we know of the available project learning data from both documented and informal sources shows that there is a remarkably consistent pattern of organization. Projects are a collection of a large variety of tasks, each with a specific objective, focusing on either topic information (e.g. researching into the history of a famous landmark), or 'real-life' operational skills (e.g. learning how to make usable audio recordings), or contact with native speakers (e.g. arranging appointments and interviewing native speakers), or practising language in terms of structure, lexis and skill (e.g. investigating the past tense, forms of narration and practising listening comprehension in order to collect oral history data), or planning and monitoring the process (e.g. carrying out group reviewing activities). How these tasks are sequenced and relate to one another depends on the main objective of the project, a central task, which we can refer to as the 'target task'. Typical target tasks in the data are:

- To produce and sell an anthology of student poetry
- To teach a class of English junior school children for a week
- To interview passengers at a major international airport
- To hold a 'jumble sale' of bric-à-brac for charity
- To design a feature film, based on a short story or a novel
- To design a brochure for foreign tourists about one's home town.

Having identified and agreed upon a target task, learners and teachers further establish the steps they need to take in order to carry out the task. In other words, they work backwards in their planning in a process referred to by Carter and Thomas (1986) as 'backward planning' to derive the tasks that lead back in time from the target task to their project starting point. Their brain-storming of ideas leads to a progressive action plan which requires joint management by teachers and learners. In the following example taken from an encounter project in the L2 environment (Hallam 1985) the target task was to visit an old people's day centre, interview some of the senior-citizen members and record on cassette any stories they wished to tell of themselves and their city when they were young. Having identified the target task, teacher and learners specified the essential preparatory steps. They would need to:

- approach a day centre and request an opportunity to interview the members – (COMMUNICATION SKILLS: making arrangements, e.g. telephoning);
- record the interviews – (MEDIA SKILLS: using video and audio techniques);

- conduct the interviews and sustain an extended conversation – (COMMUNICATION SKILLS: interviewing techniques, e.g. posing questions, asking for clarification, changing direction, etc.);
- transpose the stories into written form and produce an anthology of the material collected – (TEXT SKILLS: intensive and extensive reading and listening, transcription of text, summarizing and editing);
- understand the techniques of oral and written narration – (SPECIFIC THEME-ORIENTED LANGUAGE PREPARATION: e.g. story-telling techniques, narrative discourse, etc.);
- master relevant task-related grammatical areas – (GENERAL THEME-ORIENTED LANGUAGE PREPARATION: e.g. past tenses, descriptive vocabulary of people, places, buildings, weather, clothes, etc.).

Each area can be seen as a task module arising naturally out of the target task:

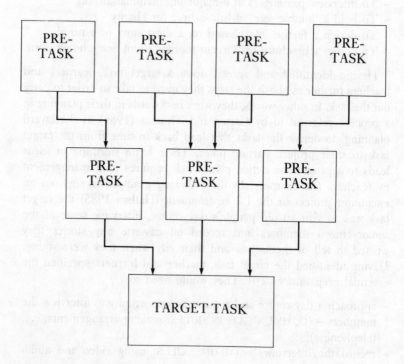

Figure 5.1 Target task as determiner of preparation tasks

At this point the challenge facing teacher and learners is to organize the modules into a feasible sequence. In order to do this they would need to take several factors into account, e.g. the necessary timing of events; the need for presentation and practice of task-related language; the availability of media within the institution, etc. For this project a particular sequence of tasks was derived (see fig. 5.2).

There are, not surprisingly, frequent examples in the informal data of on-going adjustments in the management of task execution. However the principle behind the task sequence, i.e. 'in order to achieve X, we must first do Y and Z . . .', remains constant. When learning tasks are related to each other in this way we can say that project learning is one means by which a task-based syllabus is realized.

5.3.2 Stages of a project

The diagram above shows how tasks within a project are sequenced by learners and teachers with reference to the target task. This form of sequencing is an identifying characteristic of projects. If we look again at the examples of such task sequencing in the data, we can also discern a common structure for projects which contains several clearly defined stages. This structure will differ in minor ways according to individual learning situations, but most examples seem to recognize the need to lead up to project work in a principled way. Preparation and follow up are reflected in the following stages of a project's development:

(1) opening;
(2) topic orientation;
(3) research and data collection;
(4) preparing data presentation;
(5) presentation;
(6) evaluation.

The unfolding of these stages represents the changes in the overall direction or emphasis of a project which it is the teacher's responsibility to instigate. It is the teacher's expertise in the management of learning that in general influences the change in direction, although with sophisticated and organized learners a stage can be triggered off with minimum or no intervention by the teacher. The relationship of the stages described here to the tasks discussed above is that each stage comprises a collection of tasks through which the general aims of a stage are realized.

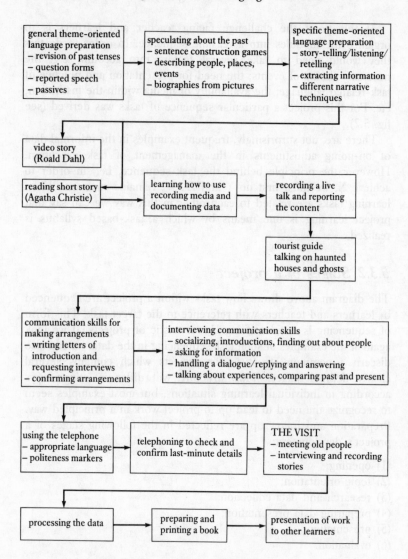

Figure 5.2 Oral history project (Hallam, J. 1985)

(1) Opening
This stage has several objectives:

- To develop a positive group dynamic.
- To introduce learners to a communicative approach.
- To give learners personal experience of using multi media.
- To introduce the live community as a resource base for language learning where appropriate.
- To introduce textual data (content materials, process materials) for research activities.

Of the data examined, this stage is a consistent feature of the Bell School, Bath, data where adult learners are drawn from diverse, multilingual backgrounds for intensive courses of English lasting up to eleven weeks. The comprehensive exploitation of this stage which the data reveals is a concentrated attempt to achieve the rapid socialization of course participants, moving from getting to know one another to an appreciation of how individuals interact with one another within their group. Learners are encouraged to become aware of their role within groups in preparation for more responsible tasks at later stages in the project. To enable such insights to be made a variety of pre-communicative and communicative tasks are set such as 'the profile task', 'the design team', and 'the geometric puzzle'. (cf. 4.2.1; 4.2.4). What both of these latter examples in particular make possible is the understanding that:

(1) Purposeful activity can take place within the group independent of the teacher.
(2) In a communicative approach to learning, skills are essentially integrated and can be practised naturally, moving from one to another.

Already at this stage, teachers introduce evaluative procedures by holding review sessions (see 4.2.9) which enable participants to articulate and monitor their reactions to the task.

Having established a basic working dynamic, it is then possible to tackle tasks which both rely on and further develop group cohesion. Tasks such as researching, writing and simulating a short TV news programme or learning and practising the skills needed to interview native speakers are included. In all of these tasks, the language input from the teacher is restricted to whatever language is required to perform them. Follow-up language work arises as a result of a post-task evaluation. There is no attempt, however, to work through a grammatical syllabus in parallel to the programme of tasks.

Since the obvious advantages of an available target language community are not present in all learning contexts, or indeed, that many non-adult learners in schools already know each other well, many of the aims of this introductory stage are inappropriate or unachievable in some contexts. Its deployment, therefore, in the form described here tends only to occur in adult learning groups in target language communities. However, opening goals must also have been pursued in school settings, as we will see later (5.4.4). Most of the data from these non-adult learning situations give very little indication of how the group of learners was turned into a project community ready to embark on a project task.

(2) Topic orientation

It is in this stage that learners focus on a possible topic and explore its interest value in terms of insights into the topic, and situations and opportunities for language practice and development. The teacher's objectives can be stated as follows:

– to sensitize learners towards the theme;
– to mobilize existing knowledge;
– to arouse curiosity;
– to allow for the exchange of personal experiences.

A typical way of realizing these objectives is through a values clarification task (see 4.2.8). In the project *Americans in the Giessen Area* (Legutke 1984), participants were asked to prioritize a list of statements relating to the heading, 'What is an American?' The ensuing discussion involved individuals explaining their own perceptions in order to process the statements. In doing so they were able to discover information that they were unaware of and also whether they collectively wished to pursue the theme further. Similarly, Carter (1986, personal communication) used photographs in both his *The Circus* (Carter 1985b) and *The Kennet and Avon Canal* (Carter 1985d) projects. In the latter, learners were asked to judge a set of photographs he had taken of the former industrial, now picturesque canal that runs through the city. The criteria he gave them were: quality of the photograph, the setting and the object. The learners were asked to arrange the photographs in an order of priority and to allocate scores to support their views, adding a short commentary under each photograph. The nature of this activity was such that there was a great deal of room for negotiation and explanation of viewpoint. It was a natural step to follow up the work in the classroom with a first-hand tour of the canal which led directly to the learners choosing the canal as their overall project topic (see also 4.2.8).

The data also reveal that local guest speakers were invited into project classrooms in order to stimulate in the learners an interest in a particular topic. Learners are able to build on the information provided by the guest speaker to find a line of inquiry into the topic which was of particular interest to them.

Seletzky (1984; 1986; 1989) calls the process of topic orientation 'opening the field of awareness' and his work outlines similar ways in which interest and motivation can be aroused in a creative way so that further research work or teacher input can take place. For example, he began his text project *The Graduate* (Seletzky 1986), by asking learners to work together in groups to develop ideas for a possible video film clip on the text of the song, 'The Sound of Silence', taken from the movie *The Graduate*. Variations of this technique are now widespread in project data, a frequently occurring example being the 'collage', an individual or group task set so that learners can create their own impressionistic view of a particular view of a particular theme, e.g. an American city or how I see the British. As Seletzky points out, any input is more effective when a personal relationship to the theme, which encompasses sensitization, curiosity and motivation, has taken place. This 'output before input' principle is inextricable from the principle that enriched understanding arises through group interaction. In other words, individual perceptions are synthesized and enlarged through group negotiation, an activity central to any process model of language teaching. The time slot devoted to this stage can be quite small, occupying only a small percentage of class time compared to stages 1 and 3.

(3) Research and data collection

In the life-span of many projects, this is the longest and most intense stage since it encompasses both the planning and the steps needed to complete the target task and the practising of the skills required, culminating in the completion of the target task itself, i.e. data collection or contact with the public. We can summarize these objectives as follows:

– Defining the nature and extent of the project tasks.
– Learning how to carry out research in the life community using appropriate means of investigation and recording, or how to research textual data and comprehend a literary text.
– Completing the target task.

Defining the target task is a backward planning procedure similar to the one carried out by the teacher in the overall planning of the possible project stages. The work of the group is now concerned with estimating the size of the task and what that will involve in terms of procedure, i.e. research to be carried out, areas of language, guest speakers and visits to be arranged, prioritizing action with regard to time-factors, availability of native-speaking contacts, refining documentation skills and allocating tasks within the group. Preparatory research can take various forms. In the 'Dear Brown Eyes' project, for example (Carter and Thomas 1986), research into forms of junior school education was carried out through interviews, question-and-answer sessions with experts and private reading tasks; in the *Keynsham* project (Lambert 1989) appointments were arranged and visits were made to local business people.

In the case of *Jumble Aid* (Carter et al. 1987) and *The Summer Fête* (Mohammedi-Lange 1989) observation visits involving informal interviews were made to other locally held jumble sales and summer fêtes. Much of the essential project research had to be carried out by means of interviews, so that the linguistic and strategic management of interviews becomes an indispensable part of skill acquisition at this stage. For learners in the airport project it was kernel to the target task and the documentation of this project indicates the considerable amount of attention devoted to it by the participants. It was no less important to the learners in the 'Dear Brown Eyes' project who spent long sessions interviewing teachers of the children they were to teach in the target task of their project. Indeed, for an encounter project in any context, the acquisition of interviewing management skills constitutes an essential core unit in the preparatory work.

For many projects the target task is the collection of the data itself, involving interviews with native speakers and research in libraries and the collection of texts and artifacts. This is true of *Airport* and many of the projects in the Bath data, as the learner documented accounts in book or video film illustrate. Others target on the documentation itself, for example *The Good Wheelchair Guide to Bath* (Fried-Booth 1981 (ed.), 1982; 1986). In school exchange and correspondence projects (Voss and Weber 1988), however, the target task is less easy to define since several intermediate steps take place before any eventual exchange between the children involved comes about. Where an exchange is not possible for many of the participants, the intermediate tasks themselves function as target tasks in their own right.

Some target tasks involve ambitious and complex interaction sequences with the local native-speaking populations. The 'Dear

Brown Eyes' project (Carter and Thomas 1986) is one of a series which has involved non-native-speaking students teaching English school children (see also Turner 1987; Carter 1988). Other projects such as *Jumble Aid* and *The Summer Fête* make great demands on the organizational, practical and language skills of their participants. The event programme of the latter demonstrates a range of tasks carried out by students before the event itself (see fig. 5.3). They sold advertising space by telephone to potential advertisers; they made decisions on the final programme of events in the light of their research and in consideration of the availability of time and staff. They had to agree on the layout of a programme, and finally, they had to type the text, print the copies and collate the pages. For the target task itself, i.e. supervising the summer fête on the day of the event was too large an undertaking for the project class alone. The group, therefore recruited help from other students in the school (see fig. 5.4).

These examples indicate the complexity of the task sequence leading up to and including the target task. Moreover, they involve actions in the outside world to realize an event which lives in the real world and is accepted by native speakers as such, or extensive face-to-face interaction in the classroom. In communicative terms, action is chained together and the language that it generates possesses the verisimilitude of life and 'communication' (see Candlin and Edelhoff 1982). It is not surprising, therefore, that teachers in the data tend to make use of few of the classroom-oriented tasks outlined in the typology during this stage, with the exception of evaluation tasks. However, evaluation often takes place, not by means of a particular process evaluation or review task, as indicated in the typology, but more in the form of working meetings by student sub-committees, to check what they have carried out in order to decide what to do next.

(4) Preparation of data presentation

The completion of the target task does not necessarily mark the end of the project. In most instances time is set aside to process and evaluate the general impact of the experience of the target task. The ways in which this objective is approached are broadly similar whatever the classroom context. Learners set about communicating their experience to others, either in the form of a direct presentation as in *Airport* or *Little Red Ridinghood* (Neumann-Zöckler 1980) or in the form of an artifact, a project end product, or both. The most common end product is a book, but there are many examples in the data of video films.

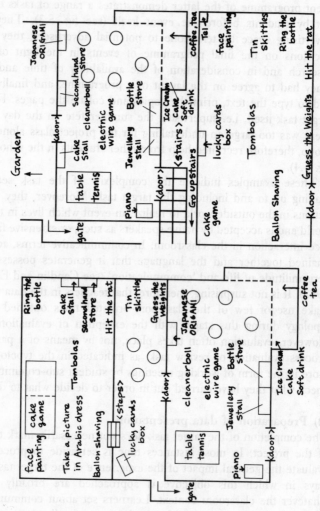

Figure 5.3 Visitors' guide in the Summer Fête programme (Mohammedi-Lange 1989)

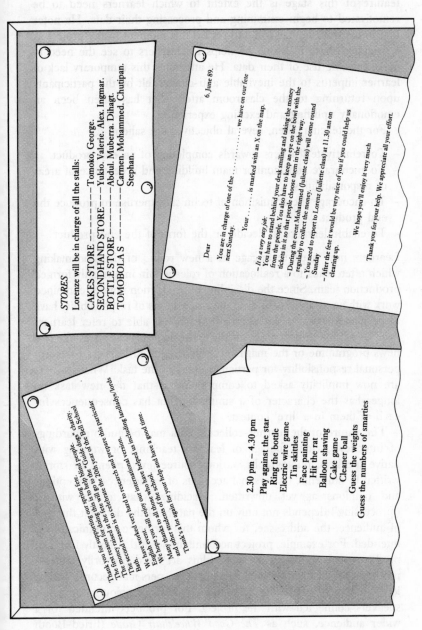

Figure 5.4 Details from the fête programme and instructions to helpers from other classes

Carter (1987, personal communication) reports that an interesting feature of this stage is the extent to which learners need to be remotivated to begin examining and processing their data. He notes that in his work he has come to regard this moment in the project as a bridging phase in which he helps his learners to see the need to make sensible use of their data. He attributes this temporary lack of learner impetus to the inevitable anti-climax felt by the participants upon returning to the classroom after what has often been an emotionally uplifting and exciting experience.

For the teacher, then, several objectives are salient:

- To remotivate learners towards completion of an end product.
- To encourage and monitor team building and acceptance of areas of responsibilities.
- To encourage the acquisition of technical expertise to produce the end product.
- To enable learners to decide on the form of the end product.

Learners now need to engage in a new round of decision-making which often leads to a reallocation of roles within in a freshly formed production team. Since the discipline of production implies combined work with an awareness of deadlines, new levels of responsibility have to be made clear. At this point the teacher is able to refer learners back to earlier project tasks in the induction stage such as the TV news programme or the magazine which required learners to accept personal responsibility for particular areas of the task. What learners are now implicitly asked to comprehend is that the new task no longer has the character of a simulation but has consequences for each of them in a 'live' context.

The nature of the learner-collected data may be audio recordings of interviews, video footage of learners teaching, or working with native speakers, photographs, various source texts, poems or stories written by students, or personal accounts of experiences, perceptions and opinions as yet unwritten. Deciding what to do with it ('processing') depends not only on the nature of the data but the type of audience, the addressee, for whom this further communication is intended. For example, project accounts indicate that costly forms of products such as books or video films are used primarily for end products which are intended essentially as personal records with a low circulation within the school, for parents, employers or native speakers connected with the project. For products intended for a wider audience, such as *The Good Wheelchair Guide* (Fried-Booth 1981); learner poetry anthologies sold for charity, e.g. *Make Life Easy,*

Try With a Smile (Thomas 1986) and *Thought and Poems* (Roberts 1988); and magazines, etc., cheaper formats such as pamphlets are used.

Whatever the nature of the end product, learners are faced with the need for team organization in order to listen to, edit and transcribe audio recordings, select usable material and produce drafts in written form. Refining text in this way makes demands on learners to perform an editorial analysis of what is usable or not. They have subsequently to decide on layout and arrange either on their own or commercially for the printing and publication of their book. Learners who opt to make a video film have to learn how to operate a video edit suite. Nevertheless, as the available data indicates, e.g. *The Circus*, *Hello is Ciao* (Carter 1985a; Carter and Cursiter (eds) 1985; Carter and Thomas 1986), learners are sufficiently motivated by the video medium to work intensively over a short period to create a viable product. They also learn to appreciate that editorial decisions have to be reconciled with what is feasible in practice.

What characterizes this stage is the reawakening of learner motivation. The data indicate that learners are largely self-directed in this stage making use of the teacher mainly for training sessions only, to help with the various technical procedures and to deal with whatever language deficits have been identified by the group. More than any other stage this part of the project highlights the shift from the classroom as a place for role-playing the outside world to being in many senses a part of the outside world.

(5) Presentation

Many projects terminate with this stage in some form of presentation or feedback to audiences external to the group. This stage provides an appropriate but different opportunity to use language as communication. The presentation itself is an event of short duration but it is preceded by a preparatory process of collective decision making, data reorganization and skill acquisition. The broad objectives for the learners are:

- to present information to a live audience using the appropriate media;
- to structure and direct the event and interact with the audience.

In the *Airport* project the presentation consisted of learners giving short oral summaries of their work to other classes. They chose their most interesting interview and wrote an account of it on large display cards which were deployed as a backdrop and a prompt during their presentation (see *Airport* film: Humburg et al. 1983). A similar format has been used by learners in the Bath data, which provides examples of short presentations given by project classes to the other classes in the school during a collective presentation session at the end of their course. Presenters also rely heavily on display material, extracts from their books or video films. The learning emphasis during this stage is on acquiring presentation skills. They must, for example, understand the need to avoid lengthy expositions and concentrate on keeping the message clear. To facilitate this task they are introduced to relevant presentation media, for example, overhead projectors and flip charts. The teacher's role here is to demonstrate and train basic techniques. For learners, the acquisition of this skill presupposes the need to understand that different communication settings require different forms of speaker behaviour. They need to know, for example, that unlike the addressee of an artifact end product, live audiences react and interact, making demands on their strategic competence. Presentations will differ according to the context of the learning situation from short 'show and tell' sessions of work done, to teaching a lesson as in the text project with Salinger's *The Catcher in the Rye* (Legutke 1988b), and Martin's didactic projects (Martin 1985; 1986), to extended events for an outside public such as the play produced by learners in the *Little Red Ridinghood* project (Zöckler-Neumann 1980). What unites them is the need for learners to change gear and adjust to a different set of communicative pressures.

(6) Evaluation
A full, concluding evaluation stage which involves an overall evaluation of:

- topic understanding;
- group and teacher interaction;
- procedural organization;
- input materials;
- language gains and deficits;
- examples of learner work;
- possible by-products, e.g. changes in learners' intercultural awareness

is not a feature of all the projects examined. Teachers in the Bath data encourage learners to keep diaries which provide vehicles to express individual reflections and reactions. Carter and Roberts (personal communication) build on the basis of this vehicle for ongoing process evaluation by asking the learners to write a draft of their own course report. Legutke and Thiel (Thiel 1984) followed a similar procedure in the *Airport* project when they asked their learners to write in their L1, their perceptions of how much they had learned in their project record books. They also supported their evaluation with a formal testing of language gains using text formats which mirrored the project task, e.g. a listening, note-taking exercise using a recorded interview. Informal teacher accounts suggest that many projects include some semi-structured overall evaluation from time to time during the project. The de Bono 'plus/minus/interesting' task (see 4.2.9), is a typical example of such an activity; elsewhere there are instances of learners defining criteria and reasons for success and failure by means of a general discussion. We include above the minimal list of areas that teachers and learners address in their final evaluation. We return to this topic critically in the discussion of the leading issues which arise out of these implementations of projects in language learning.

Appendices: Project scenarios

From our discussion of project stages above we can abstract an idealized general structure for project work (see appendix 1, overleaf) with guide questions on how to proceed. It is not meant to be seen as prescriptive but as a starting point for further classroom applications.

Appendix 2: *Scenario 1:* Jumble Aid

A group of lower intermediate/intermediate adult learners on an eleven-week intensive course in the target language country organize and carry out an English style jumble sale, i.e. a sale of old clothes and bric-à-brac, the proceeds of which are given to a charity. The stimulus for the project arose spontaneously from the group who wished to make a contribution to UNICEF to mark the International Year of the Child. The group had pursued a task-oriented programme of learning up to that point and had already gained experience of small-scale opinion survey interviewing of native speakers and had used media to collect native speaker texts and to document their experiences. The idea of exploiting the jumble sale as a way of raising money came from the teacher in his role as 'expert' in the target culture. (Continued on page 189.)

Appendix 1 General structure for project work

Inputs (teacher/learner)	PROCESS PHASES (examples)	STIMULUS QUESTIONS (examples)	ACTIVITIES (examples)	LEARNER TEXTS
– process materials – information materials	(1) OPENING * introducing learners to a communicative approach * developing group dynamics * introducing use of media for text retrieval and production * introducing texts as data for research PROJECT IDEA	* what did I/we feel doing the task? * what was the purpose for me/us of the task? * how did I communicate with others? * how did we organize ourselves? * what communication difficulties did we have?	* awareness and trust-building * information sharing * problem-solving * process evaluation * imagination gap	– posters – profiles – stories – drawings/ photographs and captions – diary entries – collages

| (pictures, words, sentences, titles)
– short texts
– slogans
– etc.
– preceding learner texts | the theme
* mobilizing existing knowledge
* arousing curiosity
* exchanging personal experiences
* creating awareness of the research area
* appreciation of difficulties
* formulation of hypotheses after evaluating prior knowledge and experience | problems, the theme as shown in pictures or texts?
* how do I react to the picture?
* what do we associate with?
* what makes us stop and think?
* what does not seem interesting at first glance?
* which of the items attract me most or least? | * awareness activities
* communicative tasks
* value clarification
* plus/minus interesting
* evaluation
* brain/heart-storming | – slogans
– collages
– posters

OHP-hypotheses
poster-hypotheses |
| and information materials
– teacher lecture | (3) RESEARCH AND DATA COLLECTION
* focusing on the theme
* articulating interest | * which of the items, topics would I like to work on?
* who could I cooperate with? | * communicative tasks (interpersonality and interaction: | – lists of themes
– project plan
– work contracts |

Appendix 1 continued

Inputs (teacher/learner)	PROCESS PHASES (examples)	STIMULUS QUESTIONS (examples)	ACTIVITIES (examples)	LEARNER TEXTS
– language input – information materials – process materials – preceding learner texts	* defining project tasks * weighing up time factors * determining areas of deficit in terms of skills and competence * carrying out the target tasks of the project	* how much time is needed to accomplish the tasks? * does the group have sufficient knowledge to go about working on the tasks? * how can I collect more information on the topic?	* value clarification) * language exercises * skill training * determined by the group themselves * interim plenary process evaluation	
– information materials – process materials – preceding learner texts	(4) PREPARING DATA PRESENTATION * selecting results for presentation * deciding on the form of the presentation * practising the presentation * allocating areas of responsibility	* which parts of our results would be interesting for the whole class? * how can we put our results across to the class? * what should we tell the others in spoken text, in writing, pictures? * what could be difficult to	* determined by the group	many types of texts: – poster/collage – minutes/essay – commentary – summary – listening text – film text – drama script

| | – preceding learner texts | (5) PRESENTATION AND SHARING
* giving a lead-in to a video film
* giving a short lecture
* acting in a drama/sketch/mime
* giving a show-and-tell session
* presenting a tape/slide show
singing a 'song' | classmates need to understand our presentation?
* do we have to produce extra worksheets?
* do we want to use media for our presentation (OHP, blackboard, tape, film)? | * determined by groups:
many forms of communicative task possible (learners as leaders and participants) | – information handout |
| | – teacher lecture | (6) EVALUATION
* evaluating process and product | * how did they project tasks, the demonstration work out? | * process-evaluation activities | – theme list for follow-up |

Appendix 1 continued

Inputs (teacher/learner)	PROCESS PHASES (examples)	STIMULUS QUESTIONS (examples)	ACTIVITIES (examples)	LEARNER TEXTS
⌐ teacher feedback - group feedback (evaluation sheets)	* extending ability to make judgements * raising cognitive sensitivity * evaluating input materials * evaluating the roles of the experts * evaluating the group dynamic processes, etc.	* which activities/presentations were particularly effective, ineffective? * what could or should be improved? * were there any language problems? * what could or should be done about them? * how did the group cooperate with the teacher? could the group make use of his/her competence? * was the textbook/workbook/resource package a satisfactory help? * etc.		

(v) FOLLOW-UP

* further work on areas of language weakness
* work on gaps in knowledge of content
* agreeing on follow-up projects
* changing to related/non-related themes as basis for new project idea

EXTENSION PROJECTS

- preceding learner texts

Appendix 2 Scenario 1: Jumble Aid

(1) OPENING

Aims: – to build a positive group dynamic;
— to assess learner abilities and needs;
— to introduce learners to 'live context of native speakers'.

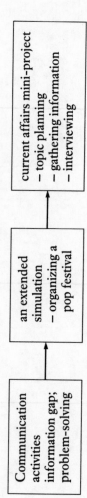

| Communication activities information gap; problem-solving | → | an extended simulation – organizing a pop festival | → | current affairs mini-project – topic planning – gathering information – interviewing |

(2) TOPIC ORIENTATION

Aim: to explore the English custom of the jumble sale.

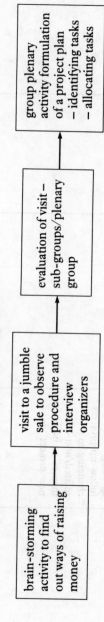

| brain-storming activity to find out ways of raising money | → | visit to a jumble sale to observe procedure and interview organizers | → | evaluation of visit – sub-groups/plenary group | → | group plenary activity formulation of a project plan – identifying tasks – allocating tasks |

(3) RESEARCH AND DATA COLLECTION

Aim: to prepare the jumble sale;
— linguistic preparation,
— organizational and material preparation.

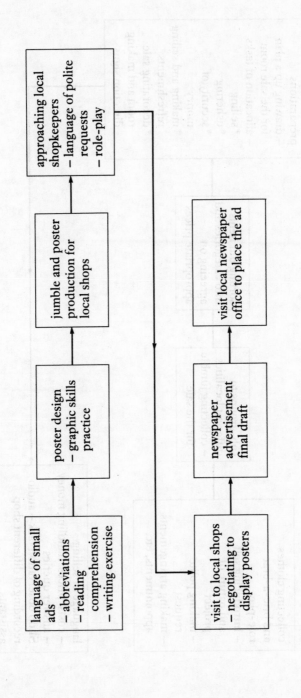

language of small ads
– abbreviations
– reading comprehension
– writing exercise

poster design
– graphic skills practice

jumble and poster production for local shops

approaching local shopkeepers
– language of polite requests
– role-play

visit to local shops
– negotiating to display posters

newspaper advertisement final draft

visit local newspaper office to place the ad

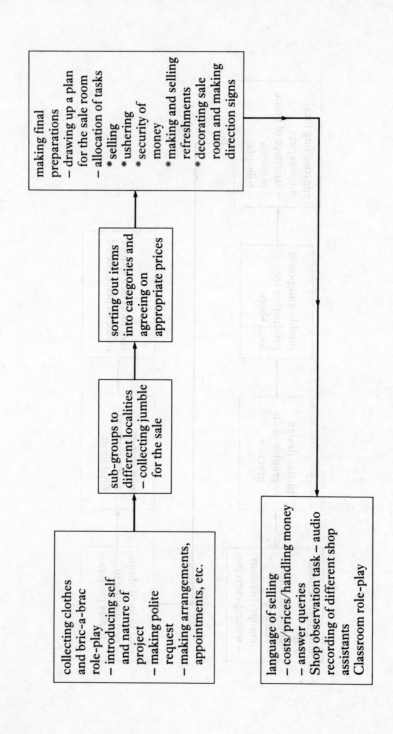

making final preparations
- drawing up a plan for the sale room
- allocation of tasks
  * selling
  * ushering
  * security of money
  * making and selling refreshments
  * decorating sale room and making direction signs

sorting out items into categories and agreeing on appropriate prices

sub-groups to different localities
- collecting jumble for the sale

collecting clothes and bric-a-brac role-play
- introducing self and nature of project
- making polite request
- making arrangements, appointments, etc.

language of selling
- costs/prices/handling money
- answer queries
Shop observation task – audio recording of different shop assistants
Classroom role-play

(4) TARGET TASK

Aims: – to carry out an English jumble sale;
       – to video record the event;
       – to obtain feedback from customers.

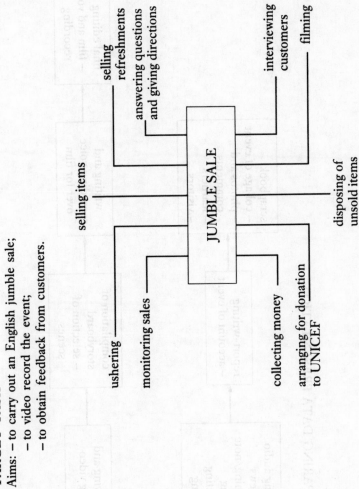

JUMBLE SALE

- selling items
- selling refreshments
- answering questions and giving directions
- interviewing customers
- filming
- disposing of unsold items
- arranging for donation to UNICEF
- collecting money
- monitoring sales
- ushering

(5) PREPARING DATA PRESENTATION

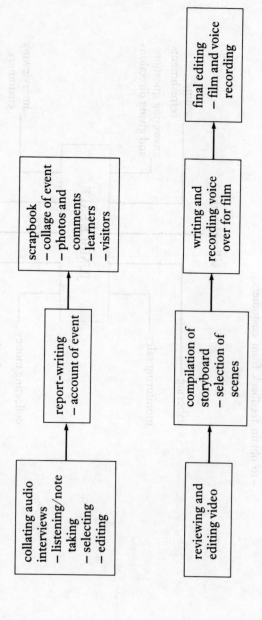

```
collating audio
interviews
– listening/note
  taking
– selecting
– editing
```
→
```
report-writing
– account of event
```
→
```
scrapbook
– collage of event
– photos and
  comments
– learners
– visitors
```

```
reviewing and
editing video
```
→
```
compilation of
storyboard
– selection of
  scenes
```
→
```
writing and
recording voice
over for film
```
→
```
final editing
– film and voice
  recording
```

(6) EVALUATION

Aim: to review the event;
    – as a cultural entity and intercultural learning experience,
    – as an opportunity for live language practice,
    – assess language input and self-assessment of performance.

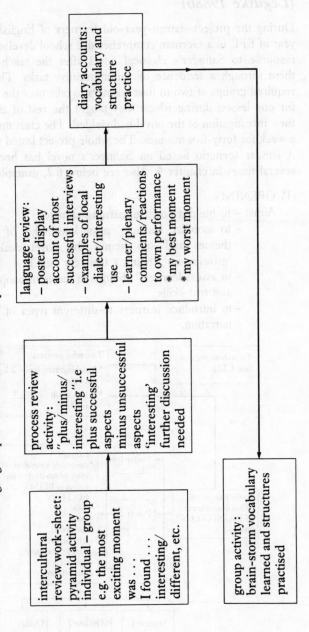

diary accounts:
vocabulary and
structure practice

language review:
– poster display
  account of most
  successful interviews
– examples of local
  dialect/interesting
  use
– learner/plenary
  comments/reactions
  to own performance
   * my best moment
   * my worst moment

process review
activity:
"plus/minus/
interesting" i.e
plus successful
aspects
minus unsuccessful
aspects
'interesting'
further discussion
needed

intercultural
review work-sheet:
pyramid activity
individual – group
e.g. the most
exciting moment
was . . .
I found . . . .
interesting/
different, etc.

group activity:
brain-storm vocabulary
learned and structures
practised

Appendix 3: *Scenario 2:* The Catcher in the Rye *(Legutke 1988b)*

During the project sixteen-year-old learners of English in the sixth year of EFL in a German comprehensive school developed their own response to Salinger's classical novel after the teacher had taken them through a sequence of communicative tasks. The target task required groups of two to four learners to take over the responsibility for one lesson during which they taught the rest of the class what their investigation of the novel had yielded. The class met three times a week for forty-five minutes. The whole project lasted twelve weeks. A similar scenario based on Salinger's novel has been mentioned several times in chapter 4. Also see below 6.2, example 2.

(1) OPENING

    Aims: – to build a positive learning climate;

          – to mobilize learners' prior knowledge of some of the themes and sub-themes the novel deals with (e.g. 'growing-up', 'being a teenager', etc.);

          – to assess learners' abilities in terms of cooperative skills, and text skills;

          – to introduce learners to different types of 'first person' narration.

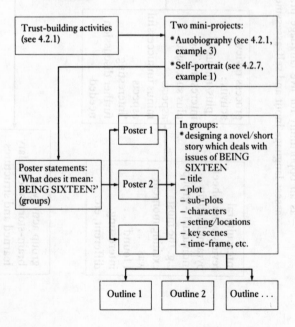

(2) TOPIC ORIENTATION

Aims: – to introduce learners to a reader-centred approach to literary texts, i.e., to introduce them to the negotiation of meaning as an essential part of a reading process in class;

– to change learners' attitudes towards reading and interpreting literary texts;

– to structure the initial phase of reading (chapters 1–7), at the same time to encourage learners to respond to the text and contribute their own understanding, through speaking, acting and writing.

Guided intensive reading of chapters 1–7 (teacher-guided)

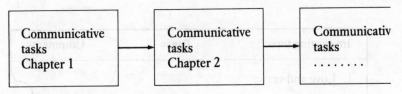

Examples for Chapters 1 and 2

'Wanted' circular:
The police have issued a 'Wanted' Statement for Holden Caulfield which is being tele-faxed to all police stations. Please write this 'Wanted' Statement.

Holden's file:
One of the counsellors of Pency Prep has kept a file on Holden. What entries does it have? Take on the role of the counsellor and write the entries. The school principal has asked for a one-page statement on Holden. Could you write the statement from the point of view of the counsellor?

Role-playing:
The counsellor of Pency Prep has asked Holden into his office. Act out the encounter between the two. Holden calls D.B. to tell him that he has dropped out of school again. Prepare and act out the telephone conversation. The principal calls the school counsellor on the phone to enquire about Holden. Stage the telephone conversation.

Reading with the body:
See above: 4.2.2, Body awareness, example 1

Parallel to teacher-guided, intensive reading:
extensive reading of novel as continuous homework, accompanied by notetaking/notemaking activity

Interesting topic	Pages	Comments
1. Love and sex		
2. School		
3. Parents' expectations		

(3) RESEARCH AND DATA COLLECTION

Aims – to plan independent research in groups;
 – to select topics for research;
 – to identify sources needed to help the researcher;
 – to process selected relevant passages from novel for the researched topic;
 – to establish research teams to meet joint (new) tasks.

A complete example is Jane the project described in Legutke (1985b):

(1) Holden's relationship with his parents;
(2) love and sex in the novel (two chapters);
(3) the meaning of the title telling, caulfield, being caught (four students);
(4) Holden/Jupiter and other failed figures (four students);
(5) Holden's attempts to communicate (three chapters);
(6) imagining what Holden life could go on to studies – Holden at twenty-five;
(7) Holden and the American 1950s (teacher-...)

 – to read novel from the point of view of the topic selected
 – summarise insights gained to give to the audience
 – prepare a 5–10 minute lesson to teach that to fulfil the problem to whole class

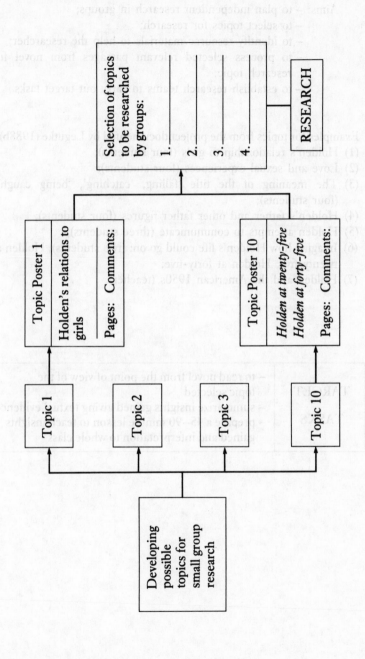

(3) RESEARCH AND DATA COLLECTION

Aims: – to plan independent research in groups;
– to select topics for research;
– to identify resource materials to help the researcher;
– to process selected relevant passages from novel for research topic;
– to establish research teams to carry out target tasks.

Examples for topics from the project documented by Legutke (1988b):

(1) Holden's relationship to girls (four students);
(2) Love and sexual experiences (four students);
(3) The meaning of the title 'falling, 'catching', 'being caught' (four students);
(4) Holden's father and other father figures (four students);
(5) Holden attempts to communicate (three students);
(6) Imagine how Holden's life could go on: (two students), Holden at twenty-five, Holden at forty-five;
(7) Holden and the American 1950s (teacher).

TARGET TASKS	– to read novel from the point of view of the topic selected – summarize insights gained giving textual evidence – prepare a 45–90 minute lesson to teach insights gained and interpretation to whole class

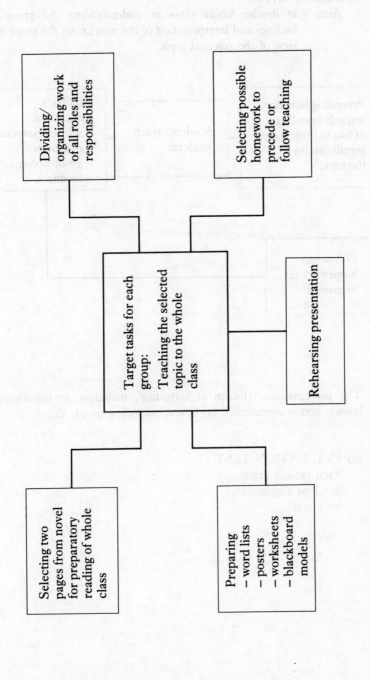

(5) PRESENTATION
   Aim: – to involve whole class in understanding the group's findings and interpretation of the novel from the point of view of the selected topic.

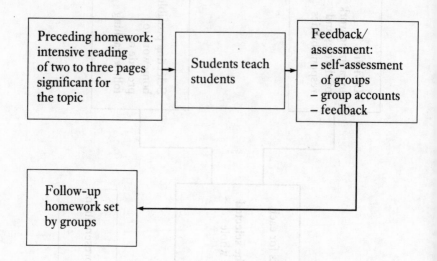

The presentation, 'Holden at forty-five', including an interesting learner text is commented on below; see 6.2, example 2.

(6) EVALUATION TEST
   Each project group
   develops suggestions
   for a test

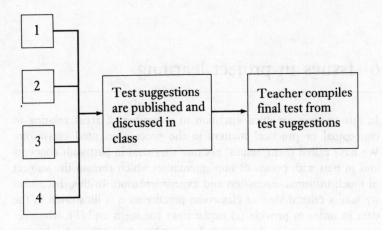

(7) FOLLOW-UP
   Possible follow-up texts from which students may select
   one or more for further investigation:
      Toni Morrison: *The Bluest Eye* (1970)
      The Graduate (File and novel, 1967)
      Charles Bukowski: *Ham on Rye* (1983)
      Encounters 1: Confidence (Bredella et al. 1984)
      – Sherwood Anderson: *I'm a Fool* (1922)
         and film adaptation
      – F. Scott Fitzgerald: *Bernice Bobs Her Hair* (1920)
         and film adaptation

6 Issues in project learning

In this chapter we draw attention to a number of areas relating to conceptual or practical matters in the process-oriented classroom. We have called them 'issues' because they deal in part with concepts and in part with points of implementation which remain the subject of much informal discussion and experimentation. In this discussion we take a critical view of classroom practice as it is illustrated in the data in order to provide (a) explanatory comment and (b), wherever necessary, to raise questions for further research into learner education and pre/in-service teacher development. The issues are:

- process
- product
- experience
- the cooperative classroom
- the individual in the group
- aspects of implementation
- the institution.

6.1 Process

There are several reasons why we may refer to learning in projects as learning within a process syllabus. Project tasks have, as we have pointed out, a causal relationship between one another, in that they are chained together in order to realize certain macro- and micro-goals. It is not possible in our experience to conceive of project learning as a series of discrete and systematic items whose direction of development can be foreseen or controlled in the way that pre-packaged materials can. Tasks are not isolated events but parts of a process whose goals are determined by the interaction between learners and their expressed interests and needs; the challenges inherent in the target task; the teacher and her assessment of learner needs and knowledge of the target culture. The project plan becomes the tool of this process (see e.g. the *Airport* project) and is itself a flexible, working plan of action which can be changed according to decisions taken by the participants for whatever reason. For example, fresh information could send an investigation along a new direction as in *The Kennet and Avon Canal* project (Carter 1985c) when research had yielded little until a very productive and interculturally interesting informant, a local aristocrat who played a leading custodial role in the upkeep of the canal, was discovered and interviewed. Similarly, failure to complete a planned activity could result in a group reappraisal of their intentions either to abandon or rethink their strategy. One group failed to film useful video data on gesture and body language in the *Proxemics* project (Carter 1986a) until participants hit upon the idea of setting up their camera on the opposite platform of the railway station and videoing passengers waiting for trains on the other side. Of the many factors which could affect the shape and direction of a project, e.g. time constraints, group dynamic difficulties, etc., the nature of the project plan and its status within the group are often overlooked sources of potential difficulty. In the data there are examples of plans, among them the *Airport* and *Circus* project plans, which provide a great deal of detail of the overall stages, action to be taken, and skill and language areas to be covered. On the other hand there is also evidence in the data of planning restricted to the short-term without any specification with regard to overall targets or possible language needed to realize these targets. Some reasons why this should be the case are immediately identifiable. For many teachers this is a new area and moving into it from a transmission model requires a great deal of assistance from other teachers who are themselves heavily engaged in 'learning-by-doing' classroom action research in their own project classrooms. There is, therefore, a great need for research and systematic data collection in this area which ultimately needs to be fed into teacher education for the task-based classroom.

We could conclude, then, that wherever project plans do not seem to be available, e.g. on display in the classroom, for constant reference and discussion, it may lead to weaker contract building between the participants, both learners and teachers. This in turn leads to possible time-wasting when sub-groups are unclear about which micro-task to do next and likewise to a possible lack of clarity about the overall direction. As elsewhere, changes in direction are only possible when a given direction exists. It follows, therefore, that fruitful changes in project direction rely on a shared understanding of the projects' macro- and micro-targets. If the working plan has identified its targets clearly, it will also provide space within the project classroom for discussion to take place on how and why targets are to be realized.

It is a characteristic of the process-oriented classroom that it directly addresses the inter-relationship of the what, how and why of learning, and makes them objects of the learning itself. We can see this particularly clearly in the opening stage, the creation of the project plan, and the on-going monitoring of the plan resulting from process-evaluation activities. At the heart of this concern for the process is also the learners' affective response to theme, task, teacher and group; how the learner reacts to his experiences of the learning process influences, as we have discussed above (see 3.4 and Underhill 1989, p. 251), his level of commitment, cooperation, contribution, resistance and rejection. We will return to this issue in 6.4 and 6.5.

A further characteristic of the process-oriented classroom is the joint concern of teacher and learners for initiating and directing tasks. There is a trend, however, in the informal teacher accounts of the Bath data which exaggerates the desirability of minimal teacher intervention as projects move through the target task stage and beyond. We consider it a mistake to see the relationship between teacher and class as one of decreasing teacher control paralleled by increasing learner independence as if it were a linear progression, as some observers have suggested (Pütt 1978). It seems that the process dimension is more accurately accommodated within cyclical models of progression, detailed versions of which have still to be developed. However, it is certainly clear from the data that the learners' scope for self-direction increases as their exposure to project work increases. Yet, bearing in mind the teacher's responsibility as the monitor of class learning, there always needs to be space for the teacher to intervene, albeit facilitatively, to introduce new language input and deal with remedial problems, to suggest further communicative activities, to name but a few instances.

We could summarize the process dimension of the project classroom as follows. It is the constant expansion of experience and knowledge, themes and language through tasks connected on a causal basis. It is also a joint preoccupation of teacher and learners with the management and organization of learning which takes place as a result of the interaction potential of the project classroom.

6.2 Product

The product of the project classroom is what emerges from the process we have described above. We can state this in terms of an end product or a summary of language learned, or as an increase in topic knowledge, or as a growth of an individual's interpersonal skills;

in other words, the product is a continuum which extends from the concrete to the behavioural. There are two issues of importance here. The first concerns the relationship between the process we have outlined above and its product. In our view, this is a dialectical one in that there is a strong interaction between the two. The teacher can influence the process positively by creating interest in and helping to define a product for learners or by creating space for learners to negotiate and define it for themselves. In this way, concern with the product generates an interest in the process of its production, and attention to the process enhances the quality of the product. The Bath data provides evidence to support this view. Here there is a tendency which indicates a marked preoccupation among learners with the end product of a learning sequence, usually a book or a video film, and with quantifiable language items, but an equally clear preoccupation among teachers with the process necessary to bring this about. This may well arise because the learner's previous experience has been in product-oriented classrooms and their new teachers are concentrating their attention on ways in which learners may achieve their product goal successfully. However, since in one sense the product is an artifact which has to be created, learners are forced into areas of learning which have an organizational and interpersonal dimension as well as a linguistic one. In other words, the key elements of the process dimension become as much a part of their focus as the product.

The second point concerns the notion of text as the product of the language classroom. Learners in all language classrooms produce texts in response at some point or another to input. We can identify them as both written and spoken, i.e. ranging from diary entries, notes, captions, letters, personal profiles, advertisements, descriptions, poems, reports, to video voice-over text, dramatic performances and contributions to discussions.

In the teacher-centred classroom texts are generally seen as ways of assessing the success or failure of the learner to master the input. The compositions, summaries, sentence transformations and even the talks and role-plays which learners create, are produced essentially for the teacher and not for themselves. There is a significant and vital difference between these texts and those for example produced by the learners reacting to the *Holden Show* (5.4, example 2), or the teaching preparation notes of the *Dear Brown Eyes* learner 'teachers' (Carter and Cursiter 1985) or those written or recorded by learners in a book, pamphlet or audio/video/slide medium. What distinguishes them at the functional level is that they enjoy a different *status*. They are conceived and produced by learners for their *own* benefit to communicate their *own* meaning. They are not principally targets for the teacher's need to assess progress but are seen as valid contributions to a mutual process of creating and making sense of the world. Hence, a wall display of text and artifacts produced as the result of interacting with the environment, or poems written as the result of an environmental or introspective stimulus (see fig. 6.1), or learner diaries, or texts which arise from the types of communicative activities discussed in chapter 4, are contributions to the learning process. They are both products of this process and they feed back into it.

Puchta and Schratz (1984, vol. 1, p. 64) describe the texts that learners create in the communicative classroom as identity-revealing forms of expression. They spring from a complex background of previous learning experiences, accumulated language data and skills, strategies and heuristics found to be successful in the past. However, we can go further and say that learner texts are also identity-forming because with each text a learner recreates his identity. (In Cohn's terms they are manifestations of the 'I' and the 'We' dimension of an interaction.) A learner can recognize who he is from what he produces. Hence the reaction of the girls in our example of the *Holden Show* (see below, 6.2, example 2) which leads them to reject the representation of Holden as an ageing punk-rocker and to write their own version can be seen as both identity-revealing and identity-forming. This process is essentially a dialectical one and characteristic of the interaction in the project classroom.

In the practical sphere of the classroom, this change of status of learner texts has had interesting consequences. Project teachers report that the amount of written and other text forms produced by learners in projects is far higher than in the conventional classroom (Carter 1986; Floyd-Sanchez 1987; Roberts 1987, personal communication). They also report that groups are generally more critical than teachers with regard to issues of accuracy, and that they develop ways of editing and correcting work to meet often stringent, internally set standards of quality. What this shows is that learners are responding to the way in which their output is valued. A learner text is now something positive and contributory, often something to be displayed in the classroom, the subject of collective discussion and scrutiny, and not something to be marked and then hidden away.

We can summarize our discussion as follows:

(1) *The notion of 'product'*: learner texts arise out of a creative process

Figure 6.1 A shape poem
Completing a sentence
A 'diamond' poem (1)
A 'diamond' poem (2)
An acrostic poem

Loneliness is: a sad way of living

a rainy day

a weekend without your friends

like me in London, far from my country

a desert between flowers

a house without doors and windows

when I stay in the park and see the sky

the moon in the silent night

Adriana is

Dreaming of

Running

It's on the clouds

Air is clean

Noon is quiet

Adriana is always in the sky.

Red

Bloody   Sad

Exciting   Loving   Trying

Stendhal   Communist   Priest   Julian   Soral

Believing   Thinking   Dying

Silent   Cold

Black
M....

England

Cool   Foggy

Potating   Wearing   Studying

English   Spanish   Passion   Nature

Dancing   Laughing   Enjoying

Warm   Marvellous

Latinamerica
C ....

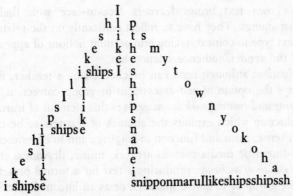

I like ships I like ships I like ships I like ships I like ships
It is impossible, of course, I like ships I like Ships ships
iful. I wanted to bring the ship to my house but
the museum of marine. The ship was very beaut
visited Greenwitch to see 'Cutty Sark' a
sailing ships. On first of November I
I like ships very much. Especially
M....

which has been at least in part self-directed. They help to reduce the alienation experienced in class by learners who only produce 'text' for teachers.

(2) *Learner individuality*: learner texts are expressions of the individuality of those who produced the text. That is to say, they communicate a meaning, an interpretation, or a view of the world which is personal to the learners.

(3) *Comprehension and the negotiation of meaning*: just as native speaker texts are reactions to the world or representations of the real world, so learner texts can be regarded in the same light. They need to be given the same status and consequently be interpreted seriously by the addressee. They are one of the forms in which learners contribute relevant content to classroom language learning.

(4) *Text as a form of experimentation*: learner texts indicate a willingness to experiment and produce 'drafts' of texts. This requires the confidence to take risks. It also reveals a level of cognitive awareness in the behaviour of learners.

(5) *The notion of reflection*: working with the foreign language to create

one's own text brings learners face-to-face with their own shortcomings. They have to reflect constantly on the relationship of text type to context, taking into account notions of appropriacy, and the sender/audience relationship.

(6) *Evaluation*: although texts can be checked by a teacher, there is always the option of self-assessment or group correction.

(7) *Playing and creating with language*: it is this element of learner text production which exploits the abilities of learners to be creative with sense, form and function in language and to experiment with non-linguistic media such as artwork, music, drawings, etc.

(8) *The notion of audience*: producing a text for a formal presentation to the group or to native speakers, or as an informal contribution to the collective learning process, means that the text has an audience and therefore a communicative purpose. This has consequences not just for the motivation of the text producer but on the composition and refinement of the text (see below).

Example

Text-project J.D. Salinger's *The Catcher in the Rye* (for details see scenario 2, 5.4.2)

After three weeks of intensive reading guided by the teacher, and extensive individual reading of the whole novel a collective planning meeting produced a set of topics for further research. Five topics were selected by groups of two to four students (Holden's relationship to girls; love and sexual experiences; Holden's father and other father figures; the meaning of the title; 'falling' – 'catching' – 'being caught'; imagine how Holden's life could go on – Holden at twenty-five, Holden at forty-five; etc.). The sixth topic was taken by the teacher who worked on 'Holden and the American 1950s'.

Here is an example of a group text – a script for a film of Holden as a television star in a popular TV show. The title page of the text bears the heading in large letters 'Script: THE HOLDEN SHOW'. There is a colour drawing of the sun setting behind a palm tree in the bottom right-hand corner. On a stylized American flag written in various letters is the phrase: 'American Award for Youngsters in the TV Industry 1980. 1980 Golden Palm of Film Festival Cannes for the best TV show of the year'. Inside the dedication reads: 'Ernst Mosch and his original Egerländer, who are clearly as idiotic as we are'. The text is copyrighted thus: 'Copyright: Sonuvabitch Moron Publishers Ltd., 1st Edition 1980'. The text is typed in two colors with the stage and camera directions given in red, with all corrections completed by the pupils themselves.

Not unexpectedly, the production of the authors and their team of actors generated new ideas. One idea consisted of adding a particularly striking soundtrack to scene two, featuring the sounds of sheep, cows, chickens, etc. and church bell, and encouraging even more improvisation from the

THE HOLDEN SHOW

Scene I

Show-Master: Good evening, Ladies and Gentlemen! This is LSD-
　　　　　　Radio International;
　　(Chorus: Halleluja . . .)

Show-Master: Tonight your special 'Discover-the-empire-of-imagina-
　　　　　　tion-Show' with our star guest . . .
　　(Beethoven, 5th Symphony.)
　　(Holden comes in.)

Show-Master: . . . HOLDEN CAULFIELD!!!

H.C. 17:　　Hi, Hello, Ilja!

Show-Master: Hello, Holden! Thanks for coming tonight. You
　　　　　　brought something with you, specially for the pets . . .

H.C. 17:　　Oh yeah, here it is:
　　(Showing up a jar of dog food.)
　　　　　　CHAPPI! The food for the happy dogs! The only one
　　　　　　with a fresh-meat-guarantee. Your butcher suggests: If
　　　　　　you really love your dog, choose only CHAPPI!

Show-Master: Thank you, Holden! And you, lovely audience, fasten
　　　　　　your seat belts and avoid smoking, 'cause the show
　　　　　　takes off!
　　　　　　Here we have Holden, 17 years of age; but he is not the
　　　　　　only guest in our show: The other one is . . . a time
　　　　　　voyager, coming out of the mysterious, magical mist in
　　　　　　which the future lies!
　　(Zarathustra.)
　　(Panning to doll.)

　　　　　　MR HOLDEN CAULFIELD, 45 years of age. Hello,
　　　　　　Mr Caulfield!
　　　　　　Now, before we start, a short introduction for those
　　　　　　poor chaps, who have never watched our fascinating,
　　　　　　exciting game:
　　　　　　At first I'm going to ask our young Holden, which
　　　　　　expectations he has for his future life. He is allowed to
　　　　　　give three alternative suggestions. At the end of the
　　　　　　show we will have an interview and an experiment, the
　　　　　　result of which even we don't know. Wait and see!
　　　　　　Soon we'll reach the peak of excitement! It's your turn,
　　　　　　Holden! Fall into the wide, majestic ocean of imagina-
　　　　　　tion.
　　(Holden looks into a glass ball.)

H.C. 17:　　I see, I see, I see . . .

Figure 6.2 The Holden Show (Legutke, M. 1988a)

Scene II

> (Holden sitting on a bench, straw hat, pipe, worker's trousers, in Vermont, deaf-mute.)
> (Farmer appears.)

Farmer: Hello, Mr Caulfield, fine weather today, isn't it?

H.C. 45:   (Typical gesture of a deaf-mute, when explaining that he is a deaf-mute, picks up a pencil and a sheet of paper, Holden nods, writes on the paper, gives the paper to the stranger again.)

Farmer: Oh, you mean the weather is just right for harvesting. Bye, Mr Caulfield!
              (Lifts his arm for a goodbye gesture, Holden too.)

Scene III

> (Holden's wife, sitting on a sofa, watches television, daughter lying on the floor.)
> (Holden comes through the door.)

H.C. 45:   Hello, my dears!
              (Wife stands up, gives him a kiss.)

Wife: Hi, Holly!

H.C. 45:   (To daughter.) Molly, would you mind gettin' me a beer or two?

Daughter: Okay, Dad! (Leaves the room.)

Wife: Did you have a good day in the office?

H.C. 45:   Oh, don't ask, Jane, it was rather exhausting. I had to defend a murderer at the Criminal Court. Poor chap, grew up in the Bronx and never had a chance in life to get out of there. He is just 19 years old and it looks as if the Prosecutor wants him to sit on a certain chair.

Wife: Similar to your first case in 1963?

H.C. 45:   Yes, but I was a greenhorn in those days. But now everybody is looking at me and expects me to get the young guy out of this.
       (Molly comes in, gives her dad the beer.)

H.C. 45:   Thanks, Molly!

Wife: Take it easy, love! Don't care what they say: I know that you do your job as good as you can.

Scene IV
  (Holden as a pop star in a corner.)

Introducer: (You can hear the applause of the audience.)
              Holly Cauly: Great, isn't he?
              You want more? You want more?

Audience: Yeah!! (Applause.)

H.C. 45:   Okay! The song I'm singing now is very personal in a
              way. I've written it for my Ma.

  (Sings Cat Stevens' 'Popstar') (Afterwards a couple of girls run up
  to the platform, trying to get a piece of his trousers.) (Applause.)

Scene V

Show-Master: Three suggestions for Holden Caulfield. There he is:
              And we, dear audience, are heading for the next step:
              ... experiment. Holden, would you please stay here for
              a little while, because the audience and me, we are having
              a conversation with you in precisely your 45th year.

  (Doing a few steps, meets a doctor, in the background
  H. Caulfield behind a grating, 45, shouting for his brother Allie,
  crying.)

Show-Master: Hello, Dr Frank'n Furter, let me introduce you to our
              audience: You are a psychoanalyst from Harvard
              University; for how long have you known Holden
              Caulfield?

Dr Frank'n   It was when Holden was 17, I met him in a sanatorium.
Furter: He was suffering from mental disorder and got out in
              the autumn afterwards. He was supposed to adjust
              himself in school or at least behave decently and he had
              a pretty good chance to make it. But for some reasons,
              he again got the obsession that his brother Allie would
              leave him alone and he was falling down a cliff, onto a
              rock, being dead. There had to be a certain reason for
              it, an event, when he relapsed into this mental illness.
              He was brought back to the sanatorium and after a
              while we got out of him that the obsession started after
              a TV-show where he had to imagine himself being 45
              and he met himself in that age .... Since that time
              he has had to spend his life in a lunatic asylum.

Show-Master: Thanks, Doc!
              And this is the right time for starting an experiment.
              Holden, would you please come over here?

  (Holden appears, sees himself lying on the floor, shouting out the
  name 'Allie'.)

Holden 17:   Is this me?

Show-Master: Exactly!

Holden: I swear to you: I'm crazy! Really!

  (Falling on the floor, shouting for Allie.)

Scene VI

(Klaus-Dieter and Andreas standing in front of the camera.)

Klaus-Dieter: Of course, these were only four possible suggestions for Holden's life story . . .

Andreas: . . . there are millions more. Imagine, for example, Holden as a soldier in Vietnam, as a hippie in 'Frisco . . .

Klaus-Dieter: . . . or could it be that a little Holden is in everybody, that a part of your life is integrated in the story of Holden Caulfield?

Andreas: Bye, and don't forget: CHAPPI is best for your dog!

Source: Legutke 1988, pp. 228–32.

actors. Another idea was to use a section of the original soundtrack from the movie 'Stagecoach' for scene three. The part the learners chose was the section where the coach is attacked by Red Indians and Peacock is killed by an arrow. This was to run as a backdrop to a conversation between Holden, a nouveau-riche lawyer, and his wife. Finally, in scene four, the popstar becomes a punk rocker.

6.3 Experience

The process orientation of the project classroom commits its participants to a focus on 'experience' as an essential and substantial element of their learning. By 'experience' we refer here both to the general past and present experiences of learners and teachers as individuals, and the specific accumulation of experience of self, group, theme and process during the project. In a classroom where language is not an end in itself but the means for learners to pursue topics and work through tasks, this focus on 'experience' is as much concerned with the learner's interaction with materials, tasks and other learners as with the acquisition of formal knowledge. We argue, therefore, that this essentially theme-centred and interactive approach represents a realization of the general notion of experiential learning as outlined by Dewey, Lewin and Piaget (Kolb 1984). Three key components of this notion are:

(1) *Learning in the here and now*: a movement away from the conventional practice of learning for some undefined future purpose towards learning for a more specific purpose which can be realized immediately; it also encompasses a holistic view of learning which transcends the traditional polarity of cognition versus affect, and intellectual versus physical activity.

(2) *Experimentation*: learning by hypothesis building and verification by experimenting, finding out by discovery, in other words, learning-by-doing.

(3) *Reflection*: learning through reflecting back on the experiment, drawing conclusions and making new hypotheses which will inform and shape further experimentation.

6.3.1 Learning in the here and now

A particularly striking feature of all the examples in the data corpus is the emphasis on learning in the here and now. Indeed it is the special advantage of project learning that it establishes a direct link between language learned and its application. The immediacy of the here-and-now experience includes for our purposes not only learning in action e.g. 'live' situations but also the pre-task preparation in the classroom. For example, the students who had to use English in formal settings either in native speaker schools in England, or in interviews at an airport or working with handicapped children, needed specific training in appropriate language forms and inter-personal skills. Both formal and informal accounts attest to the enthusiasm, excitement, energy and commitment of learners who realize that their current work has an immediate relevance. For teachers it constitutes a live dimension previously absent from the conventional teaching paradigm of language presentation, controlled practice and free practice. For learners both the pleasure and the apprehension of here-and-now learning are once more actively underscored during the creation of an end product.

In many projects in the data the here-and-now element is typically concentrated in the research and data collection stage which, in the case of encounter projects, takes place outside the classroom, e.g. the *Airport, Jumble Aid, Keynsham* projects. In text projects this element is manifest in the creativity of participants, as, for example, in the preparation and presentation of the learners' version of the Little Red Riding Hood story to a live audience; the various extensions of Holden Caulfield life-story in drama and text in the *The Catcher in the Rye* project; and the creative and editing phases of the various poetry projects.

However, we note, particularly in the informal accounts of encounter projects, a tendency for teachers to equate the 'experience' dimension of the project almost exclusively with the externally realized task, i.e. where the here-and-now dimension is most clearly in evidence. One interpretation may be that teachers justifiably identify the target task as the most salient opportunity to *experience* the L2 at first hand and use the specific term, experiential learning, to refer to this stage and undervalue its cyclical relevance to others. By doing so it could be said that they see experience not so much in process terms or as a learner-related, developmental layer running through the project, but as integral to a particular event which has to be organized.

There are several pertinent points here which we need to note in passing. The organizational burdens which befall teachers and learners when extended work outside the classroom has to be arranged and monitored are considerable. Planning is followed by communication by telephone, letter or personal visit, which in turn is followed by the completion of the target task itself. Here the teacher's role is mainly managerial, concerned with helping learners with the logistics of their undertaking. This in itself constitutes a radical departure from the traditional classroom and requires different and demanding input from the teacher. Furthermore, on the evidence of the available data the number of teachers who employ a process approach in language teaching is low. There are no clear models of process learning to follow and teachers are clearly working pragmatically, learning and researching their work as they proceed. In addition, both in L1 and L2 contexts the environment has been a seriously under-used resource for language learning, and it is only recently that descriptions have appeared in the literature of vigorous attempts to make it accessible for communication and intercultural learning (e.g. Fried-Booth 1982; Legutke and Thiel 1983; Montgomery and Einsenstein 1985; Carter and Thomas 1986), followed by explicatory analyses of its value in the literature of teacher education (Ashworth 1985; Nunan 1988; pp. 105–7).

We would suggest therefore that the reason why teachers possibly misapply the term is more as a result of their lack of a pedagogical background in experiential learning rather than a reflection of their practice in the classroom. For, as we have seen, there are many examples of a conscious attempt to equip learners to function in a learner-centred ambience where negotiation, goal-setting and evaluation take place cyclically. In the area of encounter projects, for example, many teachers follow Carter's practice in bridging the external task with a remotivating evaluation task to encourage learners to process the data they have collected (see 5.3.2). Clearly there is a need for teachers and researchers to combine to examine teacher roles and teacher perceptions of a process-oriented language-learning programme. This need, which now exists for in-service and pre-service training to provide guidelines of how teachers orchestrate a process syllabus, could more than usefully be the focus for research in this area.

6.3.2 Experimentation and reflection

There are many examples in the data of learners engaged in experimentation, reflection and re-hypothesizing. The process is typical of all text projects where learners are attempting to write drama scripts and poetry which lead to some end project, a presentation, performance or collection of work to be sold. It is characterized by the sharing of opinions and ideas, the trialling of material and the joint editing and polishing of the final version. The process is also vividly demonstrated in examples taken from encounter projects. The production of the wheelchair guide for handicapped people in the *Good Wheelchair Guide* project involved extensive exploration with a wheelchair of the urban environment and reflection on what recommendations to make. The teaching materials used by the learner 'teachers' in the *Dear Brown Eyes* project were subject to trialling *in situ*, appraisal and readjustment. The learner 'teachers' also reappraised their own performances and tried to learn from day to day from their experiences. Similarly, the team which made a film on body language and paralinguistics researched several locations, experimenting and discussing options before a final decision was made.

Learning how to conduct oneself during such tasks depends in no small measure on how learners are introduced to and guided towards more independent action by the teacher. In projects such as *Jumble Aid*, the *Holden Show* from the *The Catcher in the Rye* project, *The Kennet and Avon Canal* and *The Circus*, learners decided how to structure and organize their work accompanied by varying degrees of teacher intervention. The role which the teacher fulfilled was as a guide who helped them clarify the steps which their objective required. If, for example, collecting information on the history, construction, maintenance, use, social role, etc. of the canal was the objective, the teacher's task was to help the learners work out a sequence. This was achieved by conducting a brain-storming session to identify possible informants and sources and then to prioritize the information-gathering tasks. At this point also language needs and deficits are identified and the relevant work given its appropriate priority on the list. The organization of logistics follows, assembling recording equipment, arranging transport, and finalizing appointments. More and more of these tasks are taken over by the learners depending not only on their growing language ability but on their ability to work out for themselves through discussion what needs to be done next and who should undertake it. After the visit, however, the teacher, crucially, ensures that the learners reconvene their plenary meeting to review and assess their work. The *review session* is the recurring activity through which learners begin to accept more responsibility for their actions and to have an effect on planning and action in the project. It is an integral part of the experiential cycle (see also 4.2.9).

However, what is clear from the data is that the practice of reviewing is not uniformly applied, and it plays a larger part in some projects than others. It is not commented on to any great extent in the formal accounts of projects and tends in informal accounts to be overshadowed by reference to the 'experience' of the target task.

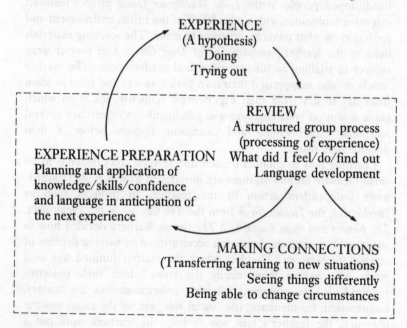

Figure 6.3 The experiential cycle (Davies 1989: 27)

Typically, teachers draw attention to any decisions or independent action taken by learners without making clear any of the processes that led up to such decisions.

In conclusion we can say that a project can provide a vehicle for experiential learning. However, it is merely an organizational construct, albeit one which provides learners and teachers with the space to explore the possibilities of the participatory classroom. Crucially, it requires an understanding on the part of the teacher of how to facilitate this process. In dynamic learning situations, moreover, self-direction and independent decision-making cannot be seen in absolute terms. The data show a necessary variation in the levels of learner participation and teacher domination, i.e. in the way in which the teacher facilitates and maintains this dynamic balance (see chapter 2). However, over and above the varying constraints of different project situations, it seems that some projects are more consciously experiential than others and that a determining factor may be the rigour of the teacher in building in a process orientation. For the present we may assert that the benefits of the project classroom depend on the extent to which learners are able to learn experientially. However, apart from the comparative work of Montgomery and Eisenstein (1985) there has been little evaluative study of projects themselves or against more conventional forms of teaching to substantiate such a claim. In the context of the continuing debate within CLT teachers and researchers need to examine both this area and the key questions concerning the roles that learners and teachers adopt:

– How can learners become active participants in learning processes, able to contribute to, manage, and evaluate their experience?
– How can teachers acquire the concepts and skills to fulfil the facilitating role which maintains the balance between task, process, product and learner?

Both of these questions will be given further consideration in chapter 7 (the learner) and chapter 8 (the teacher).

6.4 The cooperative classroom

Hardly any central project task of the learning sequences we have included for consideration in chapter 5 could be dealt with by forms of individualistic and competitive learning which have been dominant in Western education for the last decades. On the contrary, their successful completion requires learning groups, whose members collaboratively seek outcomes that are beneficial to all those with whom they are cooperatively connected. A closer look at some of the challenges posed by project tasks will illustrate this point. At the same time, the following three examples allow us to highlight some of the key issues we want to address in relation to the cooperative classroom.

In the *Airport* project (see above 5.2.1) the task which the group of elementary learners (aged eleven to twelve) had agreed upon was to interview English-speaking passengers, airport employees and visitors about their destinations, where they came from, their opinions, their jobs, etc. These interviews were to be recorded and edited so that they could function as new language in-put for all learners in the classroom. The highly complex interview situation makes considerable demands on elementary learners. Not only does it presuppose the mastery of linguistic inventories and communicative strategies, it also asks for a variety of social, managerial and instrumental skills which are not normally taught in the conventional classroom:

- Learners needed to approach possible interview partners and enlist their cooperation to be interviewed.
- They had to be able to describe the purpose of the interview in English.
- They had to 'signal' the limits of their own language abilities so that the partner could adjust to the interviewer's ability to understand.
- They had to have learnt how to indicate difficulties and ask for help, i.e. so that the interviewee repeated or clarified, or spoke more slowly.
- They were required to adjust to different varieties of English.
- They had to conduct the interview and wherever necessary take the initiative.
- Above all they had to have sufficient linguistic and communicative strategies available to get people to talk, as the success of their venture depended upon collecting as many interesting texts from native speakers as possible.
- In addition, they needed to have acquired the technical and organizational know-how to record and document their interviews, after all, their texts were to be studied and transformed into reports or portraits in the classroom.
- Last, but not least, learners were to work autonomously from the teacher for the whole of the central project phase.

It is here that the cooperative group of three to five interdependent learners plays a crucial role. The support the group offers, helps to overcome understandable anxieties about asking strangers questions in a foreign language. Group members cooperate and negotiate solutions to the problems posed by the different elements of the interview. They support each other, for example, by taking on different roles. The main interviewer may be helped by one or two others, while another learner operates the cassette recorder and a third is responsible for noting down key words and counter numbers on the recorder. There is no doubt that the effectiveness of the team depends on extensive training prior to the interview event. Apart from having learnt the necessary skills the group must have developed some positive interdependence (Johnson and Johnson 1987) which provides the emotional support to meet the challenges of the task. We will return to this issue of how this is achieved.

Helgard Neumann-Zöckler's (1980) account of her learners' work with the Little Red Riding Hood theme is a good example of how to 'open up' the language class for cooperative learning by carefully shifting to tasks whose demands can only be met by collaborative efforts. The project itself (conducted with intermediate learners in a German comprehensive school) lasted ten lessons, taking as its starting point an analysis of an audio and written version of this well-known fairy tale. The class was divided into four groups of six learners who wrote four 'new' versions of the story which they subsequently rehearsed into mini-dramatizations for eventual video filming. At the final plenary session the groups presented four strikingly imaginative adaptations: an exciting crime story, a story about opting out of society, a new, poetic version of the fairy story and a play about an imaginary escape.

In her evaluation of the written work – the scripts and narratives – Neumann-Zöckler raises the point which we feel is a common link in project work. She refers to how her learners developed the confidence to bring their own aspirations, ideas and beliefs into their work. In other words they fictionalized their own world through their own texts. It is our contention that they were able to achieve this because the cooperative learning groups had sufficient scope for independent decision-making within a framework clearly marked out by the teacher. She also made them aware from the outset of the activities they had to target on and the consequent need to make a project plan. The groupings emerged after some prompting by the teacher who made use of her knowledge of the class and the data from a sociometric test. Her aim here was to produce groups which were heterogeneous and which contained at least one pair of friends.

When work started she led the class away from the familiar ground of frontal teaching to pair work and finally to group work. The first five lessons saw a combination of teacher-led work, dealing with the introduction of new language and vocabulary as foreseen by the project plan and teacher-independent work of text-writing in groups. By approaching the work in this way the teacher made sure that even learners without previous experience of working independently in sub-groups were able to come to terms with and make sensible use of the freedom in a school environment. Having become accustomed to working on their own, the teams were now in a position to move on to the aesthetic side of their dramatization, the making of stage scenery and props.

> The extent to which the learners became involved in the project was evident in their attention to small details. Every group had taken the trouble to fill Little Red Riding Hood's basket with cookies which they had baked themselves, eating and refilling the basket for every time they worked together. One of the girls brought a white bonnet for the 'grandmother' which she had knitted herself; one of the boys created a lyrical ambience for his group by playing the guitar. Groups 2 and 4 made placards and scenery in their art class and group 4 constructed masks which gave their production additional impact.
>
> (Neumann-Zöckler 1980, p. 59)

Quite clearly the interdependent group had provided the nourishing ground for creative expression and inventiveness, thus helping learners to expand their scope of action in the foreign language. At the same time this text project raises a number of issues to which we will return later for detailed discussion.

(1) the issue of group composition and assignment of learners to the group (homogeneous versus heterogeneous groupings);
(2) the issue of learner education in view of dominant experiences with frontal classroom situations;
(3) the issue of language. As in *Airport* the question is what happens linguistically in the cooperative learning groups. What is the role of the target language and of the mother tongue;
(4) And finally, what happens to the individual learners? Who feels uncomfortable and hampered by the group because they prefer more individual styles of work?

Before we address these issues we will briefly focus on a third project report. *The Good Wheel Chair Guide To Bath*, a large-scale encounter project lasting eleven and a half weeks, was carried out by advanced learners of English (Fried-Booth 1982). The project activities involved extensive research into problems of disabled tourists and the facilities available to the disabled in the city of Bath. The research activities included interviews, telephone calls, visits to and detailed inspection of a great variety of locations, and background reading.

> The accumulated mass of scribbled notes, maps, illegible scrawls, and countless unrelated scraps of information stimulated valuable communicative interaction until agreement was reached on the need to produce a booklet for the disabled tourists which would be called *The Good Wheelchair Guide*.
>
> (Ibid., p. 100)

This impressive final product which could be given and/or sold to the disabled in Bath not only necessitated many hours of detailed language work in all four skill areas, but also involved typing, editing, copying, binding, etc., all of which required extensive group interaction focusing on negotiation and decision-making. In addition to issues of a cooperative classroom mentioned in connection with *Airport* and *Little Red Riding Hood*, the last project raises the following questions:

(1) In view of the complexity of the assignments both for the research phase and the phase of end-product production – how was the issue of division of labour and the corresponding role behaviour being addressed. Was work divided evenly? Did certain learners take over certain roles which were avoided by or denied others (the manager, the secretary, the artist), and what were the reasons for this?

(2) In what way were both the individual student and the group held accountable for mastering the assigned and/or selected tasks, since the completion of the end-product depended on a collaborative effort – or did it result from a 'tour de force' of a committed teacher and a couple of activists?

(3) How did the sub-groups deal with the pressure which might result from such a project, especially if the group was composed of learners from different ethnic and national backgrounds, with undoubtedly diverse expectations of how language learning should be best organized?

As in the examples quoted above most project reports give clear evidence that their approaches are consistent with a participatory model which utilizes cooperative learning as a major structure in the learning process. However, a number of crucial issues have been ignored by most authors, making it difficult for readers to understand the interesting outcomes of such endeavours, and even more so to implement project procedures in their own classrooms. The following issues are to some extent compatible with the five factors which have been put forward as accounting for success in cooperative learning (Johnson and Johnson 1987):

(1) the development of positive interdependence;
(2) the problem of group composition;
(3) the development of sufficient social skill;
(5) autonomy and self-direction;
(6) group evaluation;
(6) the accountability of both the individual and the group, and the issue of doability of task;
(7) language in face-to-face interactions.

Taking each in turn we can offer the following specification of our discussion on project learning:

1: Although none of the projects could do without the small 'research' team of learners mutually engaged in achieving the goals of the project tasks and thus working independently of teacher control during several of its phases, the notions of group formation and cohesion as vital factors in project learning are hardly ever addressed in the data.

Stevick (1976a) and Curran (1976) had the macro-group in mind when they emphasized the relevance of the supportive community of learners, which provides the security to the individual and the emotional safety-net in language learning. Trust and a feeling of belonging would characterize such a community. What holds true for the macro-group also applies to the small team. There is, in fact, a dialectical relationship at work. Only if the large group has become a community, are small groups able to venture out on their project tasks, whose outcomes would be beneficial to all individuals involved, and to the whole class. Conversely, only if the members of small groups have developed an awareness of their positive interdependence with each other and the group as a whole, will the macro-group become a community. To pave the road to a cooperative classroom in action teachers need to find answers to the following questions:

– How does a community of learners, both on the macro- and the micro-level of the small groups come about, especially under conditions of an evaluative situation in state schools, which are still dominated by values of competitive and individualistic learning?

– How is a climate of trust built and maintained?
– More specifically: what are the mutual goals of the group/s, how is the work divided, roles assigned and gratifications awarded?

Throughout the book we have argued that the answers to these questions have to derive from collaborative efforts within the learning process (see in particular 3.4 and 3.5) and specific interventions by the teacher using communicative tasks which have been designed with the intention of fostering a learning community (see 4.2.1).

2: In spite of a general agreement among researchers that the composition of the small group has a decisive impact on its effectiveness as a framework for learning (Schwerdtfeger 1977), only Nuhn (1982) and Neumann-Zöckler (1980) comment on this issue in greater detail by revealing their criteria for groupings. Both authors emphasize the heterogeneous group deriving from careful analysis of the teacher, as the most effective form of learning during central project tasks. The cooperative team would typically consist of at least two friends and a balanced mixture of high, average and low achievers. Research in cooperative learning has provided strong evidence in support of such heterogeneous teams which would stay together over longer periods of time ranging from weeks to months to a full school year. Whereas such heterogeneous and long-term arrangements seem to provide the most effective way to come to grips with the challenge of large project tasks, other grouping options must not be ruled out. Depending on the learning goals and the dynamics of the process in the various phases of a project spontaneous groupings (e.g. during a values clarification task or a role-playing event), or individual and/or pair work during a phase of skill training and automatization (e.g. when learners practise interviewing techniques) are not only feasible but most appropriate.

The issue here is not simply about which patterns of learner interaction are most compatible with the attainment of which learning goals, but also about who makes the decisions about forms and realizations of these patterns in the classroom. As the climate of trust can only derive from collaborative efforts of teacher and learner, so learners have an important contribution to make to grouping arrangements and group composition. Their contribution might often be in conflict with what the teacher has in mind or regards as most effective. However, a participatory classroom cannot avoid such incongruence. As a matter of fact, it is from divergent views on how to go about doing things, that it draws its major strength.

3, 4, 5: Since these issues will be given comprehensible treatment in chapter 7 where we define learner education as a path towards project competence, a short cumulative gloss will suffice here.

Once the cooperative group has been formed – be it through spontaneous decision, through teacher probing or joint efforts – the question is: how will the group go about organizing its learning? A sense of positive interdependence because of a common goal and caring about each other's learning does not guarantee the success of the group, nor does the ideal grouping constellation safeguard against possible failure, unless group members possess sufficient social skills, including appropriate leadership, communication and conflict solution skills.

For the filming of the *Airport* project (Humburg et al. 1983), the two directors (both of them experienced teachers of English) had suggested several grouping arrangements based on careful observation of previous lessons and detailed input from the group's English teacher. However, the learners did not accept heterogeneous groupings, which would have cut across established sub-groups. They insisted on meeting the challenges of the project tasks together with their friends. This led to two rather extreme constellations. One group (group A) consisted of low achievers (all of its members had scored at the bottom of the West German grading scale); group B on the other hand had four high and one average achiever.

Whereas group B performed very promisingly during the preparatory phases, i.e. they only spoke English, even in their groups at school and after school (see film), they failed initially at the airport, because they were constantly competing for leadership, and nobody wanted to take on the 'minor' jobs, such as secretary or cassette operator. Strong guidance and intervention from one of the teachers was required to help this group overcome a frustrating and unproductive situation. Group A, on the other hand, functioned extremely well at the airport, after it had mastered some linguistic difficulties (especially with formulating questions) in the lessons prior to the field trip. Of all the groups the five girls of group A brought home the highest number of interesting interviews: e.g. they had an interview with a German TV star, an American pop group (see film), and the city mayor of Nairobi (see film). Because the group had developed the social skills, they could profit immediately from their successful interviews. At the same time they were able to contribute to the learning of the whole class by providing interesting input for the others.

At least as far as the interviews were concerned, group A turned out to be extremely high-achieving and capable of managing its learning. Group B's ability to self-direct, on the other hand, was considerably hampered by the pervasive competitiveness of its members. One could certainly argue, that group A would have profited even more (especially linguistically) if it had had the help of a 'high' achieving peer tutor, conversely, group B would have needed some of the social skills of group A. Whether a teacher-induced mixture of the two groups would have produced better results, would need further investigation. What is quite clear from this example, however, is, that process competence embraces a scope of skills and abilities, which goes far beyond the traditional concept of the four skills in language learning. Thus far, the majority of project reports do not provide a coherent view on the skills and abilities which make up a process competence. We will return to this issue in chapter 7.

6: In accordance with research in cooperative learning (Johnson and Johnson 1987) most authors underscore the importance of individual accountability as a prerequisite of the successful group. Such accountability defined by the project plan and expected outcomes (e.g. the collaboratively produced book), is frequently hinted at or explicitly mentioned (Nuhn 1982; Fried-Booth 1982; Carter and Thomas 1986). What is missing, however, is a detailed discussion how accountability is framed and monitored, so that each group member can take on the responsibility for his part of the tasks without being asked to do the impossible or being bored, which would be equally unproductive for the learning process. Some authors suggest contractual arrangements between teacher and learners (Dietrich 1979a; Kaufmann 1977; Legutke 1988b).

Kaufmann's long-term project *Learning in Freedom*, carried out over eight months in Switzerland in 1977 (Kaufmann 1977), demonstrates how secondary school learners at intermediate level in French were able to work successfully in a self-directed way after they had negotiated their framework and roles in the form of a 'contract'. C. Rogers' book *Freedom to Learn* (1969) first appeared in German in 1974, closely followed by the publication of Ruth C. Cohn's *Theme Centered Interaction* (1975). Following in the wake of these publications, Kaufmann's project was an unmistakable reaction against the teacher-centred, non-interactive, unimaginative, book-oriented methodology of the time. He called the project an experiment in 'learning in freedom' and it proceeded on the basis of agreement which the class negotiated:

(1) Class members could do what they liked in their French lessons.
(2) The following conditions applied:

228 Process and Experience in the Language Classroom

(a) They remained in the classroom.
(b) Any communication was to take place in French.
(c) Working for other school subjects in these lessons was not allowed.

An external constraint was the amount of language to be covered. This was specified by the coursebook, and a short test of language skills was also planned for a later stage. Learners were free to approach the work in their own way, to decide what work the sub-groups should cover and in which order the language exercises were to be done. They were also able to choose their own forms of learning, i.e. how the group was to be organized. Kaufmann remarks upon how often the learners made changes in the work format (see also Breen 1987a). They were not bound to the text-book and they made use of this flexibility to read other French books and newspapers and listen to tapes and records. There was a certain amount of anxiety and nervous hesitation in evidence within the group at first as they realized how much freedom they enjoyed and how much responsibility came with it. However, this disappeared as soon as the work got under way.

Regular feedback sessions took place and certain elements of their freedom of operation were modified as a result. One such change was to ask one person at a time to make a presentation to the class of the grammar that had to be covered. In the end they were forced to ask the teacher to do it, not because they failed to understand the grammar point but because they lacked the didactic 'know-how' needed to make the presentation. This drew the teacher back into a more central role where he was once more guiding and directing. One could say that Kaufmann had possibly overestimated what his learners were capable of. However, this turn of events focuses upon an important area in project work and we shall return to the notion of 'didactic skills' and peer tutoring in conjunction with learner education in chapter 7.

How did the learners react to the experiment? At the end of the eight-month period a detailed questionnaire revealed that 90 per cent of them liked learning this way and that they found it successful. About 60 per cent of them thought that they had contributed something themselves to the learning process and the majority felt that the teacher's approach had been positive and helpful. They highlighted the benefits which they felt they had accrued in respect of their own language performance skills. They all felt that they could now express themselves more effectively. However, what was unmistakably clear from their comments, was that their attitude towards learning French had undergone a basic change. Kaufmann's own conclusions are quite unequivocal:

> By allowing learners to learn in an atmosphere of freedom there was a genuine chance that their general willingness to communicate and in particular their oral skills could be decisively improved. The successes achieved in the experiment overshadows anything that I have ever achieved using traditional methods.
>
> (Kaufmann 1977, p. 235)

Both teacher and student agreed that the achievements of this undertaking owed a substantial amount to the clear agreements and the framing of accountability.

Since Kaufmann's work in 1977, methodologists with a communicative bias have referred to this most encouraging and radical project, but only to note that learner-centred methods were making an appearance in the ongoing debate on language teaching methodology (Schiffler 1980; Dietrich 1984). In the early 1980s 'Learning in Freedom' was cited as the only German language account of an attempt to put the ideas of Rogers and Cohn into action. Even today we have to look hard to find any substantially documented follow-up work.

7: 'There is no magic in positive interdependence in and of itself', say Johnson and Johnson (1988, p. 10), 'it is the interaction patterns promoted by the positive interdependence that affect education outcomes'. Project data give lively evidence how the scope of action for teacher and learner is widely increased, because project tasks provide ample opportunity for meaningful face-to-face interaction within and outside the classroom. Such encounters are content-related (What is our focus of research, what do we know and/or want to find out about the target culture and its language?) as well as process-related (What is the best way of going about our research, and how can we improve our learning?).

Whereas content language is given extensive treatment, the issue of procedural and negotiatory language is simply ignored. Unless the question of how the cooperative teams go about organizing their learning *linguistically* is addressed, we will not be able to take the discussion past the level of conceptual debate into the area of classroom practice. A list of expressions for classroom discourse offered by standard 'communicative textbooks' cannot satisfy the wide range of language needs generated by the project process, requiring students to negotiate goals, understand and reformulate tasks, solve group dynamic problems, reach agreement on forms and content of presentations, and reflect on how well the learning groups are functioning – to name just a few of the functional areas involved.

Unless there is secret agreement that all this can and should be done in the mother tongue, more systematic efforts are needed through collaborative research by applied linguists, curriculum designers and classroom teachers (cf. van Lier 1988). In monolingual groups, especially at elementary level, it is our view that the role of the mother tongue as an important bridge language in procedural discourse needs to receive a fresh and undogmatic reassessment in view of project learning.

Not before the question of how and when students acquire the linguistic means to cope with the discoursal requirements of a project classroom is addressed will we be able to overcome the crucial dichotomy between theory and practice. The insight that communication about language learning makes for the authenticity of the communicative classroom (Breen and Candlin 1980; Breen 1985b; Martin 1986) needs to be complemented by documented classroom experiences which explicate a negotiated curriculum in action.

6.5 The individual in the cooperative group

I wish I could have learnt English like this!
(Camera man from West German TV during the filming of the AIRPORT
PROJECT, Thiel 1984, p. 141)

Since we will return to the individual learner in chapter 7 we shall concentrate the argument here on three issues which are related to the specific nature and dynamics of the cooperative classroom in project learning: The issues of intrinsic motivation for risk-taking, individual empowerment and divergent opinion in cooperative groups.

The learning which results from coming to grips with the multi-faceted challenges of project tasks seems to be propelled by a noticeably high degree of motivation on the part of the learner. The observation of the cameraman in the above quotation reflects the nature of learner comments made during evaluations and in diary reports. Such reactions underline the connection between the challenge of the task and the motivation to meet the challenge: the willingness to take risks in terms of social behaviour, intellectual endeavours and communicative self-expression in the target language (see below: Statements). Also teachers observing students during project processes give similar evidence (Carter and Thomas 1986; Fried-Booth 1982; Heitz 1985; Kaufmann 1977; Martin 1985; Montgomery and Eisenstein 1985; Neumann-Zöckler 1980; Nuhn 1982; Thiel 1984; Seidler 1988; Wicke and Wicke 1988).

Although extrinsic factors – such as examination requirements or parents' expectations – are always likely factors in motivating learners about to engage in classroom work, it is the project task itself which triggers and sustains motivation (Seletzky 1989, p. 45). The experience of self-directed learning during which the individual within the group gains conscious control of the task at hand by appropriating and redesigning the task-as-workplan (see above) quite obviously has an impact on the student's sense of achievement and satisfaction. This, in turn, triggers off a willingness to take new risks and embark on investigative experimentation. Davies (1989, p. 1) comments on this dialectical relationship between task-completion and motivation to take risks as follows: 'Students are noticeably more motivated. No sooner have they participated in one challenging activity than they want to participate in another. They develop an "appetite" for challenges . . .' Davies discusses the idea of personal challenges in the context of an outdoor/social education programme during which EFL students in England go canoeing, camping or mountaineering. This programme type and other specialist programmes such as drama and art, constitute long-term strands woven through a main programme of English language education. All of these 'extra-curricular' activities are conducted in the target language. Learners also realize that as they increase their level of skills and confidence they become more confident and willing to choose challenges which demand more of them: 'The idea of developing challenges works well as long as students understand that successful outcomes require a balance between the skills an individual possesses and the challenge they give themselves' (ibid., p. 6).

In the following diagram (see fig. 6.4) Davies refers to these issues to explicate the relationship between skills and challenges:

What he defines as the 'adventure' or 'peak experience' will bring out the best in the individual within the framework of the cooperative group if the conditions we have discussed above (5.4.4) are met: Individual/social skills and task challenges need to be in balance; the group needs to have developed a positive interdependence and a sense of working together for clearly defined and mutually accepted goals; every team member must be individually accountable and understand that s/he is in charge of his/her own and the team-mates'

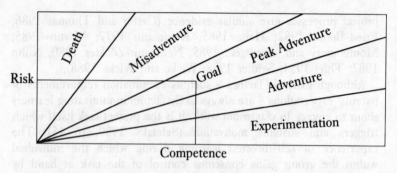

Figure 6.4 Levels of challenge in outdoor education (Davies 1989: 7)

achievements; and finally the team needs to reflect periodically and assess individual and team progress, feelings and difficulties (see Kohonen 1989, pp. 36–7).

Davies and his colleagues have observed that students transfer their appetite for challenges from outdoor education experiences to other areas of their lives, e.g. to their regular classwork within a project-oriented approach. We have already referred to the dimension of the live experience which the project task entails. It is this performance factor characterized by heightened awareness and a productive nervous tension on the part of the learner which is the common ground between the mountain experience and the contact with native speakers as in *Airport* or *Dear Brown Eyes*. It can further be argued that, although there are no differences in principle between the outdoor example and the acting phase of the Salinger project (see above), for instance, there is less at stake for the learner and therefore the 'peak experience' is necessarily different here. The latter example by no means devalues the potential of the classroom to provide moments of peak experience. Rather it highlights exactly the unique advantage of the live dimension. Indeed, most project reports at our disposal explicitly or implicitly provide examples of what critics of mainstream education have highlighted as fundamentally missing in schools, 'the exciting learning experience' (Vester 1978; 1980). Any such learning experience necessitates calculated and responsible risks of the individual within the framework of the cooperative group. The following statements taken from learner diaries and written feedback during encounter project exemplify this point.

Statements

Statement 1(a) *Eleven–twelve-year-olds learners during the* Airport Project

Kerstin (twelve): '. . . and the pilot, who we had just passed had stopped and said something in English. I brought the others back at once, and it was true indeed, the pilot spoke English. We asked him whether he would agree to an interview in front of the camera. He said "Yes". We had our first interview in front of the film camera and we thanked him for that.'

(Thiel 1984, p. 143)

Kerstin (twelve): 'Because we had not had a lot of practice in asking questions, we asked all at once and a lot of trivial things. Finally, I asked "What's your job?". He said something like "computer expert". And he looked like one. Expensive gray suit, dark sun tan and silver hair. Suddenly, I don't know, how it happened, I got going. At least five questions had I asked. My friends were stunned. I've done the interview all by myself, it flashed upon me.'

(Thiel 1984, p. 144)

Nicole (eleven): 'The city major of Nairobi was a big catch for our group. He gave us a book about Nairobi. We were very excited.'

(Thiel 1984, p. 144)

Sandra (twelve): 'We got to know many interesting people. For example there was an opera singer, who sang in German without knowing what she was singing about, because she was English or American. Then we met two funny cowboys whose hobby was drinking or better guzzling Whiskey.'

Anonymous (eleven or twelve): 'There was a lot of work we had to do. However, it was very, very, very enjoyable. I hope we can experience something similar again!!!'

(Thiel 1884, p. 145)

Kerstin (twelve): 'But a glimpse of the Airport Project will always remain in my memory.'

Statement 1(b) *Adult learners during the* Dear Brown Eyes Project (all statements are taken from Carter and Cursiter 1985)

'I never thought that I would teach children one day. As surprising as it seems I did it and I think I did it quite well. When the teacher told us about the project the first time, I didn't really understand what the aim was to teach, why and how. How a student learning English as a foreign language could teach English children? I was telling myself that it would be hard to communicate with them and I was wondering about the subjects, I had to prepare . . . . How did I feel after having taught the children? The conclusions I can give are that I was quite satisfied . . . . I am sure that I will always remember this little experience in teaching English children.'

(Zakia A. Algeria)

'If I had been asked about doing this project the day I arrived at the Bell School I would have said no. But when I realized that it would be good the experience I started to work hard on it. I was a bit afraid when we went to St Stephen's and Colerne to meet the children and the Schools I realized that it would be not difficult . . . . The most surprising thing for me in those four days teaching, was that I saw I can understand English children without asking them all the time to repeat. They were speaking with me like they speak to each other and I could understand them most of the time. They were also understanding me. I think all of them liked very much those different lessons, we can see it by the letters they wrote.'

(Christina Y. Brazil)

'Usually I loathe being in a situation where people decide for me without asking my opinion. As a matter of fact it is what happened with this experiment. The teachers came and told us that we had to teach four days at Junior Schools near Bath. Imagine that you came to England to learn English and you were asked to teach children! I was astonished. Gradually I became confident. Firstly when I met the schoolmasters one Sunday morning. We had a chat and we watched the video of a similar experiment done last year . . . . After being worried against the experiment, I started seeing the positive side of it. I prepared models to be made by children . . . . The experiment had its positive side, which is for me as a student the contact with interesting people, very broad-minded teachers and children with great abilities. I never thought that coming to learn English I should have taught British children. It was great fun.'

(Moushine G. Algeria)

'I was terrified when I heard that our project was going to teach children, but actually it was not so terrible as I thought. I even enjoyed myself very much. I think I can say that I have learnt quite a lot. But, in fact, I had some problems. I had always six children and they knew I wasn't a teacher so they tried to find a way not to work . . . . It was not easy for me to keep them quiet because I'm not a teacher . . . . Anyway, if someone asked me if I would teach children for one day, I would refuse! I had a great time but I am not the right person for that . . . but I have learned how to communicate and how to use my English. Also I learned about the school system and their way of teaching.'

(Corinne L. Germany)

In sum, the project data support claims made by several authors concerning the value of small group interaction, structured and triggered off by meaningful learning tasks and adequate challenges (Schwerdtfeger 1977; Schiffler 1980; Candlin and Edelhoff 1982). The way the group interacts quite obviously has an important impact on the intrinsic motivation of its members. Their desire for challenge increases, as well as their desire for independent mastery of similar challenges, while keeping their interest and curiosity alive. Furthermore, project accounts support the view that self-directed learning results from intrinsic rather than extrinsic sources of motivation, (although it is noticeable from the data that intrinsic motivation needs time to develop through reflection and is not always in evidence in learners' first reactions).

> The learner's feelings of competence development will increase his intrinsic motivation. Learners need positive experiences of what (and how much, in fact, even at the elementary stages) they **can** do with their language communicatively. Such feelings of success will increase their self-confidence. In an important sense it can thus be argued that competence develops through confidence.
>
> (Kohonen 1989, p. 17)

The cooperative group, therefore, can be characterized as the nourishing ground for self-empowerment of the individual.

What is missing, however, in the data is an awareness of and attention to the specific needs of the individual learner who – for transparent and justified reasons – has difficulties in coping with the demands of the cooperative classroom and the project process. There is some disquieting silence in the data about the negative experiences (doubts, pains and insecurity) learners have had to deal with. Some of the following questions need addressing if project learning is to enjoy greater acceptance as a major structure for language learning.

– What happens to the learner whose views on learning are incompatible with the behavioural and interactional demands of a cooperative classroom? Such incompatibility might result from ethnic and cultural background; it might have to do with personal idiosyncrasies, and accustomed role behaviour, etc.
– How does the group, the teacher and the whole class cope with the fact that some learners find it easy to assert themselves in a small group and profit from it, whereas others remain shy, reluctant and become lost because they are silenced by the more outspoken?
– How does the teacher, the group and the class deal with resistance or rejection which might appear in the form of boredom, but also as partial or complete withdrawal, or risk-avoidance increasing the individual's inhibition to express himself in the target language?
– Furthermore, how does the project classroom deal with possible negative implications of the division of labour for individual learners? Whereas, it is true that the diversity of project activities allows for learners to contribute their specific strengths and abilities (to be a good manager, secretary, designer, artist) to the completion of the tasks, it is also true, that individuals might find themselves confined to their areas of strength and thus fail to

develop their scope of skills and abilities.
– Finally, how can the individual achieve this within the foreign
language classroom?

The following statements from a learner's diary in the informal
Bath data exemplify the questions:

Statement 2

> *Antony (twenty-five): '. . . it was the first time I worked with other students
> together as a group and that was the most difficult point for me. However
> I'm not responsible for this thing. In Greece I've never worked with other
> students as a group. The cooperation in my country is not allowed.
> Everyone must think and work alone, because in this way the competition
> is more serious . . .'*
>
> *(Bath, October 1989)*

> *Antony (twenty-five): . . . I was impressed this term by the perfect teaching
> system . . . but also really depressed by some of my classmates who spent
> their time more to enjoy themselves than study and learn English. Most of
> the times I couldn't study in my classroom because of the music or my
> classmates' voices which were like a bee in a silent room.'*
>
> *(Bath, October 1989)*

6.6 Aspects of implementation

6.6.1 Topic and content

It is common in General English programmes to link the teaching of
a graded curriculum of language items to themes or topics whose
interest value for the learner can assist in stimulating the necessary
motivation and endurance to see the programme through. One of the
arguments in favour of the use of projects in education in general and
language teaching in particular is that, in recognizing the motivating
value of the theme they ensure the commitment of the learner by
providing him with the freedom to choose the topic and the methods
of working. Fried-Booth (1986, p. 5) comments:

> It is this sense of personal involvement that gives impetus to project work.
> For the students, the motivation comes from within not from without. The
> project is theirs. They decide (in consultation with the teacher) what they
> will do and how they will do it, and this includes not only the content of
> the project, but also the language requirements.

The question now arises as to how learners finally arrive at their
theme or topic. Earlier we discussed how theme-centred interaction

acts as a model for experiential learning and how it introduces the thematic content into the learning process as a dynamic element which takes into account the learners' interests, external requirements and also the thematic preferences of the teacher. The model also holds that any proposal for a theme (from whatever the source, learner or teacher) will be the focus of negotiation before it is adopted by the group. If we now examine what the data reveals of how this unfolds in practice, we find that the most common sources for project topics are indeed the learner and the teacher. From the learner spring not only direct suggestions, such as an investigation of children's comics and their inherent language conventions, which led to the project from the Bath data, *The Language of Children's Comics* (Carter 1986b), a survey of language in comics and children's comic-reading habits. The data also show how the observant teacher can pick up and develop random stimuli from learners into a working plan of action. This is a widely noted teacher strategy in both the formal (Fried-Booth 1986) and the informal data. The frequent comments of learners of English in the L2 environment have given rise to many surveys and group research projects, e.g. English social behaviours; eating habits; attitudes, etc. Williams (1984, p. 21) writing of project work in general education in England describes this strategy graphically:

A chance remark to an adept teacher can also trigger off an unscheduled project: the telephone kiosk survey . . . arose out of a spontaneous grumble that 'the telephone booths on our estate are always out of order', an epidemic of gimmicky mail order wristwatches that wouldn't work led to an investigation of mail order in general; the eviction of an Indian boy and his family produced an inquiry into local housing and tenants' rights . . . .

It was from a similar chance remark that the *Airport* project started (Legutke and Thiel 1983), when pupils were reading a text which purported to contain information about the life and work of an air hostess. The pupils complained about the paucity and inaccuracy of the information, correctly divining that the purpose in reading the text was to practise the formation of the question using the verb 'to do'.

A second source in the data is the teacher who chooses and researches a topic and then invites the responses of the group with a view to developing it into a project plan. Carter (1986, personal communication) demonstrates this approach in his *The Kennet and Avon Canal* and *The Circus* projects (see 4.2.8). We have already referred to the values clarification task in which he asked the learners to grade postcard photographs according to interest and photographic quality (see 4.2.8).

However, some projects which originate from the teacher require extensive pre-planning. In both the *Bath Handicapped* project and *Dear Brown Eyes* large-scale preparation took place, which involved teachers contacting institutions and making detailed arrangements. However, everything undertaken by the teacher remained provisional until the group had been given the opportunity to evaluate the proposal. It was only at the point of acceptance that the cooperative planning by means of a major project plan took place.

The justification for such teacher pre-planning is not difficult to discern. It is not a question of pre-empting student choice but a recognition that for learners, particularly on short-stay study visits in L2 environments, compiling such an undertaking would be out of the question. There is also a point at which the teacher has the direct responsibility for introducing the target language culture in any of its representative forms to the learners. She has to achieve this without prejudicing their perception of it with her own opinions. She also has a responsibility to offer choices concerning areas to explore.

We could draw some important conclusions with regard to learner choice and learner interest. In both cases the teachers did not have an opportunity before to align the topic with any stated personal interests of the learners since they were not available. Indeed the variety of their personal profiles suggested otherwise: the groups included bankers, engineering students, young architects, language students and designers. It seems clear from the process in the data that learners' interests are neither static nor definitively predetermined, rather that they are negotiable *in situ* with the nature of the challenge contained in the tasks and the teacher's presentation of the project as the determining factors. In other words if the task is appealing as a means of realizing personal learning goals, which may include improving particular linguistic or non-linguistic skills, or widening their experience of the target culture, the ostensible or surface relevance to their personal backgrounds has little bearing.

There is an abundance of evidence in the data as instanced in the two examples above which suggests that arriving at a topic choice is subject to a particular process and is not a simple 'take it or leave it' matter. When learners bring forward suggestions they do not normally do so until they feel confident enough to raise questions and make proposals in the knowledge that they will be listened to and taken seriously. This presupposes that they will have had experience of collective negotiation and become familiar with the communicative classroom. The data shows that teachers try to take this requirement into account. Working from the premise that most learners have come from transmission-based classrooms they conduct a training or induction phase to provide experience in exploiting the enlarged scope of the learning space. The implication of the data is then that the teacher's proposals need to be introduced at a time when learners are capable of making reasoned decisions. However, while the timing of the topic introduction and its acceptance is discernible from the data, there is still a dearth of accounts providing detail on topic negotiation and on the actual process of topic refinement. It would clearly be of benefit to teachers to have well-documented examples of how successful outcomes may be achieved here.

We can make one final point in passing. When learners research aspects of the target culture it seems that despite the stereotypic views or impressions they hold, which generally concern the exotic elements, e.g. the British Royal family; film or pop stars; provocative lifestyles such as punk fashion, or the fantasy world of the aristocracy or high society, it is the everyday topics which hold learners' attention. The evidence for this comes from the many topics researched in the Bath data during which learners have interacted with ordinary citizens and have made important personal intercultural discoveries concerning attitudes, lifestyle and perceptions of the world. The other source is the data from the Contracts sans Voyages initiative, involving school children who exchanged a series of audio and written texts about themselves and their everyday lives. The results gave rise to vivid interest on the part of the children in the world of their exchange partners and a range of insights demolished many fixed stereotypic views (e.g. 'the English eat fish and chips all the time' – their surveys revealed that most of the English children asked preferred to eat chilli con carne or pizza), (see Jones 1984).

Our discussion of content of lessons as seen via theme or topic has pointed to the importance of the topic as the focus for learner motivation in projects. Our earlier discussion made it clear that the topic also provides the impetus for the learner end product. However, as we have noted from the process in which the topic is derived, the topic also created another area of content in the classroom, the process of negotiation, which includes organization, decision-making, action and evaluation of both the managerial and affective dimensions. In company with Breen (1987b) therefore we would identify two forms of content in the process classroom: content as theme seen through the topic; and content as learner development seen through the process.

6.6.2 Long-term planning and the sequencing of projects

For teachers who wish to move away from a transmission approach towards a process model, there is a serious organizational consideration to be faced in the area of long-term planning. It is the problem of programme continuity. Prespecified curricula and guidelines contain inherent ordering and grading according to given notions of language difficulty, topic applicability and relevance, coverage of core knowledge, etc. Whether the teacher uses published or personally produced materials to realize the curriculum, the organizational difficulty of sequencing the long-term programme for the learner has been overcome. If one envisages a project as a substantial unit of learning in a learner's overall programme, the question facing the teacher is how and on what basis is the next unit of learning to be constructed and what will be its relationship to what has gone before.

In L1 contexts the recognition of the constraints of externally applied curricula may paradoxically lead to greater freedom to introduce a process orientation than might appear to be the case. Williams (1984, p. 19), writing of project work in general, comments:

> Many countries, though not Britain, have a core of essential subjects which
> students are obliged to study. In India, for example, the school leaving
> certificate is based on the total number of marks students get in maths,
> science, language and social studies, with language subdivided into Hindi,
> English and the state language, and social studies subdivided into history,
> geography and physics. Compulsion in itself is not an obstacle to project
> work, since in those countries where it exists the range of subjects includes
> all those where there are already opportunities for active, investigative
> learning. The key question is whether these opportunities can be seized.

The projects *Airport* and *The Americans in Frankfurt* are examples of how such opportunities can be taken. The question remains of how often this may be done and with what consequences for learners and teachers who are bound to an externally ordered programme. In both of these instances the classes returned to a conventional form of classroom teaching, not without, however, the learners in both cases requesting further project work. A possible way forward has been proposed by Seidler (1988). He foresees a series of 'Projektinseln' (project islands) which would be built into the given longterm (three to five year) curriculum to exploit the themes and initiatives of classwork. It recognizes the sequencing difficulty facing the teacher while at the same time providing a means of progressively training learners towards a greater degree of self direction as one project experience follows another. It is to be hoped that more liberally framed curriculum arrangements such as the Rahmenrichtlinien Neue Sprachen for the German region of Hesse (Hessische Kultusminister 1980) may extend the scope for proposals such as Seidler's.

In L2 contexts the majority of learners are usually adults who study on a voluntary basis bringing with them a wide range of motives for learning. Many wish to pass recognized examinations as stepping stones in their own career development. Some have specialized instrumental ESP needs, others need English to pursue full-time education at secondary or tertiary level while for a considerable number the desire is simply to learn to speak or improve their English. The courses which meet these demands are typically organized against the background of needs analyses and specific curricula to meet the identified target of examination success or language skills acquired. Many of them are complete in themselves so that learners leave when their unit of study is complete without experiencing advancement from one level to another. Where learners remain in the L2 context long enough to experience more than one unit of organized learning, the issue of sequencing and arranging for the reasoned and planned continuity of their programme become apparent.

The data indicate that those learners who move from a project unit of learning into a following unit invariably come together with new students who in turn need to be given the opportunity of adapting to a process mode of learning. This is the role of the opening stage, that is, to train learners and to create a new working group dynamic. In order not to repeat tasks for the benefit of continuing learners, teachers make careful selections from existing material banks and make active use of the didactic involvement of the learners who are more experienced in project work. To arrive at possible project topics, the informal data shows that teachers take account of individual learners' stated needs to instigate group, sub-group, or individual projects. Since the mode of learner research is often through interview and information or opinion collection, there is also a need to create opportunities for text projects of different types to widen the focus of language text type and level of language analysis. The Bath project data include a range of text projects involving the making of documentary films, the creative study of literature through poetry, story-telling and the novel (often in connection with external examination targets), and a focus on non-fiction texts through topics such as advertising, history, communication, social issues, cultural and social institutions, etc. Teachers also report informally that they make use of existing viz. conventional syllabus checklists, exam criteria and their own observation of learners' deficiencies to influence the choice of possible input or the topic area of the project.

A more challenging sequencing problem for teachers and the institution is the problem of the learner who opts for a consciously product-driven programme after a project course. The reason appears to be not so much a failure to learn but an inability or reluctance to continue in a learning context where the learner has to share the burden of taking some of the initiatives. There may be many reasons why such a reaction occurs but there is clearly the need for closer observation of the learner training process and the conduct of project courses in which physical and/or emotional over-involvement, rejection by the group, and disaffection caused by working arrangements could be factors. Such difficulties suggest that greater attention could be paid to the process dimension of learner training (see 3.4 and 6.1). However, the experiential approach to learning must also allow for disaffection as a possible product of the learning process, just as the transmission-based classroom needs to recognize its capacity for alienation. It is clear that the regulation of this affective dimension by the teacher is an area for further research and development when examining teacher roles. Similarly the process classroom needs further research support to help teachers to resource their work with language and topic guidelines to cope with the challenge of moving from one unit of learning to the next.

6.6.3 The role of automatization

Teachers in the informal data when considering what may be appropriate as teacher input for an experientially conducted learning programme tend to underplay the role of automatization. With the emphasis on live communication with native speakers and on the creative use of language, it seems to be assumed that a process orientation obviates this need to focus on language form. However, as both Kohonen (1989) and Clark (1987) point out, this may be a mistaken policy, not just because there can be no guarantee that the language they will encounter in their experiential phase will be appropriate to their needs. A more important reason is that a focus on form which also involves automatization is an essential element in building language proficiency and being able to communicate without having to memorize large chunks of language. For Kohonen, in order to play their full part in experientially organized learning, learners must develop 'an incrementally fine-tuned understanding of the system and an increasingly automatized use of it in meaningful communication . . .' (ibid., 1989). In the *Airport* data there are clear examples of practice leading to automatization as a preparation for the visit to the airport.

Our contention thus far is that the process perspective made possible through a project allows language learning to be organized according to the causally related requirements of the target task and not according to externally specified syllabuses. It allows learners space to explore their own self-concept. However, while such features exploit the inherent potential available in the 'I', 'We' and 'theme' dimensions of the classroom, it would be misleading to describe a project orientation as a clear break with past practices. Although the projects introduce a substantial change in emphasis towards the nature of classroom interaction, they nevertheless still rely on techniques and insights accumulated by teachers over years of experimentation and practice. We agree, for example, in this connection with Nunan's conclusion (1988) that teachers build on what they know, so that in compiling a syllabus as work plan they start with tasks that have been successful for them in the past and, significantly, not from items on a syllabus list. In the data, particularly those examples from an L1 context, there is a clear role for the conventional paradigm of dealing with language input by means of presentation, and controlled and free practice. It lies in providing the linguistic means to complete ensuing tasks successfully. As such we can say that conventional forms of language teaching have a logical position in the sequencing of activities within a project because they are directly related to tasks. Such a role creates a constructive relationship between one of the products of the language classroom, knowledge of language as system, and the way it is put into use in the execution of the tasks. We use the term 'product' here in the sense that Nunan (1988, p. 20) presumably has in mind when he calls for the 'due consideration' of a product dimension as well as process in curriculum design and not in the sense of learner products which we have described above (see 5.2).

6.6.4 Evaluation and assessment

We have stressed throughout our discussion so far that ongoing evaluation of learning goals by learners and teachers is integral to a process syllabus, and it is the mechanism through which learning can become consciously experiential. It is formative and addresses itself to all the components of learning tasks, language input, topic content, the affective climate, methodology and the syllabus itself. We have tried to indicate through examples from the data that such formative evaluation in Breen and Candlin's words (1980), may not only indicate 'the relative successes and failures of learner and curriculum, it can also indicate new and different directions in which both can move'. Moreover, as we have suggested in our discussion on process evaluation (see 4.2.9) a growing number of tasks are now available which provide the means to conduct critical monitoring and reviewing of the teaching–learning process. Tools for self-evaluation of the syllabus and learning arrangements, such as learner diaries as in the data corpus and self-evaluation questionnaires (see Davies 1989; Hunt and Hitchin 1986; Nunan 1988, p. 132–4), are also gaining acceptance in the learner-centred classroom. We have suggested earlier that process evaluation takes place in the data, albeit with variations from project to project. Further, the focus is mainly on parts of the process with the purpose of influencing the future work of the project. The evidence of learner and teacher evaluation of the syllabus in its entirety, on the other hand, is slight. It may be that documented accounts, which include evaluative reviews of the whole learning process in a project, may well appear as a consequence of more rigorous application of process reviewing tasks.

While an agenda has been set, as it were, for the role and practice of evaluation in the learner-centred classroom, the question of assessment, which we take to mean the summative evaluation of learners' progress against a set of targets, remains problematic. It is still the case that national curricula require in the main quantifiable measures of progress, despite, as Brindley points out (1989), the large body of educational opinion which argues that a product-oriented view is an oversimplification of the educational process. Learners in both L1 and L2 situations may also come with expectations that not only will their progress be assessed in terms of a grade, but that this will form the main focus of their work. The versions of process syllabuses that we have mentioned from the available data are evidence of this dilemma. They seem to be torn between a process orientation on the one hand and the need to provide a quantifiable, product-oriented assessment on the other. We have to say from the outset that in this data corpus there is no systematically collected information dealing specifically with the assessment of achievement which would allow us to construct detailed arguments. What we offer below are therefore brief comments only which have the status of anecdotal evidence. Assessment within process syllabuses is clearly an area for further research. (However, as van Lier (1988) has pointed out, in the complex world of the classroom with its abundance of variables we may need to exploit forms of research that can regard the classroom not as a laboratory, but as a culture. It follows from this view therefore that a perspective which will include teachers' subjective reports, learners' diaries and collections of anecdotal evidence may be a more appropriate form of handling the data.)

Dealing with the question of the efficacy of a process-oriented classroom presents particular problems since the criteria for such an evaluation need to be specified. First of all there needs to be agreement on the competence model from which specific criteria can be derived. Swain (1984) comments: 'Competing claims about the efficacy of communicative language teaching programs . . . cannot be verified unless we can agree upon what is meant by communicative competence and performance' (p. 189). In this context we recognize that the debate surrounding the issue of communicative competence is still active. However, we will use for the purposes of this discussion the general outline of communicative competence offered by Canale (1983) on the basis of Canale and Swain (1980) which consists of four categories:

(1) *grammatical competence*, concerned with the mastery of grammatically correct language, with language code, etc.;
(2) *socio-linguistic competence*, concerned with what is socially accepted language, i.e. with decisions about appropriacy of language in context;
(3) *discourse competence*, concerned with the ability to decode – in negotiation – and encode coherent written and/or spoken text;
(4) *strategic competence*, concerned with the knowledge and ability of how to use language to communicate intended meaning and how to repair breakdowns that occur in communication.

For the data in this survey, we are able to say from the evidence of learners' performance in public examinations, i.e. formal school set examinations for learners in L1 settings or those offered by the University of Cambridge Local Examination Syndicate, e.g. the First Certificate in English or the Certificate of Proficiency in English (UCLES, Cambridge UK), there is no indication that learners were disadvantaged. These examinations are strongly biased towards testing grammatical competence, although discourse and socio-linguistic competences are also examined variously by means of tasks relating to various text types in the four skill areas. Learners seemed to perform in accordance with informal teacher expectations and in line with other learners from non-project-based classes who were judged to be parallel in level of attainment. However, teachers report that their performance in certain skill areas, particularly listening and speaking, improved considerably (Legutke and Thiel 1983). With regard to the fourth category of the model, strategic competence, Carter and Thomas (1986) make specific reference to the abundance of informal observation and feedback on the growth of each learner's capacity in this area. This ability to deal with discourse and cope with unpredictable language difficulties, new contexts and situations has been a consistent feature in the Bath data subsequent to this initial reference. The most salient feature of learners' improved strategic competence seems to be their level of personal confidence in dealing with native speakers and all manner of formal, e.g. presentations, and informal situations. A further, and by no means insignificant source of feedback in this respect is also learners' accounts of their own progress. What others have noted in the example over is confirmed by learners recorded on film in the project *Hello is Ciao* (Carter 1988), a later version of the *Dear Brown Eyes* project. These sources of feedback on learners in projects suggest therefore that at least two categories in the model of communicative competence are positively affected, grammatical competence and strategic competence. Yet, as we have already emphasized, it requires specific and detailed research to discover whether such statements have any substance.

It is not the purpose of the discussion thus far to imply that summative tests assessing grammatical competence or performance in skill areas are undesirable. Not only do they represent a high level of face validity for many learners they can also be said to provide a necessary test for a part of the communicative competence that learners develop. We have, moreover, already referred to the necessity of taking this dimension into account. What teachers tend to question, however, is the dominant role such tests have in their relationship to language programmes. They do not reflect teaching and learning procedures and tend to produce a negative 'washback' effect. However, examinations were formulated in Britain and known as the UCLES CUEFL (Communicative examinations in English as a Foreign Language) examinations, originally developed by a team led by Morrow (1984) for the Royal Society of Arts (RSA 1980, 83), in order to meet this objection. (This collection of tests was updated in 1990 and is now known as the UCLES CCSE examinations, i.e. Certificates in Communicative Skills in English.) The tests, set in their new version at four graded levels, are defined against a set of performance criteria detailing degrees of skill required by the learners. The tests are characterized by the clarity of the specification of tasks which learners have to perform (in a British context), filling-in forms, reading railway timetables, understanding news bulletins, etc. They also make use of text data drawn directly and without adulteration from native speaker sources. The oral test offers greater scope than other available oral tests for learners to demonstrate all four categories of the communicative competence model, since it envisages a three-stage interaction involving learner and an inter-locutor engaged in a semi-structured conversation; two learners involved in a problem-solving exercise and the learners and the interlocutor to whom the learners report their findings. The assessor remains a silent observer of the whole procedure.

No comparative studies have been carried out to gauge the effect on the test on classroom practices but the informal feedback suggests support for the claims made for it. There is considerable informal support for the view that it reflects much more accurately the content and methodology of the mainstream EFL classroom in many L2 (predominantly British) contexts. While this situation may represent progress in 'washback' terms it could also be said to provide further evidence for Howatt's view that the majority of the profession has opted for a 'weak' form of CLT. However this comment is not intended to undermine its value for the process classroom. It offers a further dimension of testing untouched by other types of test by introducing the concept of skills as sets of operations carried out by native speakers for particular purposes of decoding and encoding and it has reinforced the use of materials from native speaker backgrounds. In process terms the effect of criterion-referencing as a basis of measurement may also contribute to the shift towards a cooperative classroom in contrast to the norm-referenced test associated with the ranking and competitive element of the traditional classroom.

A major reason why the CCSE tests were developed was to reflect changes in classroom practice not shown in examinations existing at the time. By the same token such tests no longer reflect what is happening in the project classroom. Learners in projects have opportunities to develop communicative competence by means of a wide range of teacher and self-directed activities through which they acquire inter- and intra-personal skills, instrumental skills and/or media skills. The competence they achieve in these areas which we call 'process' competence is, we believe, part of their overall communicative competence and should be regarded as additional to the model outlined above. We shall return to this concept in greater detail in chapter 7. It is in the absence of any available test which recognizes such learner activity that native speaker test formats such as those current in secondary schools in England and Wales are considered by some teachers in the data as valid alternatives to standard language examinations for their learners. These examinations provide a role for the learner's product and require a learner or a group of learners to present the product, e.g. a book, display or film and explain its provenance. (See English GCSE examination in Communications, Associated Examining Board.) In this examination learners are assessed according to how well they understand the concepts inherent in the subject and how well they have translated them into a product. The examination recognizes that processes play an important part, but still relies on a product to reach an assessment. At this stage of development of the learner-centred classroom, however, it is still debatable as to whether we really should assess those parts of a learner's process competence that a product-oriented test cannot reach.

The more immediate concern for proponents of the communicative classroom is to find ways which can legitimately reflect learners' progress in areas which pay due respect to the need for accountability towards the outside world. The solution may lie in the combination of various types of test. Doyé and Rampillon (Doyé 1989) for example make use of the information-gap principle in their examples which aim at generating learners' pragmatic use of language. Their test item where two learners exchange information on the uncompleted versions of a map is similar to drawing exercises in the Bath data and the task typically found in the oral part of the CCSE tests. A potentially rich area for development is the collaborative approach outlined by Brindley (1989) who cites criterion-referenced tests produced as part of the National Curriculum Project in Australia (Nunan 1987a). The approach is based on the distinction that teachers, learners and native speakers often use different criteria to judge the oral production of a non-native speaker. Brindley astutely points out that a teacher may emphasize communication success while a learner may desire correction of inaccurate forms, and native speakers in turn look for overall intelligibility. As a result all three parties are involved in the assessment using rating scale assessment sheets to provide a rounded picture. For the learner the self-assessment sheets are a way to judge progress against discernible goals (see Brindley 1989, p. 141).

In contrast, the Bath data in which learners write their own end of course report underlines the value of learner involvement while at the

LISTENING

1. I can understand most Australians when they speak to me. ✓
2. I can understand people in business (formal) environment. S
   e.g. bank, C.E.S., library, doctor.
3. I can understand the radio news. S
4. I can understand the T.V. news. ✓
5. I can understand people when they are talking in a group. ✓

USING THE TELEPHONE

1. I can understand simple information on the phone. ✓
2. I can ask for something on the phone. ✓
3. I can take a message for someone. ✓
4. I can ask someone to pass on a message to their friend. ✓
5. I can ask someone to repeat the information. ✓
6. People can understand me on the phone. S
7. I feel happy and confident about using the phone. S

READING

1. I like reading.
2. I can read most forms e.g. for C.E.S., Medicare etc. ✓
3. I read magazines (e.g. *Dolly*, *New Idea*, *Cleo*). S
4. I read the newspapers (write the name/s .Telegraph lenghst.+ arabc
5. I read the news in English (names of papers: daily.tele,. Sun ..
6. I can find information in the paper e.g. house/units for rent,
   things for sale; jobs; entertainment. S
7. I can use a street directory or map to find places. ✓
8. I can use a dictionary easily. ✓
9. I can read a business letter. ✗
10. I can read a book or novel. ✓

Put a tick (√) for Yes; a cross (✗) for No; and an S for Sometimes
or a little to answer the above.

Figure 6.5 Self-assessment of skills for office skills course (de Reuver
1987)

Language skills

I think I have been given the opportunity to speak English, however, my English is not so skilled. This course might be good for the student who can understand what the teacher expect from the student. My English level was not enough to respond to it.

Application and Progress

As I was not interested in the *Circus*, I did not take part in this class actively. But this was good to me that I noticed my vocabulary was few to express my opinion.

(Rie M)

Language skills

Making this project, especially the book, has helped me to improve my english writting and to learn a lot of new words. I think I have improved in the way that I can express myself when not knowing a specific word, and understanding is not a problem for me anymore.

Application and Progress

I have worked really hard not only for improving my english but for getting our aims, our book and our video. I got very interested on this work and tried to do my best in every way. I think that this is the reason why i have made a great progress, and now I am able to correct my own mistakes but of course four weeks are not enough and I have a lot to learn yet.

(Maria S)

Language Skills

My general impression was that I improved quite a lot in listening and especially in understanding. I can't really say how much I've progressed as far as speaking is concerned, anyway at the end of the month I realized that one month may not be enough for really improving one's language skills.

Application and Progress

I think that the idea of the project was indeed good. In fact it has really made me responsible for what I was doing and helped me lot in building a better and better cooperation behaviour. There is no doubt that the project could have changed my approach to English, it has made me more sure even when I've to do with the worse difficulties you find when you've to speak a foreign language.

(Gino A)

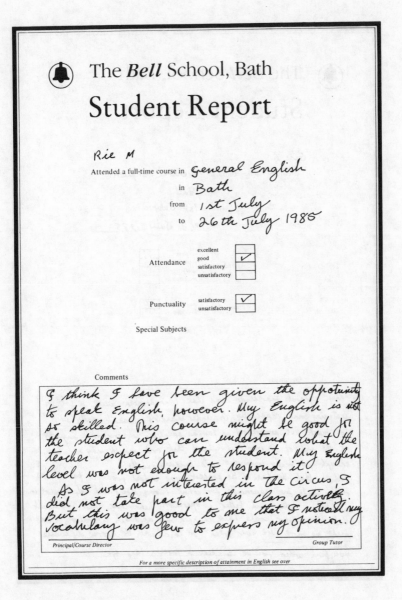

The *Bell* School, Bath

Student Report

Rie M

Attended a full-time course in General English

in Bath

from 1st July

to 26th July 1985

Attendance
- excellent
- good ✓
- satisfactory
- unsatisfactory

Punctuality
- satisfactory ✓
- unsatisfactory

Special Subjects

Comments

I think I have been given the opportunity to speak English. however. My English is not so skilled. This course might be good for the student who can understand what the teacher expect for the student. My English level was not enough to respond it.
As I was not interested in the circus, I did not take part in this class activity. But this was good to me that I noticed my vocabulary was few to express my opinion.

Principal/Course Director   Group Tutor

For a more specific description of attainment in English see over

Source: *The Circus* (Carter 1988).

Figure 6.6 Student reports (Carter 1986)

The *Bell* School, Bath

Student Report

Gino A

Attended a full-time course in   General English

in   Bath

from   1st July

to   26th July 1985

Attendance		
excellent	✓
good	
satisfactory	
unsatisfactory	

Punctuality		
satisfactory	✓
unsatisfactory	

Special Subjects

Comments

My general impression was that I improved quite a lot in listening and especially in understanding. I can't really say how much I've progressed as far as speaking is concerned, anyway at the end of the month I realised that one month may not be enough for really improving one's language skills.

I think that the idea of the project was indeed good. In fact it has really made me responsible for what I was doing and helped a lot in building a better and better co-operation behaviour. There is no doubt that the project could have changed my approach to English, it has made me more sure even when I've to do with the worse difficulties you find when you've to speak a foreign language.

Principal Course Director   *Group Tutor*

For a more specific description of attainment in English see over

The *Bell* School, Bath

Student Report

MARIA S

Attended a full-time course in GENERAL ENGLISH

in BATH

from 1ST JULY 1985

to 26TH JULY 1985

Attendance		
excellent	✓
good	
satisfactory	
unsatisfactory	

Punctuality		
satisfactory	✓
unsatisfactory	

Special Subjects

Comments

Making this project, especially the book, has helped me to improve my english writing and to learn a lot of new words. I think that I have improved in the way that I can express myself when not knowing a specific word; and understanding is not a problem for me anymore.

I have worked really hard not only for improving my english but for getting our aims, our book and our video. I got very interested on this work and tried to do my best in every way. I think that is the reason why I have made a great progress and now I am able to correct my own mistakes but of course 4 weeks are not enough and I have a lot to learn yet.

Principal/Course Director   _Group Tutor_

For a more specific description of attainment in English see over same time indicating that learners may need more specific assistance to identify the extent of their progress than is offered on the report form.

6.7 The institution

6.7.1 The location

The examples we have described to illustrate our discussion of project work have been drawn from both L1 and L2 settings. We have argued that for learners in either setting the opportunity to make contact with native speakers in live, open-ended communicative situations introduces the dimension of learning in the here and now into their learning. Clearly, providing such conditions is a relatively easy task for teachers in the target language environment. The ready availability of a range of potential contacts and the teacher's own knowledge of local conditions are undeniable advantages. However, while these factors do not pertain outside the target language environment this is not to say that it is either particularly difficult or unreasonably onerous for teachers in L1 settings to undertake project work. The *Airport* project is a case in point which serves as a well-documented model for the L1 setting and which has subsequently been copied and adapted in a variety of L1 locations (e.g. Thiel 1983; Ferragati and Carminati 1984; Bicker and Swanenvleugel 1985; Fleck 1988). Making use of native speakers of the target language from the immediate L1 locality in this way has been referred to as 'exploiting airports around the corner' (Edelhoff 1983). This is a reference not just to isolated individuals such as the German-speaking senior citizen, resident in Oregon whom a German class from the local high school interviewed (Maurer, forthcoming) but also to companies, banks, hotels or other transport contact points such as railway and bus stations. For Nossenko and Garkusha (1990) the notion of 'airports around the corner' extends beyond native speakers to other users of the language with whom the relevance of the here and now element is demonstrably clear. They have identified for their learners, students of English at a Russian university, a 'secondary' target-language community consisting of:

(a) teachers of foreign languages (including retired teachers);
(b) peer students learning foreign languages;
(c) other members of the source-language community who had a

chance to visit the target language country and who are able to speak its language;

(d) native speakers who visit the USSR.

(Nossenko and Garkusha, 1990)

They report that students have conducted a variety of questionnaires relating to topics covered in the classroom and have contacted speakers of English, including former students and retired faculty members. Speaking of encounter projects directed towards information gathering, they write: 'Our conclusion is that projects of this type are indeed possible even outside English-speaking countries, and that to be successful, project work does not always need to be conducted by highly trained, confident native-speaking teachers who have a lot of technical resources at their disposal' (ibid.).

The availability of 'airports around the corner' or a 'secondary' target-language community will clearly vary with each learning situation and will in turn determine the extent to which project learning can become part of learning in an L1 environment. However, these examples show that encounter project learning need not be ruled out on grounds of location but remains open to consideration for teachers possibly everywhere.

Encounter projects wherever they take place in L1 or L2 settings make a bridge between learners and the community at large. Learners and teachers benefit from this contact, but also find themselves in positions where certain responsibilities befall them. Learning in live situations such as interviewing members of the public not only implies observing normal courtesies of punctuality and acknowledging cooperation. It also means that the teacher in particular needs to monitor how much learners exploit the community as a resource base so as to avoid 'overfishing the sea'. The experience of large-scale encounter project work in Bath, for example, has led to close links with the community but also to an awareness that demands made by teachers and learners should be responsible and moderate. As Ashworth (1985) points out, learners who reach out into the community also take themselves beyond the role-play world of the classroom. The latter is a place for them alone and is a place where mishaps involving language system or appropriacy can be analysed and adjusted. When they take themselves into the cut and thrust of the real world, the disappointment of an unsuccessful interaction resulting from a linguistic or cultural misunderstanding must be allowed for as a possibility, despite careful preparation by learner and teacher. Beyond establishing that learner's linguistic resources are adequate to the task, the role of the teacher lies in ensuring that learners understand the nature of their responsibilities as seekers of information or as contributors to the community.

6.7.2 Institutional adjustments

(1) The time factor

Institutions impose their own constraints on how learning proceeds because they are charged with managing the learner and his learning in the light of many variables. In the conventional, somewhat atomized school curriculum where language learning is one of many subjects taught, it has to fit in with what exists, often competing for time and attention and resources with other subjects. It is not infrequent, therefore, in L1 settings that the foreign language will be given, for example, a maximum of up to four lessons per week, either as four separate units or possibly in two blocks of two lessons. Such non-intensive language learning is also the norm for many institutions offering courses to adults in L1 contexts because of the limited availability of the learner owing to demands of work or suchlike. Language learning is severely constrained by the time factor and in such circumstances the lesson has a high profile as a unit of planning. By this we mean that a major concern for the teacher will naturally be to plan tasks which can be completed in the short time available. If external tasks are foreseen which require longer sequences then special arrangements have to be made, as in the case of *Airport* for example, when students went out for a day to complete the target task. A possible answer for the high-school context is to introduce a project week ('*Projektwoche*'), a practice now common in parts of West Germany, where learners opt for the subject in the curriculum on which they wish to concentrate. Such an arrangement recognizes that tasks need to be carried out in a more realistic time frame. In other words, tasks last as long as they take because of deadlines inherent in the task or external constraints, e.g. the processing of taped data or the readjustment caused by a postponed interview. Accordingly learners work until tasks are finished to an agreed level of acceptability. This means that they do not necessarily work within a time-scale of lessons but of working days.

The advantageous conditions which apply to the project week are easily transferred to those institutions teaching the foreign language intensively in the target language environment. Such an approach to time planning has been adopted at the Bell School, Bath (Thomas and Walters 1988), where project learning is conducted on a widespread basis. Here the project target task and its many subsidiary tasks are managed in large blocks of time, normally all or most of the working day, which allow for considerable flexibility in the 'learning space'. It represents a shift from the lesson to the task as the salient unit of planning time. This change has had interesting consequences in several areas. Whereas before teachers were allocated to classes so that each class had a main teacher and other teachers who provided additional 'skills' teaching in fixed timetable slots, teachers are now allocated to one class only. This arrangement allows learners and teachers to develop a relationship and plan their course together within a larger time-frame. Teachers teach in other classes whenever an individual's specialist expertise is required by another colleague, for example, a video specialist will give an introduction to the equipment in one class while a computer expert will guide another class. Such arrangements may be made according to the needs thrown up by the demands of the various project plans current in the school at any one time. This contrasts with previous arrangements where classes changed teachers according to a change in the focus of their learning from, for example, grammar to listening, or reading to writing.

Such informality in the sharing of human and material resources has consequences also for the working relationships within groups of teachers. It requires a level of tolerance and cooperation not normally necessary when timetables legislate for and to a large extent define how teaching is to be organized. This is particularly true when dealing with fixed resources and equipment. Whereas on previous, more rigidly constructed timetables, resources such as the language lab, computer room, video equipment, library, etc. were available at set times, they are now available on a flexible booking-out system. Fixed timetables are still published as a guide to establish parity of access but use is open to negotiation. Such flexibility is essential because courses tend to require equipment at more or less the same time. It is often necessary in project work to allow for the fact that learners tend to work beyond formal classroom time limits and frequently have informal, timetabling agreements for after-school or evening work.

(2) Rooms and equipment
Attitudes towards and the exploitation of classrooms differ in the many settings in which language learning takes place. Learners may leave their own classroom for the modern language room as, for

example, in many British and American schools, or they may remain in their own room in which they are taught the majority of subjects. In the latter case, all equipment must be brought in and taken away with the inevitable loss of time and disruption. More crucially, however, there may be restrictions, particularly in L1 settings, which prevent learners and teachers from using the walls as display areas for learner texts and products. Legutke (1989a) has pointed to the need for a reconsideration of such situations, comparing the West German with the American norms. The basic freedom to display learners' work is in our view a fundamental advantage. In an institution such as the Bell School, Bath, which like many other similar institutions in the L2 setting makes use of video and audio support equipment, it was the relatively basic step of providing extensive display space in the form of cork noticeboards on every available wall which has had a decisive and positive impact on learner-centred learning.

Wherever classes are able to benefit from such a facility, as in this example taken from the L2 situation, remaining in one room can be positively advantageous because it can become the project room for the class. Here the project learners have unlimited and uninterrupted access to their learning facility, a luxury not possible in other contexts or settings. However, as the *Airport* example shows (see Humburg et al. 1983), it is possible to replicate quite easily the other advantages of such project room conditions. The display of learner texts relies on the availability of graphic materials such as coloured pens, large card, scissors, pins, etc. Both the *Airport* and Bath examples provide powerful evidence of what learners may achieve when they are able to present their work regularly in such a creative form (see 6.2). In contrast to expensive media equipment, project boxes containing display and graphic materials may indeed be more feasible and productive acquisitions in less well-equipped institutions where teachers may have to compete for limited resources.

7 Learner education

7.1 Broadening the concept: process competence of language learners

Throughout the book we have discussed the language learner from a number of perspectives. We will now pull together the various strands from earlier chapters by concentrating on the learner. In doing so, we will proceed by discussing example target tasks in the light of the demands they pose for learners. This will lead us to define more clearly the areas of knowledge and abilities which the process-oriented classroom both requires and aims to develop. The examples: (1) an encounter project in an L1 environment with elementary learners; (2) a text project with intermediate students; and (3) an encounter project with advanced learners in an L2 environment; will help us to illustrate what we would call *process competence* in language learning (7.2). Finally, we will ask how process competence embracing both knowledge and the ability to use this knowledge can come about through learner education (7.3).

Example 1: The guest-speaker (see Maurer, forthcoming)
The location is an American high school in a small city in Oregon with about 30,000 inhabitants. The students, third-year learners of German as a foreign language, have explored the city with the intention of locating German-speaking citizens who might provide interesting partners for target language encounters either inside or outside the classroom. The students have made more than fifty contacts and have realized that their target language is represented surprisingly well in their community. Whereas most of the contact partners will be interviewed by small teams outside the classroom, the owner of the local Volkswagen shop has agreed to come to the classroom and give a presentation in German on his business career and his experiences as an immigrant to the USA. This seemingly simple event might entail the following range of activities, which in turn require the training of a wide range of interpersonal, linguistic, socio-linguistic, discoursal and media skills:

– Two learners prepare a letter to the guest speaker with a formal invitation; they present the letter to the class for approval, changes, etc.

- Two learners make a telephone call a few days later to confirm a date, time, etc. They make inquiries about the topic of his presentation.
- Groups of learners prepare questions for the question and answer session.
- On arrival of the speaker, two students meet him and have a short interview with him to collect some data for a formal introduction to the class.
- The same students introduce the speaker in the class.
- The presentation is recorded both on audio tape and video by two teams of students.
- A question-and-answer session is conducted.
- The recording team edits their recordings by selecting the most interesting passage(s).
- A brief summary of the event is presented as sample text for all students' project books.
- Two students write a thank-you letter which they present to the whole class before sending it off.
- Several teams of students write an article about this event for the community paper of the continental club. The whole class decides which of the products to send to the paper.

All these activities take place during regular contact time in class. Students make use of their text-books and of a variety of support materials according to the needs of their respective tasks. Since the visit of the guest speaker is a part of a larger project, some students might be simultaneously involved in preparing other interviews or working on their own reports.

Example 2: Richard Wright's 'Almos' a Man' – from text to film
Supported by a sequence of imagination gap, values clarification and creative expression tasks (some of which we have referred to in 4.2.1 – 4.2.9) a group of intermediate EFL students (ages fifteen to sixteen) of a West German high school had read and attempted to understand the short story 'Almos' a Man' by Richard Wright. Before the students were presented with the film adaptation of the short story, the teacher introduced the opposite project scenario.

The students were informed that after the first phase of 'research', the group would be reorganized so that one or two members of the original grouping would change to a new team. It was, therefore, of

You are part of a team which has been given the task and the necessary funding to make a film of Richard Wright's short story 'Almos' a Man'. First of all, some research needs to be done. Conduct this research in teams of four:

Team A: Think about the difficulties of using a short story to make a film. Which parts of the story need to be changed? Which scenes or passages must be omitted? What scenes must be added? Please redesign the story line for the film.

Team B: We need to know more about the setting of the film. Use your school library, geography and history books, encyclopaedias and film strip materials from the American Studies Media Center for your research. Please come up with detailed suggestions for the setting (landscapes, vegetation, climate, housing, etc.) and the life-style of people during the time of the story. One question you need to address is whether you want the film to take place at the same time as the story.

Team C: Your task is to choose actors you want to work with. Write a profile for each character. These profiles should function as guidelines for your casting.

Team D: It is your special task to study some basic concepts of film language. You should be able to explain some functions of camera angles, camera movements, types of shots and editing techniques. Which of these techniques would be most effective with which scenes of the story?

primary concern to the teams to make sure that each member could explain and pass on the suggestions for story-line development, setting, casting and film editing during the second stage of the scenario. So, in their new groups, learners were given the following tasks:

(1) Develop one or two scenes of the film. Write a script and comment on the actors and the setting of the scene(s).
(2) Develop detailed suggestions for the beginning and/or the ending of the film. Write the outline of the scene(s) on a poster.
(3) Develop a complete treatment of the film (poster).
(4) Write one scene of the film which you act out in front of the class. Note: For the presentation in class, each group had no more than ten minutes.)

The demands of the three-stage scenario (the presentation in class is the third stage) are concomitant with a range of abilities we expect learners to have developed after about five years of high school language learning following a project and process-oriented model. Some of these skills are as follows:

- They need to have learned to operate productively both in flexible social settings and in stable teams.
- They need the ability to make responsible and independent decisions concerning task execution, learning strategies, and topic refinement.
- They must have gained considerable mastery of how to combine linguistic forms and meaning to achieve spoken and written text of various or different genres. What is required, therefore, is more than a knowledge of the unity of text which is achieved through cohesion in form and coherence in meaning (Widdowson 1978). Learners also need the ability to produce such text in a variety of types using different media and creative ways of expression. Under these conditions, the learner texts (e.g. the poster with a film treatment, the script for the opening scene of the film) will optimally reveal their double function. They will stimulate interpretive activity with reference to themselves and at the same time throw new light on the original text.
- Therefore, learners need the ability to participate actively in processes of negotiating meaning which again necessitates a wide range of personal, linguistic, socio-linguistic and subject-matter skills.
- In addition, students must have the ability to act in the roles of mediators and teachers. After all, the teams during the second stage rely upon the knowledge passed on by the specialists on setting, casting and editing.
- Furthermore, presentational skills are required for the successful completion of the public demonstration of the team's product.
- Intermediate EFL students who have learned in project classes for some time would at least be expected to have mastered most of the classroom discourse in L2. Even if there are still limitations in notional and functional areas, they will, however, have gained the strategic competence which allows them to cope with the unforeseen demands of communicative action.

Example 3: Small town America – intercultural learning with advanced students (see Burke and Legutke, forthcoming)

The elementary encounter project in the L1 environment with *Airport* has a more demanding counterpart at the advanced level in the following exploratory project into the L2 and its culture.

The twelfth grade intensive EFL course (seventh year of language learning) of a West German small town high school is planning a five-week study trip to the USA where it intends to spend three weeks at a partner school. Since the partner school is in a small town itself, the teacher has defined the semester topic of the course as 'Small town America. Values and Lifestyles'. As the course will use the Easter vacation, the group has about six weeks to prepare for the journey. During this time, the course develops an orientation framework which manifests itself in a number of hypotheses and questions in relation to the topic. These hypotheses synthesize prior knowledge, new knowledge gained in class and value-judgements of students and teachers. Parallel to reading and interpreting a number of expository and literary texts dealing with the topic, the group has created a fictitious American small town in Washington State for which they used, in addition to the content materials mentioned, materials they could get from school libraries, travel agents and private sources. Students drew a town map; designed, named and placed buildings; and created a whole range of characters who live in this town, have the usual relationships with each other, love and hate each other; do jobs (accepted and legal ones), solve problems, etc. The imaginary small town represents both (pre)knowledge and values of the students. At the same time, it provides the framework within which the group will approach the real small town and its people in Washington State during their encounters and research. For the letter, the following research topics were formulated and agreed upon:

(1) the role of sports in small town America;
(2) the role of churches and religious institutions;
(3) teenage careers;
(4) dreams and escapes;
(5) family life;
(6) important events in the life of the families – how they are celebrated: birth, graduation, weddings, birthdays, deaths;
(7) school;
(8) life stories older people can tell, moments of oral history;
(9) local politics;
(10) women in small town America.

In addition, the group negotiated a three-part project task which had to be completed by small groups of at least two but not more than four students.

(1) Each group would select a topic and conduct research on this topic in the partner town. Three tape interviews were to be conducted (each not longer than ten minutes), which had to be technically good enough so that parts of them could later function as text input in class.
(2) Each research team agreed to document its work with the help of a project book, with photos, gathered texts and regalia of all kinds.
(3) After returning to West Germany, each team had to prepare a presentation of its findings. For the presentation, making use of all media available, the group would take over the role of the teacher by structuring and conducting up to two full lessons. The following aspects had to be taken into consideration:
   (a) new insights gained which challenged, changed or broadened the hypotheses;
   (b) difficulties in communicating with the Americans (misunderstandings, breakdowns in communication, things which were surprising, unexpected, painful, annoying);
   (c) significant examples of American English;
   (d) each team had to select a short text (e.g. an interview, an article from the local paper, etc.) or write one which could function as an introduction to the topic. If necessary, support materials had to be designed which could facilitate the work in class (theme-related word fields, tables, surveys, posters, transparencies);
   (e) furthermore, each team was responsible for making sure that the other groups and the teacher (who was an equal participant in the learning process) were actively involved in the presentation.

Apart from self-access, media, organizational and didactic skills, 'Small town America' requires and fosters the ability for intercultural communication and understanding.

Learners who participate in such scenarios need to have developed the necessary skills and abilities and have access to areas of knowledge which are not included in the conventional concept of communicative competence. Throughout the book our argument has implied that there are limitations in the conventional view. We must now address the following questions:

(1) Do we need to add to the conventional concept?;
(2) How do the areas of competence relate to each other in view of the process model of teaching/learning we have outlined in the previous chapters?

7.2 Components of process competence

We referred in 6.6.4 to Canale's instructive explication of communicative competence. This 'underlying system of knowledge and skills required for communication' (1983, p. 5) embraces as we have seen four major components: (1) *grammatical competence*; (2) *socio-linguistic competence*; (3) *discourse competence*; and (4) *strategic competence* (ibid.).

In view of the project classroom, two major changes to this concept seem necessary. The first change is quantitative in the sense that we would add intercultural competence as a fifth component to Canale's communicative competence. We also propose to add a separate domain which inter-relates with communicative competence. We will call this new domain process competence. Process competence represents knowledge and the ability to use the knowledge of three areas:

(1) *the individual*, i.e. knowledge about 'self' and personal growth; the ability to respond and to be responsible (cf. confluent education, chapter 3.3);
(2) *the group*, i.e. knowledge related to the dynamics of the group, the ability to interact, cooperate and work things out with others;
(3) *the learning process*, i.e. knowledge about learning and the learning process; the ability to learn, to manage learning and to teach others.

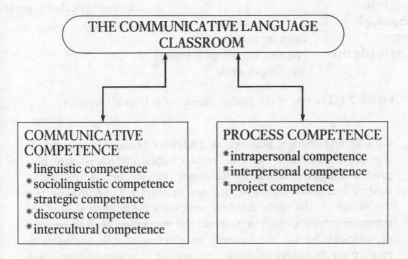

Figure 7.1 An outline of competences for the communicative classroom

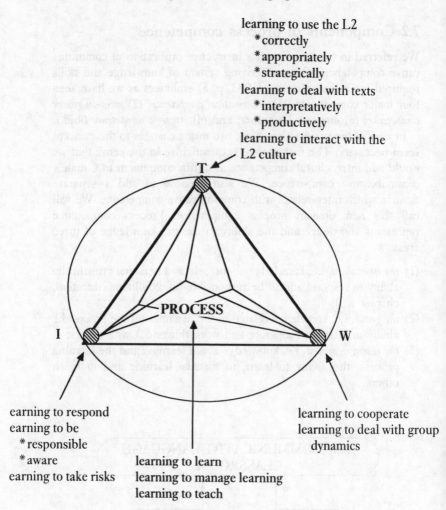

learning to use the L2
* correctly
* appropriately
* strategically
learning to deal with texts
* interpretatively
* productively
learning to interact with the
L2 culture

T

PROCESS

I   **W**

earning to respond
earning to be
    * responsible
    * aware
earning to take risks

learning to learn
learning to manage learning
learning to teach

learning to cooperate
learning to deal with group
dynamics

Figure 7.2 The role of the process dimension in language learning

This second change, however, is qualitative because it responds to the question of how these different components inter-relate in a process-oriented classroom. Returning to our model of theme-centred interaction which we outlined in chapter 2, we propose that the triangle in the circle also best represents the primary goal of the communicative approach: to facilitate the integration of all these types of competencies for the learner, 'an outcome that is not likely to result from the overemphasis on one area of competence over others throughout second language programme' (Canale 1983, p. 18). The triangle in the circle – in addition to conceptualizing the areas of knowledge and abilities – also provides the critical instrument for our final section in this chapter. It will guide our discussion of 'learner training' and 'learner education'. 'Good language learners do not just come about . . . they must be educated' (Kohonen 1989, p. 40).

7.3 Learner education and learner training

7.3.1 Experiences – expectations – beliefs: what the learner brings to the classroom

The learner does not come into the project classroom knowing nothing. Rather, he brings with him a range of previous learning experiences, of values, views and expectations. Anecdotal accounts (e.g. Bath data, 5.2) as well as a number of different research studies suggest that learners, because of what they bring to the classroom (their implicit contributions, see above 2.3.2), not only have rather fixed ideas about which activities are most appropriate for them, but also, how the teacher should go about her teaching, so that learning can be valued as profitable (see Nunan 1987; 1988; 1989b; Wenden 1986; Kleppin and Königs 1987). Several authors have pointed out that there are frequent mismatches between learner and teacher expectations as to what are 'legitimate' classroom activities (Nunan 1988; Kleppin and Königs 1987). Learners' hidden agendas (Nunan 1989b), expectations and counter-expectations may exert a powerful influence on what is possible in the classroom.

Whereas the transmission model of teaching and learning may at best cater to learner expectations through a pre-course needs analysis collecting data *about* the learner, the project approach fundamentally depends on contributions *from* the learner. Furthermore, the latter may, because of the prevailing dominance of the transmission model in language teaching (see chapter 1) challenge or even contradict what learners expect to happen in the classroom. American and British ESL teachers attempting project work with multicultural groups of adult learners have reported informally that they sometimes felt like having opened a Pandora's box when inviting their students to engage in project work. There are accounts of breakdown in communication between a Swiss and a Brazilian group of students, because of mutually incompatible views on accountability, learning management and culturally mediated learning styles. One teacher comments on resistance and even hostility of an Arab male, whose concept of himself and of learning did not allow for a group situation in which a Portuguese woman was in charge of the managing role. A Mexican student found project groups problematic because they lacked the competitive element he believes should be part of serious learning. Project teachers have also reported that it is not unusual for learners who have made significant progress to complain fluently and accurately about their 'poor' fluency.

Although multicultural groups of adult learners pose specific demands on the project teachers with regard to what they bring to the classroom, the culturally more homogeneous classroom has similar problems. West German EFL teachers working in the upper stream of the high school system, for instance, report that the implementation of a project approach into the everyday routines of the language classroom has to deal with, among other things, the scepticism of administrators and parents. Such implementations also have to come to grips with what learners in this college-bound stream regard as good and appropriate ways of learning. For the most part, their views have been formed by their learning history, which has been dominated by the transmission approach.

Yet what appears to be a major problem of project work, i.e. the diversity of learners and what they bring to the classroom, is at the same time its strength. For, what the learner brings, can also be understood as an asset, making up the richness of the classroom's culture. Managing this diversity in a joint effort of all those who are involved in collectively creating this culture (see 2.1) is the challenge we will now be concerned with. We will focus on the following issues:

- personal growth and interpersonality
- learner strategies and autonomy
- text production and presentation
- peer teaching.

7.3.2 Personal growth and interpersonality

Although the influence of personality factors and group dynamics on language learning is difficult to isolate and measure statistically, there is consistent evidence to suggest that motivation and attitudes towards oneself and the group play a crucial part in learner achievements (see Kohonen 1989; Scovel 1978; Solmecke 1976; 1983). The project data unanimously reiterate this evidence by underscoring the significant role of ego-involvement, sense of ownership of learning and awareness of positive group interdependence. However, we have also highlighted the considerable risk for the individual to be prevented from reaching a state of being motivated, i.e. energized for action, by a variety of distractions and disturbances. These may result from both inside the learner (e.g. his previous learning experiences, his views on learning, and his personal values) or from outside – the teacher or the group. The teacher disregarding what the learner brings to the classroom may encroach upon his private sphere with manipulative interventions, or may negatively affect his self-esteem. The group may infringe upon the individual's space of self-expression by threatening his self-image and inner balance. We have referred to these issues in great detail during our discussion of the critical criteria in chapter 3 (3.4). Whereas the learner can hide to some extent in the goose-step formation of the transmission classroom, he can no longer do so in view of the constantly changing demands of the project classroom.

The proponents of humanistic education have broadened our concept of learning by emphasizing that meaningful learning has to be self-initiated. Even if the stimulus comes from outside, the sense of discovery, however, and the motivation which that brings has to come from inside driven by the basic human desire for self-realization, well-being and growth. In our discussion of the critical criteria (3.4) and the evaluation of project data (chapter 6) we have pointed out that in terms of personal and inter-personal competence the process-oriented classroom revolves around issues of risk and security, cooperation and competition, self-directedness and other-directedness; and meaningful and meaningless activities. We have also tried to make clear that 'teachers who claim it is not their job to take these phenomena into account may miss out on some of the most essential ingredients in the management of successful learning' (Underhill 1989, p. 252).

Developing personal and inter-personal skills requires not just techniques (see: 4.2.1; 4.2.2; 4.2.4; 4.2.7; 4.2.8; 4.2.9) but a background of educational principle. We have argued for the creation of a supportive learning climate as a collaborative effort making use of behavioural rules and procedures deriving from the study of group dynamics and assertiveness training (3.5). Whatever the techniques we chose, their employment needs to be consistent with the principles of theme-centred interaction. We will return to this point once again at the end of this chapter.

7.3.3 Learner autonomy

No school or university can provide its students with all the knowledge and skills needed to deal with the requirements and challenges of their adult lives. For this reason it is imperative that when leaving their formal educational experience, students are equipped to continue learning beyond school without the help of teachers and a specifically structured learning environment. In view of the complexity and rapidity of change worldwide, the issue of life-long learning has moved from a side show to centre stage of the educational debate since the 1970s (see chapter 2).

In the field of second language learning this general debate has given rise to two inter-related directions of research which have a direct bearing on the process-oriented classroom. Researchers of the first one (mainly in Europe) have committed themselves to the development of *learner autonomy* as a primary requisite of learning beyond school in democratic societies (Dietrich 1979b; Holec 1980; 1988; Dickinson 1987; Kohonen 1987; 1989). Representatives of the second direction (mainly in North America) have focused on solving the secret of the *good language learner* by emphasizing *learner strategies* and the notion of *learning to learn* (Wenden and Rubin 1987, with survey of research background; Chamot and Kupper 1989; Oxford et al. 1989; Prokop 1990).

Following the European debate, we understand autonomy as the ability to assume responsibility for one's own affairs (see Holec 1980). In reference to the learner, it is the ability to act in a situation in which he is totally responsible for 'all the decisions concerned with his learning and the implementation of those decisions. In full autonomy there is no involvement of a 'teacher' or an institution. And the learner is also independent of specially prepared materials' (Dickinson 1987, p. 11). If we accept the promotion of such learner autonomy as a relevant educational goal, project-oriented approaches to language learning should be more explicitly and systematically attempted, because they provide the principled and practicable passage towards this goal:

- Projects, as we have seen, increasingly include the learner in the decision-making process about topics, content and process materials, about learning and the management of it.
- They encourage independent decision-making and shift a great deal of responsibility for these decisions to the learner and the cooperative group.

– The experiential cycles (if they take a micro-level format when realizing a communicative task or a macro-format during a full-scale project over days and weeks) constantly heighten the learners' awareness for understanding, improving and directing their own learning.

The project data contribute to the debate on learner autonomy by helping to clarify two important aspects of it. On the one hand the accounts exemplify the various degrees of learner independence as part of process competence ranging from short moments of self-directed group interaction in a values clarification activity to independent research over several weeks requiring decisions in almost all areas of theme, group and process, including media and texts (example 3 above 7.1). On the other hand, the data vigorously support the claim that learning to be responsible for one's own learning is not a privilege of the gifted/college bound students in the high-school system nor can it be restricted to adult groups. No doubt, forms of fostering learner autonomy will vary according to age, institutional constraints and experience. However, given the appropriate guidance and encouragement *all* learners can become more responsible and self-directed – even under the conditions of second language learning.

One major study of learner autonomy deserves detailed comments here because it systematically addresses the issue in reference to heterogeneous groups of learners – most of them from non-academic backgrounds – within the public school system. Whereas most project reports, which we discussed above, refer to learning sequences of six to twelve weeks, Dam (1982); Dam and Gabrielsen (1988) conducted and evaluated a six-year experiment starting in the learners' first year of English (students at the age of eleven). Using the freedom which the Danish compulsory school system allows in terms of syllabus realization, the two educators focused on three questions when they started the experiment in 1980:[1]

(a) whether it was possible *at all* for eleven-year-old learners to become involved in planning, organizing, managing and evaluating their own learning;
(b) *how* such a process should be structured, maintained and expanded into the following five years of schooling;
(c) which *effect* such a process would have on the development of learners' *communicative competence*.

The experiment which was accompanied by an intensive teacher-training programme eventually involving more than 100 teachers over several years (see Breen et al. 1989) had a number of interesting results in relation to the issue of learner autonomy:

(1) The first question (a) was answered positively.

(2) Learners were also positive in accepting responsibility for their own learning and for the management of social interaction in the classroom. They felt that what they were asked to do was demanding, but relevant and participated actively in negotiating decisions concerning selection of materials, methods and classroom management (Dam and Gabrielsen 1988, p. 28).

(3) It was found that a wide range of different materials supported this process of expanding learner autonomy. Materials were brought in by children (children's books, posters, stickers, books from parents) and by teachers (e.g. dictionaries, readers, films, etc.). Pre-fabricated and conventional teaching materials such as textbooks only played a marginal role.

(4) Once learners had grasped that the quantity of interesting materials was not important, but *how* to access these materials in order to unlock (i.e. *interpret*) their meanings and *express* what they themselves had to contribute in the L2, the active involvement of learners increased considerably. Thus, process criteria helped in independent decision-making.

(5) Teacher-guided and learner selected activities for the interpretation of texts and the expression of meaning mutually supported each other. By emphasizing the expressive abilities of learners in the L2, the experiment gave a new role to learner-produced texts (plays, poems, posters, drawings, paintings, collages, etc.). Activities leading to such learner texts, because they had an immediate transparency, i.e. a recognizable purpose of communicating meaning, were preferred by learners, whereas non-transparent activities of conventional textbooks were rejected. Expressive possibilities obviously increased the learners' willingness to invest themselves in the decision-making process.

(6) Over the years a number of questions used by learners when choosing/planning activities emerged. The typical questions during the first year such as 'What do I feel like doing?' or 'What would I find interesting?' were at a later stage augmented by 'What do I want to be better at doing?', 'What do I want to know more about?', 'What do I need to learn?' Further criteria, mainly introduced by the teacher, were 'Does the activity in question allow teacher and learners to focus on the process rather than on

the product? Does it give scope for differentiated processes *and* for differentiated products?' (ibid., p. 25).

(7) In constantly expanding cycles students learnt to meet the following challenges in day-to-day classroom work:

- to focus on their own learning, registering progress made, means and mode of learning, deciding on the next step, if possible choose between alternative routes to learning;
- to justify decisions made as to immediate aims and objectives for learning, to discuss and justify changes in overall strategy;
- to focus on and be responsible for interaction in groups, and the learning opportunities of others;
- to negotiate plans for work and decisions made as part of that work with other learners and the teacher;
- to be willing to review and evaluate their work, to be interested in that of others, and to accept responsibility for the outcome of cooperative ventures (ibid., p. 27).

(8) The contracts which learners made between themselves and the teacher covering the work they had decided to do and regular evaluation were a key part of the experiment.

(9) Difficulties reported by teachers mostly had to do not so much with learner resistance and inabilities but with teacher roles. Redefining the latter constituted considerable challenges because established power-relationships were at stake here. Some difficulties were caused by the resigned attitude of learners who were used to a predominantly receptive mode of learning. They were often, but not exclusively, learners who had at some point been diagnosed as 'academically weak'. For them to build up confidence in their own capacity to cope and to define their own 'aims for learning' required 'time and persistence' (ibid., p. 28).

For our discussion, the most important insight gained from the Danish experiment, however, is that its positive outcomes in terms of learner involvement and language ability cannot be attributed to specific techniques (e.g. the contracts) or certain training elements (e.g. learning to decode/interpret audio-texts). Rather, it is the whole process which accounts for the learners' development – their education as responsible and self-directed language learners. Although skill training was essential, particular skill areas received constant attention through teacher inter- ventions zooming in on key elements such as progress reports, self-assessment and evaluation (Dam 1982) – justification for such training did not derive from the need for training as training but from the necessities of the educational endeavour as a whole embracing the complex interdependence of theme, group, individual and process.

None of the other project accounts we have referred to deals as directly with the issue of helping learners to become better learners as the Danish experiment does. Yet even this encouraging attempt lacks conceptual precision of what is to be understood by a good language learner. Moreover, it is unclear in its terminology when dealing with *learner strategies*. This shortcoming, which, by the way, characterizes all project reports, comes as no surprise, since research in and debate about learner strategies in language learning has only gained momentum since the mid 1980s when the issue began to surface at TESOL and IATEFL conferences and in language journals (Wenden 1986a; 1986b; Wenden and Rubin 1987). In the meantime, researchers have discovered dozens and perhaps – depending on how they are classified – hundreds of such strategies which may be used consciously and with effort, and which can become habitual and automatized (Oxford et al. 1989; Prokop 1990). Furthermore, initial attempts have been made to develop materials and activities for learner training in the use of cognitive and metacognitive strategies (Wenden 1986a; 1986b; 1987).

Whereas there is no longer any doubt about the validity and impact of informed learner training, there seems to be a somewhat disquieting lack of an educational framework within which to train the learner and for what goals. Consequently learner training is in danger of being technically reduced and regarded as a means in itself as recent publications indicate (see below). It seems to us that both movements mentioned above, the movement towards learner autonomy and the research in learner strategies, could mutually benefit from each other. Their meeting ground for further research activities and implementations of classroom innovation towards the life-long and responsible learner could be the project-oriented classroom where learning to learn and learning to manage one's learning are inseparable parts of the learner's foreign language education. We will once again return to this issue at the end of the chapter (7.3.6).

7.3.4 Text production

Since we have commented on the status and function of learner texts in the project classroom above (6.2), a few additional remarks shall suffice here. One could argue that the conventional concept of discourse competence (7.2) in principle requires the learner to become both a proficient interpreter *and* creative producer of L2 texts of different genres, opportunities for which are made available in the project classroom. Beyond the knowledge of text types, textual conventions and functions, and the ability to use this knowledge for decoding and encoding meaning, the project classroom calls for, and at the same time, teaches a wide range of media skills without which classroom work would not only be dull but simply impossible. All three examples at the beginning of this chapter show this quite clearly. Media skills include:

- using the OHP
- using blackboard and flip charts
- using audio and audio-visual recording equipment
- using computer programs for text production and editing
- using print facilities and print shops
- using photo equipment
- using artistic skills: drawing, lay-out, collaging, etc.

It goes without saying that classrooms do not magically become text-producing workshops unless learners are either encouraged to utilize and share the media skills they already have or to acquire them through training. We have found that the training of media skills provides unique opportunities not only for language work (see *Airport* film, Humburg et al. 1983), but also for peer tutoring. It became evident very often during projects that students who either had a strong affinity for working with media and/or had learnt to work with them in some other context became involved in the process because their input was needed and because they saw a chance to do things they liked. As with any other form of special skill training in the FL classroom, media training also only makes sense as part of the overall project process. Of course, learners needed some basic practical understanding of video equipment before embarking on the *Airport* project. However, without the application of the media during the encounters with English speaking passengers and for the presentation of parts of the interviews in class, the training would be a waste of time. As well as in reference to other skill areas, the classroom implications of a fundamental principle that there is no usage without use must not be ignored.

7.3.5 Peer teaching: learning through teaching

Process competence consists, as we have seen so far, of a range of knowledge areas and abilities required by the learner so that he can be profitably engaged in project work. It includes self-awareness and knowledge of group processes, meta-cognitive and strategic knowledge; the ability to cooperate with others, organize one's work, and to set one's own learning targets. It implies that learners will want to determine their own forms of learning. However, process competence also implies a high degree of 'didactic' capabilities, i.e. the ability to make insights and findings available to others – the ability to teach one's peers. For successful project work to take place, the teacher in charge must make the acquisition of skills in these areas a priority in her pre-project preparation. The data indicate (see, for example, Kaufmann 1977; Nuhn 1982) that this important area of skills has been widely ignored so far. What do we mean, then, by didactic skills?

A constant and important feature of work done in a project is that sub-groups focus on related but separate areas of the project theme. It is an effective and time-honoured division of labour. However, everyone needs to share the information gained by each sub-group and this step is achieved by feedback and presentational procedures. It would not be fruitful if reporting back simply became a tedious verbatim account of work done. What learners need to be able to do is to select the main points, summarize and comment on them. They need to learn to give presentations with the skill of a teacher, otherwise they run the risk of losing the attention of the others and the information will be useless. They have to take on the responsibility for assuring that as many of the class as possible understand what they have to say about the insights gained during their group work. In doing so, they may have to design tasks themselves, prepare information and support materials and/or manage phases of skill training. However, it is not only in the relationship between groups and the whole class that project work requires teaching skills and meta-communicative knowledge, but also among group members peer teaching is both a necessary, and highly productive activity, as the above example of Richard Wright's short story demonstrates (7.1, example 2). Within the group learners will take over the roles of a helper, facilitator, demonstrator – in short those of a teacher.

Just how many of classroom activities, traditionally monopolized by the teacher, can be taken over by learners is shown by Martin in his long-term study of pupils learning French as a second language within the West German school system (Martin 1985; 1986; 1988). Martin's starting point is the fatal imbalance between teacher and learner activities in language classrooms which – as several studies have shown (Solmecke 1984; Dinsmore 1985) – severely limits information processing and learning (Martin 1985). Martin concentrates on showing how organizational and didactic activities (in the transmission model solely in the responsibility of the teacher) can be transferred to the learner. In four video documents he demonstrates convincingly how to achieve such a redistribution of classroom activities by allowing, encouraging and training learners to introduce new vocabulary, present texts, explain new grammar, manage language exercises and drills, set up role-plays, give dictations, check vocabulary, etc., but also to lead more complex, independent research projects similar to *Airport* or *Dear Brown Eyes* (FWU 1983; 1984; 1987a, b).

Martin proposes a clearly defined step-by-step approach transferring didactic and organizational activities to the learner. On the basis of the overall repetitive structure and the ritualized procedures of most textbooks the transference is a fairly straightforward job. Starting with guided attempts to manage drill and exercise phases, learners have acquired all the basic teaching skills ranging from vocabulary introduction to grammar presentation by the end of the first year of high school. It goes without saying that learners predominantly use the target language while they function as peer teachers. The necessary speech functions are therefore introduced simultaneously with the exploration of texts and topics offered by the textbook.

The issue of whether students are allowed to and are capable of progressing past copying what they have experienced during many contact hours with a teacher, i.e. whether they can go beyond their internalized concepts of teaching and thus become didactically innovative, is not addressed in Martin's initial study (Martin 1985). In the last two films, however, he points out that with growing experience as peer teachers, learners become didactically more daring and innovative – gradually transcending traditional forms of presentations. His findings are in keeping with our observations of project classrooms that learners not only develop the skills of becoming teachers astonishingly fast, they may also surprise the teacher with unexpected and creative ways of teaching.

The weak point in Martin's work is that with his concern for process he seems to ignore the issue of the quality of text and task input offered by the textbooks, especially for the first three years. In his examples of these first years (FWU 1983; 1984), learners act as teachers but the material they use is largely contrived and devoid of relevant content coupled with uncontextualized language exercises. Learners are neither encouraged to make use of their knowledge of the world (because textbook design makes no allowances for this) nor are they able to write their own texts. We hold that more challenging content and process materials would probably increase the validity of Martin's work. Nevertheless, these objections apart, Martin has pinpointed four essential aspects of learning through teaching:

(1) In company with Breen and Candlin (1980) and Breen (1985b) he has emphasized the fundamental authenticity of the language classroom: '. . . talking about organizational and teaching matters represents a considerable and important achievement in so far as it is situationally appropriate and takes place in the target language' (Martin 1983).

(2) More than anything else he has demonstrated that learners by dint of their proximity to their peers in terms of psychological development and background are capable of intellectual and emotional empathy towards others in the group. Given guidance, they could not only substitute for but in fact perform better than the teacher. For the teacher often fails to pick up what is difficult for learners. Littlejohn (1983) makes a similar point when he says that learners role-playing teachers can make a very positive contribution to the learning climate because of their ability to empathize. At the same time they are much more finely tuned to notice possible disruptions or lack of attention by their fellow learners quite simply because they see what is happening from a different perspective than the teacher. Disruptions can be defused at a much earlier stage than is often the case with the teacher.

(3) Martin presents convincing data that learning through teaching not only enhances the learning climate, stimulates readiness of learners to be involved but also has a major impact on the development of their linguistic and socio-linguistic competence. Learning through teaching seems to stimulate language acquisition because it provides the opportunity for learners of being able to negotiate input and meaning through speech modification and conversational adjustments. Martin's findings are compatible with Long and Porter's study of group work and interlanguage talk (Long and Porter 1985) and Long's analysis of the role of

conversational adjustments for the promotion of comprehensibility (Long 1985).

(4) We also agree with Martin's insistence on the mutually supportive nature of content-related and meta-communicative knowledge. The ability to explore the target culture and its language under classroom conditions is greatly enhanced by procedural routines (e.g. 'project routines') which the learner has developed through gradually taking over the task of teaching his peers (Martin 1988).

Although classrooms in public school settings may be at a disadvantage in adopting project formats as the general structure of learning (see 6.7), they do have the advantage of a continuous group experience which may last for three to six years. Martin's findings concerning the development of didactic skills and project routines depend on such continuity in long-term processes. However, even if different institutional constraints and respective settings need to be taken into consideration when implementing peer teaching, the latter is not only feasible but also indispensable for unlocking the language classroom's communicative potential. The scenario below from the Bath data illustrates this point within the context of a short term intensive EFL course (see page 282).

7.3.6 Learner education – an integrated approach

We can say that the cyclical and cumulative development of experiential learning in the communicative classroom relies on seven inter-related types of learner capacities:

- a capacity in respect of content
- a capacity in respect of process
- a capacity in respect of intrapersonality
- a capacity in respect of interpersonality
- a capacity in respect of resource
- a capacity for experimentation
- a capacity for critique.

We will now briefly summarize a number of 'tools' which have emerged as useful for the development of these capacities and the encouragement of learners' active and conscious participation in their education as learners.

THE GRAMMAR WORKSHOP

Background: This procedure was used during two-week intensive courses for IBM managers in which their basic communication skills in English were improved. It was important to devote some time to a focus on grammar because both teachers and students saw the necessity to correct basic errors which led to faulty communication. In addition, work on grammar corresponded to the students' atavistic notions of language learning. The workshop lasted three hours and was structured as follows:

Step 1: The teacher asked the class to write down those areas of grammar which they found difficult or constantly got wrong.

Step 2: The teacher then explained that they, as individuals, would be given time (up to two hours) to study one of the grammatical points in detail. Their task was to locate it in the support materials (grammar books, pedagogic grammars, etc.; textbooks, grammar aids); study the explanations; formulate some simple rules; find examples to explain the rules; and locate a series of practice exercises or devise one themselves. Having done this, each participant would prepare to teach his/her grammatical point to the group later. If they wanted, they could form pairs, assuming there was a common interest.

Step 3: In the research phase learners made use of books *and* the teacher as a resource.

Step 4: This was an optional step in which some learners sought the advice of others as to how to structure their teaching slot. It was important that the teacher also monitored this activity but not to the point of imparting advice and tips too freely.

Step 5: Three points of grammar were chosen because of time factors, and each individual/pair was/were given up to twenty minutes to teach the class. The cooperation of the class was readily given.

Feedback: The IBM executives all found that the process of independent research with the goal of trying to explain a grammatical problem to others, or, more accurately, to find ways to make it clear, taught them the grammar point very effectively. Having understood it they felt confident about teaching it to the group. Even if they had not grasped it completely, the group usually picked that up and dealt with it appropriately. Furthermore it was apparent that the IBM managers enjoyed the opportunity and challenge of presenting to others. The teacher was always there, however, as a 'backstop' observer.

(a) Communicative tasks

On the basis of the fundamental premise of clarity/reflexivity (see above 3.5) any communicative task or any sequence of communicative tasks are means of enhancing learners' awareness of how and why they learn and in which way they could contribute to the improvement of their learning. As we have discussed in some detail (see chapters 4 and 6) any communicative tasks or sequence thereof represents an experiential cycle in itself if accompanied by forms of self or group monitoring, or if evaluated in terms of workplan, re-interpretation through action and anticipated versus real outcomes. However, we have also highlighted certain types of tasks which are ostensibly well suited to focus learners' attention on their learning. Such task types are *awareness training* (4.2.2) *values clarification* (4.2.8) and *process evaluation* (4.2.9).

(b) Project plans and work contracts

Building on Dewey's and Kilpatrick's ideas, and a long tradition of pedagogical reform movements (see 5.1) teachers have – with conspicuous success – used detailed project plans and contractual work agreements, which may even be formalized contracts between teacher and learners and among learners. They increase not only the accountability of all parties involved, but also the understanding of the learning process and its components and requirements. Both plans and contracts deriving from joint action and negotiation provide the reference points for self-monitoring, group assessments and retrospective accounts (Dam 1982; Dam and Gabrielsen 1988; Kaufmann 1977; Dietrich 1979a; Legutke and Thiel 1983; Legutke 1988b).

(c) Progress and retrospective accounts

Related to jointly constructed plans and mutually accepted contracts are different forms of formalized self-assessment (see 6.6.5) and structured progress reports, which learners write either at the end of the course or at the end of longer sequences (Oskarsson 1980; 1984; Clark 1987; Brindley 1989) or at the end of the course (see Bath data in Figure 6.5). These can result from individual and group activities; they may or may not involve the teacher.

(d) Learner diaries and project books

A further powerful tool for learner development and training is unstructured, first-person accounts of the learning experience in the form of a diary. We do not mean here systematic diary studies as a mode of classroom research (see van Lier 1988), but rather, more or less continuous notes accompanying other classroom activities. Such accounts, personal comments and reflections on all aspects of the learning process could be part of larger documents, which we have called project books. The project book, as we see it, not only serves as a place to compile interesting L2 texts (be they from native L2 speakers or from the learner himself), it serves a series of additional purposes. That is to say, it is an exercise book, a scrap book, a resource for language notes as well as a diary. Project books belong first and foremost to the students who maintain the right to share their notes with other students and/or the teacher. Even if the written accounts and personal notes are kept private they will indirectly provide important input during regular feedback and circle sessions where students can draw upon their notes. Whereas the personal entries will have to be in the L1 at the elementary level, L1 comments could gradually be replaced by attempts in the L2 which would provide an additional incentive to experiment with the use of the target language.

(e) Circle and feedback sessions
Regular feedback and circle sessions (see 4.2.1 for example) drawing on data provided by formal assessments and informal notes are indispensable components of the project classroom. Here modifications of goals, variations of procedures, and new directions of focus can be determined as well as disturbances in group dynamics discussed and repaired.

(f) Peer teaching
Since the project classroom depends to a great deal on learners taking over organizational and didactic responsibilities by becoming teachers themselves (see 7.3.5), peer teaching in its various shapes constitutes a further passage towards learner development. As with any other tool we have mentioned so far, such activities cannot be reduced to operations only rendering meta-cognitive and meta-linguistic insights or training respective skills and strategies. They simultaneously pertain to matters of content, of the individual and the group. This is not to say, however, that the understanding of how to learn and communicate in the L2 classroom is not a major outcome of such endeavours, as we have shown in our discussion of Martin's research (see 7.3.5).

(g) Learner training sessions and programmes

Although we have called for an integrated approach to learner education we do not exclude explicit training in cognitive and meta-cognitive strategies, in instrumental and managerial skills at appropriate moments in the learning process. There is also an advantage in specially tailored, informed training sequences (see Wenden 1987). Indeed, we have, when discussing the stages of a project, characterized the 'opening phase' as both a tool and a location where learner training can and should take place. The same holds true for the 'bridging phase' (5.3.2). Some of the mini-projects in the Bath data (Carter and Thomas 1986) and the task-sequences in text projects serve – among others – the purpose of making learners aware of their views on and beliefs about learning, of the scope and limitations of learning strategies, etc. A possibly provocative and unfamiliar communicative task or task sequence might be the first step towards reconstructing the group members' previous learning experiences and lead to careful experimentation with new ways of going about learning and thus help the implementation of change, which has been described as a 'gradual deconditioning process' (Wenden and Rubin 1987; Holec 1980).

There is an important caveat, however. One can accept that intensive ESL/FL programmes with adult learners of diverse ethnic, cultural and educational background call for concentrated efforts at the outset of a course to establish some common denominator and group coherence by making them aware of their expectations towards and beliefs about learning. However, it does not imply that such initial awareness raising can replace learner training as an integral component of the whole course. In a pioneering study on what 'L2 learners know about their language learning' Anita Wenden (1986a; 1986b; 1987) working with students in a seven-week intensive ESL programme at university level concluded that 'learner training was not considered relevant in its own right' by the majority of the students involved (Wenden 1987, p. 164). In fact, isolated learner training concerned with the development and refinement of meta-cognitive awareness, providing students with concepts that were intended to help them focus more precisely on various aspects of language learning, created considerable resistance among students. In concluding her study, Wenden therefore suggested that training materials and tasks required a far more integrated approach (ibid., p. 165). What seems to be called for is an infusion model of continuous learner training as has been proposed and practiced by Dam, Gabrielsen and Martin (see above 7.3.3 and 7.3.5).

Recent attempts to offer course-books in learner training under-score the significance of this caveat. It seems that the fragmentation of the learning process which went along with decontextualized and thematically arbitrary grammar training of the past, is resurrected or continued in new and fashionable clothes, such as: *Learning to Learn English* (Ellis and Sinclair 1989a; 1989b):

- Why should learners be interested in listening unless there is something or someone worth listening to?
- Why should they want to learn reading unless there were texts which engaged their curiosity, stimulated their imagination, and provoked their responses?
- Why should they learn writing strategies unless they had something worth writing about?
- Why should they want to speak unless they had something to say?
- Why should they learn to use self-access centres unless there were tasks and projects requiring the use of such resources?
- Why should they enthuse over learning video skills unless they actually used them to convey meaning and document experiences during their encounter and correspondence projects?
- Why should they feel enticed to become autonomous if the course materials prescribed or dictated the path towards this autonomy?

The challenge therefore is not helping learners to think about learning and offer learner training so that they become good learners and *then* teach them a language. Rather, the task is to teach them to communicate in the L2 while helping them to learn and think about their learning. Learning to learn is not a solipsistic enterprise but a collective experience with a request for action aiming at revising, improving and thus changing what is perceived and given. It is an integral part of language education based on a critical, reflective and explanatory pedagogy (Candlin 1989). There are, unfortunately, no simple and global choices that can be made if we are to maintain the integration of knowledge and experience argued for in the foregoing. We need the best and richest not the worst and most impoverished grounds upon which to choose progression within the curriculum. After all, ultimately, it is learners who have their own curriculum, often independent of that of the textbook or the class; to keep in touch with learner curricula we need, ultimately, to keep in touch with learners.

Note

1. Unfortunately, this extensive experiment which proposes as radical changes in language learning as Kaufmann's project in Switzerland (Kaufmann 1977; also see above 6.4) or Prabhu's work in India (Prabhu 1987) has only marginally been discussed outside of Denmark. See Dickinson 1987, p. 61–6 and Breen et al. 1989. It seems to us that the Danish approach deserves at least as much attention as the Bangalore Project which has challenged many scholars (Prabhu 1987).

8 Teacher education

8.1 Teachers and the experiential classroom

We have implied at various points that experiential learning is not compatible with a transmission approach to teaching. In this chapter, we will outline the roles that teachers who attempt to work in process-oriented programmes fulfil. In order to delineate the general and specific areas of action and responsibility of the teacher our reference point will be the data corpus. Subsequently we will be able to specify more clearly the nature of the teacher's *process competence* which underlies her ability to unlock the potential of the communicative classroom. Finally, we shall briefly discuss ways in which teachers in service have been given opportunities to become aware of what it means to work within a process-oriented learning arrangement.

It is without contention that the teachers responsible for the examples of projects and learning sequences quoted thus far have received little or no training in process learning. In common with the mainstream of the profession, they have pre-histories as learners and, to some extent, as teachers firmly rooted in the tradition of the transmission classroom. As Wright (1987a), referring to research by Barnes (1969; 1976) points out, the characteristics of this tradition are that teachers are all powerful and knowing, set high standards, and exercise tight control over the dissemination of learning and knowledge. Learners on the other hand conform to such standards or fail and are ultimately judged, as are their teachers, by their results in examinations. It is very apparent that the practice of teachers in the data corpus reflects a different type of teacher. In Barnes' (ibid.) terms, such a teacher would be termed an 'interpretation' teacher, i.e. one who

> . . . would prefer to disperse responsibility for learning among the learners. Control is maintained by persuasion and appeal to the better judgement of learners. The teacher's position is, in the terms of the amount of control he exerts over the learners, weaker than that of the transmission teacher. Learners develop their knowledge of the subject and also refine their personalities. Understanding is the criterion of the teacher's success.
>
> (Wright 1987a)

Such a profile is compatible with the nature of the task setting, control and learner/teacher interaction displayed in the data. As individuals the teachers concerned have clearly made their own journeys towards a learner-centred approach to their work and for a variety of possible reasons, e.g. changes in their beliefs regarding language learning, confirmation of intuitive feelings from various current ideas, peer pressure, willingness and enthusiasm for experimentation, a supportive working atmosphere, etc. have arrived at their individual ways of approaching the potential of the communicative classroom. The slight differences in their approaches which we noted in chapter 6 may be due in part to the fortunate absence of a researched, abstracted and tightly delineated paradigm, in place of which teachers were busy learning by doing and from each other. These differences may also be due to natural variations in local approaches or teaching styles which could account, for example, for the varying levels of teacher control discernible in the informal data from project to project. (In this respect, we concur with Wright [ibid.] when he describes teaching styles as 'a complex amalgam of belief, attitude, strategy, technique, motivation, personality, and control' and when he states that 'teaching style lies at the heart of the inter-personal relationship between teacher and learner'. We shall look later at ways in which this relationship can be positively enhanced through particular teacher intervention strategies.) Yet such differences apart, there are strong similarities in the data in the way in which the defining characteristics of a process-oriented classroom are managed, e.g. learner training for the open classroom, the introduction of and the development of project plans in conjunction with learners. We will derive a specification of possible roles and how the process classroom is managed therefore, from what teachers in the data discernibly *do* as a group.

8.2 Teacher roles

8.2.1 The general role of the teacher as coordinator and facilitator

The general role of the teacher in the project classroom is as the coordinator of the learning process. However autonomous learners become in their own task setting or execution, the teacher carries the responsibility for the learning process as a whole and retains the right to intervene with help, advice or to set fresh targets. The projects in the data, however, not only show a reliance on the teacher for coordination of the 'whole', they are often initiated by teachers who present suggestions for projects to the class or help learners to build their own interests and ideas into a project plan (see 6.6.1). If it is fundamental to the process teacher's role to act as 'generator of learning space' (Stevick 1980, p. 20) so that learner initiatives and self-directed learning can unfold, then what the data reveals is that this space exists within frameworks created by the teacher. When teachers and learners come together, it is the teacher who has to stake out the ground or invite the learner to help her to do so.

The data also shows that coordination of the process on its own is not enough. The process dimension of learning within the space provided by a project needs to be facilitated in order that learners can understand and discover self-experience, the dynamics of the group, and also how to articulate their needs and feelings. Learners cannot normally undertake this for themselves. Young learners often lack the maturity or institutional freedom while older learners may be constrained by traditional concepts of role. They need to be shown how to do it and encouraged to believe that bringing themselves and their input into a language-learning lesson contributes positively to how and what they learn. Opening up this opportunity for learners is the responsibility of the teacher in her role as facilitator.

Coordinating the learning process involves, therefore, both the basic managerial and instructional roles of the teachers in a way which is in sharp contrast to the traditional classroom. As we have seen (5.3.2 and 7.3.5), the process classroom makes a break with the conventional monopoly of roles by making it possible for learners and teachers to exchange roles. The data examples illustrate teachers acting with great flexibility in their response to learning situations and recreating on their learners' behalf a qualitatively different and humanistically influenced learner/teacher role relationship. It is a relationship which empowers learners to take on responsibility and to work cooperatively with each other and the teacher to achieve project target goals. It is also clear from the data that the role of the teacher has expanded to encompass previously neglected elements of classroom experience such as learner education for autonomy, experimentation, reflection and evaluation, text production using difference media forms, and providing means for inter-cultural learning.

In chapter 2, we referred to the enlarged and qualitatively different role of the teacher in terms of the model of the communicative classroom as the setting for theme-centred interaction. We can use the model to illustrate the general role of the teacher as the project coordinator and facilitator of the learning process. The model sees the teacher as someone who maintains a dynamic balance between the various elements of the learning situation (see Figures 2.1–2.6) by ensuring that this relationship is altered according to the needs of the situation. Hence at any time there may be a different orientation, i.e. towards the individual, the group or the content as theme, with emphasis towards different types of learning materials.

The model also clarifies the central importance of the teacher in the learning process. Project learning does not imply that the teacher becomes a slave to the real or imagined needs of the learners, relegating her own needs or responsibilities beneath theirs. She still maintains both her managerial and instructional role. It depends crucially on how it is defined and interpreted. She does not, for example, lose her controlling role or the right to take the initiative even at times when learners have taken responsibility for their own learning and are pursuing their own plan. As Cohn (1984a, p. 284) and Stevick (1980, 17ff.) point out, the centrality of the teacher is not in conflict with learner autonomy, provided the teacher adopts a suitable role.

8.2.2 The teacher as manager and organizer

8.2.2.1 Creating the project framework
There are various approaches evident in the data which indicate the degrees of teacher initiative and pre-course preparation.

Teacher pre-course preparation
In (6.6.4) we discussed how projects in the target language environment need to rely on the teacher's pre-course organization. In the target language environment, certain arrangements such as visiting schools to teach, helping handicapped children and interviewing prominent local people need to be in place well in advance to fit the pressures of the world outside. For learners in the L2 context also, certain project experiences require both the teacher's knowledge of the target culture to identify possible fruitful areas for learner activity and her proactive work to set up provisional arrangements before they come together to learn. For instance, complex and lengthy pre-course organization is a feature of the preparation required to set exchange projects between learners of different

countries. Voss and Weber (1988) and Jones (1984) recount that the structured and progressive exchange of cassette and written texts (profiles, questionnaires, feedback comments, collages, etc.) and artifacts required extensive negotiation with their opposite numbers abroad including pre-project visits and discussions. It should not be overlooked that setting up project work often requires enthusiasm, stamina and commitment if learners are to experience learning in the here and now. It often requires teacher initiative for it to take place at all.

Learners' stimuli

Sometimes the teacher can develop the framework for the project from suggestions or ideas articulated by the learners. We have already discused how *Jumble Aid*, *Airport* and *The Summer Fête*, for example, arose in this way. The teacher's role at this point is to identify the parameters of the undertaking with the group, supplying essential practical and cultural information and acting on their behalf, making contacts and opening social or administrative doors. At such moments we can note how the participatory role of the teacher grows, parallel to her role as a frameworker.

Using communicative tasks

We have discussed the wide ranging applications of tasks as tools for learner training and for constructively intervening in the learning process as a whole. Many projects arise out of working with a particular communicative task, e.g. *The Kennet and Avon Canal* project, which sprang from a values clarification task (4.2.5) or the poetry anthology project *Make Life Easy, Try with a Smile*, which grew out of several imagination gap tasks (4.2.5). In the text film project *Almos' a Man*, the project was structured as multi-layered tasks set inside a project scenario which envisaged the class as part of a team. In one sense the task framework was a simulation – in this case a film team – but guided by the objectives of each micro-task, there was considerable freedom for experimentation and negotiation. In all three examples, the tasks are project starting points which provide a framework and are, despite their interventionist function, open-ended in that they offer space for learners to exploit.

Teacher presentation

Some projects begin with a simple proposal by the teaching which, of course, runs the risk of rejection by the group. There are many possible factors involved in the issue of rejection or acceptance, not least of which may be the open-mindedness of the group, the nature of the presentation, the appeal of the topic and the complexity of beliefs within the group regarding the role of the teacher. Clearly an acceptance of the teacher as an initiator of action is a pre-requisite. Many of the projects requiring pre-course teacher preparation fall in this category. The following observer commenting on *The Circus* project indicates not only how learner acceptance grows but how the project idea sets in motion the framework for the learning programme.

> ... the stated aims of the project – to make a book and a film about a part of the town – were clearly and unequivocably laid down. The business of deciding WHAT should be investigated was explored to an extent (with the ordering of possible sites in terms of interest) and the HOW was discussed in some detail, but the question of WHY was shelved for the moment with the answer, 'because it's there'. (The rationale for why project work rather than any other form of language teaching arose daily and became a familiar topic of discussion for participants.) Once it was established that the whimsical nature of the first decision about the order of popularity of the sites had not decided the very basis of the project, but that thoughtful pre-planning and previous experience had actually brought them to this point, there were few doubts about the overall objective.
>
> (Paine, 1985)

8.2.2.2 Creating and managing the learning climate

Experiential learning as we have understood it so far takes place in an atmosphere in which the learner is encouraged to involve himself as a contributor to and as an evaluator of the learning process. Reflections on how he relates to task, group, teacher and materials, followed by decisions for future action require a learning climate which values and prioritizes such learner activity. Such reflections pre-suppose further an inter-personal relationship between teacher and class based more on cooperation than hierarchy, and on mutual respect and acceptance than on antagonism or distance. Detailed information in the data of how teachers created their learning climates in their classes does not exist and there are dangers in drawing very specific conclusions from the products or teachers' feedback. However, one can infer certain levels of cooperation, and learner initiative, and contribution from the nature of the written and video products in the data. We can identify three key areas which teachers address when creating the psychological atmosphere for learner growth.

Creating trust
It is self-evident from the foregoing data that teachers will wish to

start their learning programmes with an emphasis on building trust. In the stages of a project (5.3.2) tasks which help create a positive relationship between learner and teacher are seen as part of the opening stage and are often the first activity undertaken together. In 4.2.1, all three tasks outlined emphasize this element of the teacher's agenda by inviting learners and teachers to share personal information. Since all the participants could decide how much they wanted to reveal, a level of personal control was retained and the possible level of threat reduced. A crucial element in trust building is the participation of the teacher as part of the group. For many learners, this defines a new role for the teacher forcing them to adjust their concept of the traditional role-relationship. Writing on the teacher's involvement in *The Circus* project, Paine (ibid.) comments:

> The element of mystery about having a real product to create together permeated the group as a whole (teacher and students). The challenge and genuine interest in the outcome was equally shared by all participants. This appeared to break down the power imbalance, so commonly accepted in a class, where the teacher has the 'answers' and simply allows the students to go through the motions of 'discovery'.
>
> (Paine 1985)

What is noticeable here is how the notion of the product galvanized a group which now naturally included the teacher whose new role as guide *and* participator broke with the traditional hierarchy.

Dealing with power

The issue of power and how it is mediated is a crucial one for the project classroom. We would claim that a fundamental part of the teacher's managerial role is the empowerment of the learner. By this we mean not only the ability to undertake tasks but also the enjoyment of an atmosphere of security and acceptance. We have indicated that using specific communicative tasks which encourage learner action on the one hand (4.2.5, 4.2.5 and 4.2.7) and reflection of the other (4.2.9) may encourage learners to redraw their relationship with regard to other learners and the teacher. However, this is a complex issue which is often difficult to manage in the cut and thrust of the classroom. Writing from a humanist background, Underhill (1989) has lucidly demarcated the pitfalls by drawing attention to four types of power observable in the classroom:

(1) *Authoritative power*: this is power aimed at helping learners to become autonomous and is typically to be seen in areas where learners cannot function without the teacher's help, e.g.

developing text comprehension skills, understanding and manipulating grammatical structure, learning how to learn, planning visits, exchanges, and using unfamiliar media equipment. It is used to help learners towards their next phase.

(2) *Autonomous power*: this is power exercised by the learner who possesses the expertise to identify tasks and carry them out at the appropriate level. The role of the teacher is to facilitate this autonomy, e.g. learners interviewing native speakers, organizing their own events, making films, etc.

(3) *Authoritarian power*: this is power used by the teacher to carry out activities which are not in the learner's interests, e.g. to follow an imposed syllabus or undertake a task which does not engage the learner.

(4) *Abdicated power*: this is the 'degenerate' version of autonomous power in that it is given to the learner because the teacher is unwilling to accept responsibility for an initiative or unable to facilitate autonomous power appropriately. As Underhill (ibid.) points out, 'implicit in this may be the teacher's own confusion and discomfort with his or her role, and the projection of that confusion onto (the learner)'.

Such a picture of power we take, however, to be dynamically available in the classroom in that it is possible for a teacher to set a task and use authoritative and authoritarian power at the same time since it may impact on different learners differently. Likewise, learners working together in a group may be susceptible as individuals to both autonomous and abdicated power. The informal project data corpus has not infrequent examples of individual learners who either reject participation in tasks or find themselves uncomfortable and needing more guidance than has been given. This is clearly an area which will benefit from greater attention and reflection by teachers presently involved in project learning. In doing so, they will be able to draw upon the growing body of work on experiential learning now available in the fields of adult and continuing education. Here, as Heron (1989) points out, theory and practice have undergone a radical change, the premise of which is that 'student learning is necessarily self-directed: it rests on the autonomous exercise of intelligence, choice and interest'. In this new paradigm, teaching is redefined as facilitation of self-directed learning and the teacher a facilitator who helps learners to learn in an experiential group. Heron's work, that of Underhill in the UK who seeks to build a bridge between the mainstream of experientialism and language learning, and Allen (1989) in the USA who has drawn attention to changes in the leadership and power paradigms of organizations, could form the focus for further in-service education in this area.

Facilitating the learning process
The process competence of the teacher is, we maintain, the determining factor in the extent to which learning can become experiential. It has to do not only with the selection and application of tasks but crucially with the issues of power and with how the teacher behaves and interacts with learners. Specifications of what this might involve for language teaching are at present only programmatic. However, in our discussion of teacher style above, it is noticeable that Wright's (1987a) list of factors which form the basis for how teachers interact with learners are not necessarily static components. While we agree with Rogers' (1983) view that it is not possible to force teachers to introduce a particular climate if they do not feel it themselves, we conclude that, in company with Underhill (1989), teachers can change their beliefs, attitudes, strategies, techniques, motivation, and levels of control, if they have a mind to. That is the task facing ongoing teacher education (8.4).

We can identify, however, at least the following characteristics from the data:

(1) the capacity to set tasks and allow learners to proceed without necessary interference;
(2) the capacity to judge when an intervention is appropriate (When teachers intervene to complete tasks for learners unnecessarily, it takes away from learners opportunities for learning and effectively disempowers them);
(3) the capacity to negotiate with learners what and how they wish to learn;
(4) the capacity to conduct feedback which is both honest and supportive;
(5) the capacity which allows the teacher to devote time to listening to individuals;
(6) the capacity to assert oneself without being drawn into arguments;
(7) the capacity to accept and respect other viewpoints and tender one's own.

In Underhill's (ibid.) terms, these capacities would represent movement between the authoritative and autonomous uses of power.

8.2.2.3 Structuring and guiding the learning process
Initiating events during the project and helping learners to decide for

themselves how they wish to proceed is a basic element in the teacher's managerial role. We have already discussed how teachers create the overall framework within which learners can become self-managing. It is clear, however, from our discussion of the various stages of a project (5.3.2) that teacher intervention is often necessary during the learning process, with the teacher acting in her 'authoritative' role. Tasks may be set which relate to work outside the classroom, e.g. learners making a film for themselves as researchers; or editing and processing audio, video and written text collected from native speaker informants (5.3.2), and which function as mini-projects. Examples of process-structuring tasks for use inside the classroom would be, for example, topic orientation to indicate the direction of learner activity. This effect may be achieved by a range of task types, e.g. awareness and sensibility (4.2.2), imagination gap (4.2.5) or values clarification (4.2.8) tasks. Similarly, teachers in text projects can create clarity and remove blocks to comprehension by the type of tasks outlined in 4.2.6 role-playing and creative dramatization and 4.2.7 interaction and interpersonality. Scenarios which take the form of simulations, e.g. the TV news programme from the induction stage in the Bath data or the film crew from the *Almos' a Man* example or the *Holden Caulfield* film scripts example, can also determine future work because learners may wish to continue working with media on a different topic or re-evaluate the content element of the theme as a result of insights gained. Evaluation of the learning process itself, which in turn will produce further initiatives for future action, can also be set in motion by the tasks outlined in 4.2.9.

8.2.3 The teacher as instructor

8.2.3.1 Teaching learner autonomy

A key role of the teacher as an instructor is to show learners how to learn experientially. Creating the conditions and opportunity to do so is part of her managerial role and conducting and participating in tasks is part of her instructional role. For many learners, the way in which teachers conduct themselves in their involvement in tasks – working side by side with learners, encouraging learners to follow their intuitions and express opinions – is likely to set the teacher in a new light and contrast with previously held notions of classroom role relationships. In this new relationship, the teacher acts as a guide who encourages learners to become proactive contributors breaking away from their traditionally more passive and receptive role. Being active and directive also means, of course, accepting responsibility and effecting this change in learners is also integral to the challenge facing the teacher.

In 7.3.3, we referred to the two strands of the learner autonomy debate and concluded that they are by no means mutually exclusive. Apart from the Danish example (Dam 1982; Dam and Gabrielsen 1988), there is no specific reference in the data to the strand concerning learner strategies for better language learning as an individual. The other European examples which make up the majority of the data reveal a preoccupation with learner autonomy as a means of equipping the individual to manage his/her behaviour within a social grouping. This second, inter-personal dimension which educationalists such as Kohonen (1989) consider to have key significance for the development of a democratic society, plays a lynchpin role in the communicative classroom. Since most teaching takes place in groups, it is not surprising that exploiting the potential of the group and finding ways for the individual to relate to, contribute to, and where necessary withdraw from the group has received the attention it has. Indeed, the communicative classroom is by nature a group-oriented entity in that it focuses on how individuals can express themselves within and through the group or subgroup rather than outside the group. Learner autonomy, in this context, means concretely learning how to function in a group and take decisions often independent of the teacher and learning how to negotiate and articulate opinions and feelings.

The following observations from the Bath data corpus indicates the typical action taken by a teacher in the crucial opening stage when the agenda for learner autonomy is being created.

Physical separation from the teacher

  The students got away from the classroom and the teacher at an early
  stage, during the Bath walks task. The physical separation of the
  participants from the teacher as they explored in twos and threes remained
  a constant feature. However, before and after each activity there was a
  period when the teacher held their attention in class to explain the reason
  for the activity in terms of the contribution to the final objective and to
  debrief or share and compare results. This pattern of setting up a firm
  framework within which the students had autonomy, seemed to serve as a
  kind of syllabus. The locus of control over given activities constantly swung
  between the teacher and students without being insisted on dynamically.
  (Paine 1985)

The purpose of the task in this instance was to make observations of the local environment which required learners both to negotiate in their sub-groups the exact aims of each sub-task and to seek help from native speakers. In doing so, they were obliged to start to make decisions for themselves and act upon them and thereby become accustomed to coping without the teacher.

Working in different social groups

Filming – at this stage the teacher could afford to step back and allow greater student autonomy, as guidelines were clearly laid down by the nature of the task. The roles were defined for each member of the group, e.g. cameraperson, editor, floor manager.

(Paine ibid.)

This kind of learner activity is a general feature in the data. Neumann–Zöckler (1980) e.g. documents how her secondary school learners were first introduced to pair work before going on to group work to produce their reworked dramatization of the Little Red Riding Hood story. In other examples, *Dear Brown Eyes*, *Jumble Aid* (5.3.3) pair work using information-sharing tasks (4.2.3) is employed as a fore-runner to more ambitious simulation work. Such tasks also serve the purpose of introducing the learner to speaking for himself without waiting to be corrected by the teacher.

Learning how to negotiate

When the teacher and learners meet for the first time to learn, atavistic notions of how teachers and classes behave are likely to determine the way they might negotiate with one another. We would maintain that for traditional, institutional reasons the interface between teacher and learner is an unequal encounter. It would also be overstating the case for working in projects to claim that this will always be removed. Each learner/teacher relationship is very individual to the learning setting and in many cases, institutional roles may be more dominant. What can be claimed, however, is that the process of negotiation between teacher and learners and among learners themselves can substantially alter the traditional balance. In order to achieve this learners need at least space, a role model, and encouragement, to feel secure enough to participate in a new relationship.

Following a game necessitating group cooperation a useful debriefing session was conducted by the teacher (nominating turns to get the ball rolling). It served as the opportunity to bring out into the open the issues of responsibility, leadership, apathy, etc. as well as the more detailed background of the methodology of CLT.

(Paine ibid.)

This extract does not indicate that what emerged was a result of the teacher's own agenda or whether the issues mentioned were brought forward by the learners. However it was standard practice in this project that such debriefings followed each talk serving to establish the appropriacy of creating space for discussion and negotiation. We can discern from this example and the data in general that *each* task provides an opportunity for learning how to negotiate and that succeeding tasks provide cyclical opportunities for developing and refining this part of a learner's process competence. The project target tasks are evidence that learners are able to achieve a high level of negotiative ability. We may be justified in deducing this from project accounts in the data but we still lack detailed knowledge of how teachers develop this ability. In particular, there is no reference in the formal data and little discussion in the informal data of the language skills involved: that is, the way in which learners articulate their needs and feelings and whether teachers undertake to provide further resources with regard, for example, to the development of register. If learner autonomy is going to be taken seriously, we propose that this area should not be neglected within the teacher's instructional role.

8.2.3.2 Providing language resources and monitoring language use

Language input

It is this part of the teacher's role which is heavily underscored in the transmission-oriented classroom since the teacher's efforts centre on delivering language in discreet terms according to a pre-specified syllabus, i.e. with a focus on language as system and with minimal concern for the process dimension. We have described language learning in the process-oriented classroom on the other hand as a learner-shaped, task focus where language is a means not an end.

Here input by the teacher is task related as the discussion in 5.3.2 and the examples in 5.3.3 demonstrate. A further comment from the observation data from *The Circus* project helps to illustrate how language preparation was integrated into the task (see also the *Airport* project).

A TV news bulletin was analyzed in order to replicate it on video next day. All aspects of the film were discussed, including the language used. This reduced the emphasis on the code by giving it equal weighting with other categories. Allowing language to become a tool, to be sharpened at times in order to achieve another purpose more efficiently, reassured the learners with radically different previous language learning experience and kept the sense of progression towards the terminal objective . . . language input was always closely allied to the overall aim, e.g. polite forms of address before interviews or notetaking exercised before a talk. The need for the skill was always apparent. Worksheets and handouts were available and clearly organized and presented . . . they served as indicators of progress, as chapters in a book . . . .

(Paine ibid.)

Project tasks are not the only reason for language input, however. Many project accounts describe how learner diaries, in addition to their role in the process, are used as a diagnostic tool to identify learner deficits. Follow-up work takes the form of a group task in which learners are asked collectively to iron out grammatical errors which the teacher has collected over a period of a week and re-presented as anonymous examples. This form of error correction workshop might lead on to a grammar research workshop of the kind described in 7.3.3. What many formal or informal data accounts do not provide, however, is information of instances where learners cope inadequately with dealing with their own deficits. It would not, in our view, be inconsistent with the teacher's role in experiential learning to meet such needs with a transmission *oriented* lesson since learners could identify its purpose and not necessarily misconstrue its effect on their relationship with the teacher. It is a moot point how often such instances may be necessary but the data, apart from Nuhn (1982), makes no mention of it.

It is a commonly held view that project activity cannot take place until learners have reached a given level in the target language. Working from this premise, it would be difficult to imagine meaningful project activity with groups of beginners. It would be difficult to disagree with this view in absolute terms since learners need language forms and a given level of resources before they can proceed to use. However, informal accounts from the Bath corpus suggest that adult beginners enjoy the challenge of using what little English they have mastered in the live context. It seems, therefore, that definitive statements in the area of applicability cannot be made without further observation and research.

A further, potentially productive area for research by teachers is how to bridge the lacunae in learners' language competence which teachers may identify from time to time. These would typically arise when teachers measure learner needs against existing syllabus specifications (exam syllabus, textbook inventories, etc.) and the language product of particular projects. Teachers in their role as language expert may also identify from their general experience such shortcomings or areas which need attention. It is not clear how, and to what extent, existing project teaching considers this point. Although the informal data suggests so far that the multiplicity of tasks generated by projects overcome the difficulties suggested above (even with reference to examination needs), there is a dearth of retrospective syllabus accounts of how teachers deal with it to indicate whether this is indeed a problem area or not.

An important function of the teacher's role as provider of language resources is making available tools and materials for independent learning. We have referred to the need for abundant information materials in 2.3.1. It is part of the teacher's responsibility to make these accessible and to help build learner's self-access competence (Dickinson 1987; Sheerin 1989). In doing so, they would be able to draw on cognitive and metacognitive strategies (Wenden 1986a; 1987) which promote individual language awareness (7.3.2). We have also indicated (in 6.2.2) that it is part of the teacher's responsibility to provide opportunities for the automization of language forms. Since projects promote *par excellence* language in use as opposed to language as system, it is not surprising that many accounts do not refer to the role of automization. It may well be that future evaluation of learning in projects may support Prabhu's thesis (Prabhu 1987, 1–2) that such work is 'unhelpful to the development of grammatical competence and detrimental to the desired preoccupation with meaning in the classroom'. This is undoubtedly an area for closer investigation, both to examine Prabhu's claim further and to look at the nature and effect of automization on learners in projects.

Informal monitoring

One of the purposes of the communicative classroom is to maximize the amount of interaction between learners. Such an aim runs counter to the aim of careful control by the teacher of learner language production prevalent in the transmission classroom. While few observers would dispute that CLT both in its weak and strong form has been successful in bringing about a freer use of language in the classroom, it has brought with it the dilemma of how to react to a potentially higher level of error in code and appropriacy. Forming more constructive attitudes to error is a difficulty for learners and teachers alike since both have to reconstruct the view that frequent correction is an effective classroom response. While teachers can find clarification and guidance from the body of work on 'interlanguage' (Corder 1967, p. 81; Selinker 1972; Tarone 1988), they are still left with the vexed question of how to deal informally with error in class. Refusal to correct on the basis that the error is part of the learner's 'approximate system' (Selinker, ibid.), and will disappear with use and exposure to target language input, can sometimes be counter-productive. The learner may become frustrated and the error may indeed become fossilized. Correction on the other hand could not only reinforce unhelpful attitudes but increase dependency on the teacher to the detriment of self-correction.

While the data yields little detail on how teachers cope, however, certain general practices have emerged. We have already pointed to the use of learner diaries as an ongoing means of monitoring learner output. Other written informal work such as interview accounts, e.g. the *Airport* film (see Humburg et al. 1983), or learner profiles (4.2.1) may be displayed (uncorrected by the teacher's red pen) principally for peer- and self-monitoring, but the teacher can also take advantage of them. Monitoring of oral work, on the other hand, seems to be more effectively carried out during group work when the teacher is not ostensibly engaged on a monitoring exercise. Paine (1985) in her observation of *The Circus* project notes:

> . . . the teacher was often occupied 'documenting' the class in such a way that he was present but not 'available' for consultation because he was filming or taking notes. This served several purposes. It allowed the teacher to keep in touch with the stages of development of the students, both linguistically and socially, without appearing to monitor them, as sitting inactively might have done. It also gave the students the confidence to proceed, knowing that the teacher was on hand to step in . . . .

How teachers handle error in oral interaction will, however, ultimately be a function of the ground rules that they define together with the group on the basis of their style and experience. One positive strategy for monitoring language which is present in the Bath data is the teacher emphasis on 'quality' of text production, e.g. when written or video text is being produced for a given audience. It is a form of 'pre-emptive' monitoring and works by arranging for learner editorial teams to vet drafts of written work for errors of any kind before it is included in the final product. Learners invariably become involved in researching language information materials (grammar resource books) and discussion with group colleagues as a result of this task. The role of the teacher here is to function as final arbiter if advice is sought.

Formal monitoring
We have discussed this point in 6.6.5, indicating the inadequacies of current practices and the lack of a principled approach to formal assessment in the project classroom. We would add here, however, that the role of the teacher as an assessor of learner progress is by no means in conflict with her participational role within the group. Even in teaching contexts where teachers have institutional and social responsibilities for younger learners, or where their assessment of adults' progress may affect employment prospects or social standing, this is a resolvable dichotomy. The root of the solution, we believe, lies in the relationship between learner and teacher created by the facilitation of the process dimension; that is, whereby the learner can accept the teacher's monitoring role within the context of her role as a supportive helper. The increasing dialogue between learner and teacher, evidenced in the data, has meant in practice greater opportunity for interviews during which educational and personal counselling takes place. This leads in turn to degrees of mutual trust out of which learner self-assessments supported by teacher input emerge (6.6.5).

8.2.3.3   Providing technical expertise and presentation skills

Providing didactic expertise
We have referred in 7.3.5 to the value of learners acting as teachers. In her role as an expert in didactics and communications, it is the teacher who can advise on technique and presentation skills. What learners can experience here is the creation of a form of text designed for a live audience which requires them to consider how best to formulate and mediate it to their addressees. The event provides an opportunity for learners to enhance their understanding not only of the content but also of a form of communication which places particular emphasis on clarity and dealing with an audience which can interact and make strategic demands on them. Formal presentations are a familiar feature of ongoing project work in the data while for some project examples teaching and presenting are central, e.g. *Dear Brown Eyes, Hello is Ciao, Airport,* or *The Catcher in the Rye.* In the Bath data (5.3.2), many projects conclude with a group

presentation to a school audience and others from outside the school community.

Providing technical expertise

Part of the teacher's expertise which needs to be made available is how to work with multi-media. Within institutions, teachers may need to share expertise in this field and act cooperatively to meet the needs of learners (6.7). In adult groups such expertise may even be available from the learners whenever professionals from other fields meet to learn languages. However, it is, in our view, not an unreasonable expectation of learners that they should have the benefit not only of learning with technical and challenging forms of text creation but that teachers should possess the basic skills to show them how to exploit this facility. Media skills can be seen as an extension of the basic role of a teacher in tandem with the development of the communicative classroom. The comment in our example of observation data (Paine 1985) underlies this point:

> The teacher now stepped in to help out with the technical matter of control of the camera . . . . This timely 'intervention' helped to ensure that the desired end product was available by the end of the session. The group obviously had a serious interest in improving the product but might easily have become disheartened if the technical problems had not been cleared up in time. It seemed that the trust in the teacher as the one who can 'produce the goods' had been transferred from the usual role of final arbiter on the language (a walking grammar and dictionary) to an expert in the field of film and book production.

8.2.4   The teacher as investigator and researcher

In company with Breen and Candlin (1980) and Wright (1987a), we would propose that the role of the teacher in the communicative classroom contains a third area of responsibility, namely to engage actively in researching what is happening in the classroom with the view to understanding its processes more clearly and to bringing about improvements. Such work can lead to further professional and personal development for the teacher and improve learner and teacher performance. It may begin with the need to get to the bottom of a problem; for example a negative classroom atmosphere or the incompatibility of some individuals in their sub-groups. It could also impact on learners as another type of communicative task if, for example, they were asked to participate in an experiment on which type of learning style they preferred. Similarly, it could involve the use of learning materials, i.e. as to how they affect learners' competence, or teacher/learner roles, or it could lead to collaborative work with colleagues, team teaching or observation. Wright (ibid.) advocates using a range of data collection methods, e.g. questionnaires, lesson observation, diary-keeping, audio/video recording and interviews (see 8.3.2.2) He further stresses the need to formulate research questions clearly, limit one's investigation to a manageable area and record the data accurately and regularly. Clearly, any form of research or experimentation needs documentation if it is to demonstrate rigour. Sharing results can feed into staff development and help to maintain the professional awareness of those involved. A common outcome of classroom action research of work considered to have application beyond the context of its origin is the publication and dissemination of results. The Dam and Gabrielsen investigations (1988) are a case in point. The SIGS (special interest groups) of teacher organizations (such as IATEFL and TESOL) also provide for the outcome of much teacher-conducted classroom research. What is at stake for teachers in widening the scope of their classroom roles in this way is a form of professional development which will lead to the renewal of their curriculum and of themselves as interpreters and creators of curricula. For the importance of teachers being placed once more in the role of learners lies not only in being able to empathize with the learner but that they may experience the benefits of change within themselves. Underhill (1989) is surely correct in his view that we can only facilitate processes in others that are already going in ourselves. Further, for language teaching in general, the result of using communicative tasks as additions to a repertoire of techniques and materials acquired over years in the profession *without* an accompanying inner change of attitude would be to negate any advantages of the communicative classroom and amount to 'more of the same' of an exhausted paradigm of language learning.

8.3 Teacher education for the process-oriented classroom

8.3.1 Pre-service teacher education

We have noted earlier that teachers presently engaged in process-oriented teaching are themselves breaking new ground and learning by doing. Generalized models of learning in the form of a method do not thankfully exist and, we stress, in company with Pennycook

(1989), should not. This is an area of difficulty for pre-service education in particular, which would need to take into account the criteria and selection of tasks for learning and the facilitation of the learning process in addition to equipping new teachers with the basic skills of classroom language teaching. Corder (1986, p. 189) makes reference to this point:

Allwright: Previously teachers using a book or following a clear-cut syllabus weren't asked to make decisions about what to teach at a particular time. The problem in teacher training is now that, with a task-oriented approach, teachers are not going to be asked to teach any particular language item at any time, but must select tasks according to criteria that up to now have hardly been included in teacher training: 'conceptual readiness' and 'interest readiness'.

Pit Corder: ... Task-based approaches will require a total rethink of teacher training ... teachers will need to be trained in task development and task selection, and to recognize when a particular task is appropriate for a particular group.

Rossner: ... it is still not clear ... how the teacher, working in the context of formal education, which is permeated with the notion of 'systematic progress', is to adjust to the apparent randomness of task-based approaches ... .

Pre-service training is not our concern here but we would note that solutions to the difficulties outlined above will, in part, depend on the progress made in experiential forms of in-service education (Edelhoff 1984; Nunan 1989b).

8.3.2 Initiatives in in-service teacher education

The question therefore which we wish to raise at this point is: What preparation and training do teachers require in order to be able to facilitate learning in the process classroom? If we accept that the teacher's own experiences as a learner exercise a powerful influence over her future beliefs and interaction with learners (Edelhoff 1989), it follows that a basic component of this preparation must be the opportunity to learn experientially oneself. In other words, the preparation of teachers for the experiential classroom needs to mirror in its procedures and methodology the experiential classroom. The examples below indicate ways in which this has been attempted thus far and point to possible directions which future work in the field may take.

8.3.2.1   Teachers as course participants and learners

The in-service course type developed by Edelhoff in 1981 for German high school teachers of English and held annually in the target-language countries (Edelhoff 1984) has the particular advantage of giving its teacher participants the opportunity to learn as learners. However, they do not carry out simulations or exercises which could necessarily be transferred into the classroom. Instead they are given the chance to carry out information-gathering tasks which relate to their personal and professional interests, and which are appropriate to them as adults. The course aims are given as follows:

– to practise a wide variety of communicative language skills in an English-speaking environment;
– to become familiar with information gathering techniques for later individual use;
– to gather and process a wide variety of authentic language material on project topics (written, video, audio);
– to look at language used in the material (Edelhoff 1984).

Teachers proceed in small sub-groups, carrying out research by interviewing contacts from the local native speaker population and assembling a range of multi-media texts. Each contact and interview provides not only information but the chance to gain first-hand intercultural insights.

Working intensively in this way over a period of ten days mirrors the activities which learners also undertake in projects. For many teachers this is their first real experience of the kind of group work they might ask their learners to carry out. They are faced therefore with the challenges of making group decisions, negotiating, representing one's opinion and accepting others', resolving interpersonal difficulties, evaluating action and making fresh decisions. They also discover that they have a personal investment in what they do which emerges when they experience the excitement of learning in the here and now. For example, it is a common occurence for participants to return to the course centre elated after a recording a particularly stimulating interview. Acquiring new skills is also a matter of involvement. Those who practise and experiment with the media equipment, for example, learn how to use it, and of course the reverse is also true (Roberts 1988).

We do not yet know the long-term effect of experiential in-service education of this kind and several questions still need to be addressed: e.g. whether or not this kind of individual experience can bring about institutional changes. Nevertheless, Edelhoff and his colleagues (Edelhoff et al. 1990) are assembling a body of data in support of the view that for the individual at least the experience has led to a revision, in some cases fundamental, of attitudes and practices.

8.3.2.2 Teachers as course participants and researchers of their own work

We have already discussed (see 7.3.3) the Danish CLT project led by Dam and Gabrielsen (1988). It repays further scrutiny from the perspective of the long-term, in-service project from which it grew. We have seen from the learners' gains (7.3.3) what may be achieved when their teachers are given the opportunity to articulate and work upon their problems in collaboration with their trainer/facilitators. In their report on the project, the trainers (Breen et al. 1989) describe how their approach developed from (a) training as transmission, through (b) training as problem-solving, to (c) training as classroom decision-making and investigation. Their description of it as 'emergent and reactive rather than planned and proactive' illustrates the emphasis given to the evaluation of succeeding phases to determine strengths and weaknesses. For example, the evaluation of phase one brought about significant changes in phase two, in which teachers' own classroom problems became the theme of the workshop instead of material brought in by the visiting trainers. At this stage a sub-group of teachers also initiated their own classroom research to be shared later with colleagues – making use of teacher diaries, video recordings of lessons, learners' work and learners' own evaluation of their work and of the classroom process. In phase three the project progressed towards solving the problem of the perceived hierarchy between the teachers and the trainers by 'encouraging teachers to interact with themselves and with the trainers as equal participants with equally innovative ideas'. The ensuing workshops relied solely on data which the teachers provided. 'Trainers, teachers and learners are placed in an interdependent role relationship. In a way it is the learners who now act as the source of training, and the workshops are a forum for teachers and trainers to plan cautiously and thereafter to share and evaluate what has been achieved and uncovered by the learners (Breen et al. 1989, p. 133).

In changing teachers into researchers (see 6.3.4) the Danish experience has profoundly changed the in-service paradigm for its participants. Its significance can be seen not only in 'product' terms: insight into learning, research methodology and the confidence to represent what they do as of equal value to theorizers' contributions. It represents also an 'experience' of experiential learning in which reflection, evaluation and action underlie the compilation of the in-service programme.

8.3.3 Teacher education: a final statement

Our purpose in this section has been to look briefly at two examples of how teacher development has been taking place against the general background of the communicative classroom. We wished to draw attention in particular to (a) how teachers can be given a first-hand experience of process learning and (b) trends in teacher education which seem to indicate that the relationship between teacher-educator and teacher is being reconstructed. Such trends reveal a growing awareness that teacher-development at the individual level and change at the institutional level is more likely to occur when teachers are involved in articulating their needs and shaping how such change may take place (see Thomas and Walters 1988). This concern for the actualities of the classroom and the direct preoccupations of teachers parallels the way in which teaching in the communicative classroom is seeking in turn to involve and exploit the needs and contributions of learners (4.2.1–4.2.9; 5.3.2, 5.4.2; 6.2, 6.4, 6.5; 7.1, 7.3.2–7.3.4). We would suggest that this is a natural and appropriate change of focus in teacher education. However, while such a reorientation means an emphasis on a 'bottom-up' approach and a movement away from the traditional transmission model of learning and training (Clark 1987, p. 92), it would be an oversimplification to see new developments conveniently as polar opposite reactions to what has gone on before. What the examples above indicate is that while the need for fresh input of insights and ideas from educators has not diminished, the reason for that input is being more closely coupled with the needs of the classroom. In conjunction with this realignment, there are signs that the role relationship between teacher-educators and teachers is becoming less hierarchical and more heterarchical. In other words, the role of teacher education is now not to deliver sacred principles to a grateful profession but to facilitate change by helping teachers to become self-directing and researchers of their own work.

Bibliography

Abbs, B. and Sexton, M. 1978 *Challenges. Student's Book*. Longman, London.
Alderson, C. (ed.) 1985 *Evaluation* (Lancaster Practical Papers in English Language Education, Vol. 6). Pergamon, Oxford.
Allen, K. 1989 Diverse voices of leadership. Emerging harmonies and different rhythms. Paper given at the American Educational Research Association SIG, San Diego, CA. November 1989.
Alix, C. and Kodron, C. 1988a Deutsch–französiche Schulkooperation: Lernen im Dialog. In Edelhoff and Liebau (eds).
Alix, C. and Kodron, C. 1988b *Zusammenarbeiten: Gemeinsam lernen. Themenzentrierte Zusammenarbeit zwischen Schulen verschiedener Länder am Beispiel Deutschland–Frankreich*. Bad Honnef: Deutsch-Französisches Jugendwerk.
Allwright, R. 1984 The importance of interaction in classroom language learning. *Applied Linguistics* 5: 156–71.
Ashworth, M. 1985 *Beyond Methodology. Second Language Teaching and the Community*. Cambridge University Press, Cambridge.

Bach, G. and Molter, H. 1976 *Pychoboom. Wege und Abwege moderner Therapie*. Rowohlt, Reinbek b. Hamburg.
Bach, G. and Timm, J.-P. (eds) 1989 *Englischunterricht. Grundlagen und Methoden einer handlungsorientierten Unterrichtspraxis*. Francke, Tübingen.
BAG. Bundesarbeitsgemeinschaft Englisch an Gesamtschulen (ed.) 1978 *Kommunikativer Englischunterricht. Prinzipien und Übungstypologie*. Langenscheidt, München.
Barnes, D. 1969 Language in the secondary school classroom. In Barnes, D. et al. *Language, the Learner and the School*. Penguin, Harmondsworth.
Barnes, D. 1976 *From Communication to Curriculum*. Penguin, Harmondsworth.
Bastian, J. and Gudjohns H. (eds) 1986 *Das Projektbuch. Theorie, Praxisbeispiele, Erfahrungen*. Bergmann und Helbig, Hamburg.
Bicker, N. and Swanenvleugel, J. 1985 Verslag van een Project voor Engels in een Hetergene Brugklas. *Levende Talen* (Netherlands) 399: 148–53.
Black, C. and Butzkamm, W. 1977a Sprachbezogene und mitteilungsbezogene Kommunikation im Englischunterricht. *Praxis des neusprachlichen Unterrichts* 24: 115–24.
Bleich, D. 1978 *Subjective Criticism*, Johns Hopkins University Press, Baltimore.
Bohnsack, F. et al. 1984 *Schüleraktiver Unterricht*. Beltz, Weinheim.
Bolte, H. and Herrlitz, W. (eds) 1983 *Lernen im Fremdsprachenunterricht. Berichte aus alternativen Lernkonzepten*. Utrecht.
Brandes, D. and Phillips, H. 1979 *Gamesters' Handbook. 140 Games for Teachers and Group Leaders*. Hutchinson, London.
Bredella, L. 1984a Lebendiges Lernen im Literaturunterricht. Vorverständnis aktivierende Methoden und Selbsterfahrung bei der Interpretation

literarischer Texte. In Schratz, M. (ed.).

Bredella, L. (ed) 1984b *Die USA in Unterricht und Forschung*. Kamp: Bochum.

Bredella, L. 1985 Leseerfahrungen im Unterricht. Kognitive und affektive Reaktionen bei der Lektüre literarischer Texte. In Bredella, L. and Legutke, M. (eds).

Bredella, L. (ed.) 1988 *Perceptions and Misperceptions: The United States and Germany. Studies in Intercultural Understanding*. Tübingen: Narr.

Bredella, L. 1989 Die Mitwirkung des Lesers beim Verstehen literarischer Texte und die Aufgaben der Literaturdidaktik. In Edelhoff, C. and Candlin, C. (eds).

Bredella, L. and Legutke, M. (eds) 1985a *Schüleraktivierende Methoden im Fremdsprachenunterricht Englisch*. Kamp Verlag, Bochum.

Bredella, L. and Legutke, M. 1985b Ein interaktives Modell für das Verstehenlernen einer fremden Kultur am Beispiel der 'American 1920s'. In Bredella, L. (ed.) *Das Verstehenlernen einer paradoxen Epoche in Schule und Hochschule. The American 1920s*. Kamp, Bochum.

Bredella, L. et al. 1984 *Encounters. Confidence*. Kamp Bochum.

Breen, M. 1983 How would we recognize a communicative classroom? The British Council (ed.) *Dunsford House Papers*.

Breen, M. 1985a The social context for language learning – a neglected situation? *Studies in Second Language Acquisition* 7: 135–58.

Breen, M. 1985b Authenticity in the language classoom. *Applied Linguistics* 6: 60–70.

Breen, M. 1987a Learner Contributions to Task Design. In Candlin, C. and Murphy, D. (eds).

Breen, M. 1987b Contemporary paradigms in syllabus design. Part II. *Language Learning* 20: 157–74.

Breen, M. 1989 The evaluation cycle for language-learning tasks. In Johnson, R. (ed.).

Breen, M. and Candlin, C. 1980 The essentials of a communicative curriculum in language teaching. *Applied Linguistics* 1: 89–112.

Breen, M. et al. 1989 The evolution of a teacher training programme. In Johnson, R. (ed.).

Brindley, G. 1989 *Assessing Achievement in the Learner-Centred Curriculum*. National Centre for English Language Teaching and Research, Sydney, NSW.

The British Council (ed.) 1982 *ELT Documents 113: Humanistic Approaches. An Empirical View*. The British Council, London.

Brocher, T. 1967 *Gruppendynamik und Erwachsenenbildung. Zum Problem der Entwicklung von Konformismus oder Autonomie in Arbeitsgruppen*. Westermann, Braunschweig.

Brown, G. 1971 *Human Teaching for Human Learning. An Introduction to Confluent Education*. The Viking Press, New York, NY (Penguin 1977).

Brown, G. (ed.) 1975 *The Live Classroom. Innovation through Confluent Education and Gestalt*. The Viking Press, New York, NY.

Brumfit, C. 1984 *Communicative Methodology in Language Teaching. The Role of Fluency and Accuracy*. Cambridge University Press, Cambridge.

Brumfit, C. (ed.) 1984 *General English Syllabus Design. Curriculum and Syllabus Design for the General English Classroom* (ELT Documents 118) Pergamon, Oxford.

Brumfit, C. and Carter, R. (eds) 1986 *Literature and Language Teaching*. Oxford University Press, Oxford.

Bundesarbeitsgemeinschaft Englisch an Gesamtschulen (BAG) (ed.) 1978 *Kommunikativer Englischunterricht. Prinzipien und Übungstypologie*. Langenscheidt-Longman, München.

Burke, J. and Legutke, M. (forthcoming) Kleinstadtgespräche, Kleistadtbegegnungen. Ein Modell für interkulturelles Lernen. In Legutke M. (ed.).

Canale, M. 1983 From communicative competence to communicative language pedagogy. In Richards, J. and Schmidt, R. (eds).

Canale, M. and Swain, M. 1980 Theoretical bases of communicative approaches to second language teaching and testing. *Applied Linguistics* 1: 1–47.

Candlin, C. (ed.) 1981 *The Communicative Teaching of English. Principles and an Exercise Typology*. Longman, London.

Candlin, C. 1984 Syllabus design as critical process. In Brumfit, C. (ed.).

Candlin, C. 1986 Explaining communicative competence: the limits of testability. In Stansfield, C. (ed.) *Towards Communicative Competence Testing. Proceedings of the Second TOFL Invitational Conference*. Educational Testing Service, Princeton, NJ.

Candlin, C. 1987 Towards task-based language learning. In Candlin, C. and Murphy, D. (eds).

Candlin, C. 1989 Language, culture and curriculum. In Candlin, C. and McManara, T. (eds) *Language Learning and Curriculum*. National Centre for English Language Teaching and Research, Sydney, NSW.

Candlin, C. and Edelhoff, C. 1982 *Challenges. Teacher's guide*. Longman, London.

Candlin, C. and Edelhoff, C. (eds) 1989 *Verstehen und Verständigung. Festschrift für Hans-Eberhard Piepho*. Kamp, Bochum.

Candlin, C. and Murphy, D. (eds) 1987 *Language Learning Tasks*. Prentice-Hall International, Englewood Cliffs, NJ (Lancaster Practical Papers in English Language Education. Vol. 7).

Canfield, J. and Wells, H. 1976 *100 Ways to Enhance Self-Concept in the Classroom. A Handbook for Teachers and Parents*. Prentice-Hall, Englewood Cliffs, NJ.

Carter, G. 1985a *Dear Brown Eyes*. Video film. Bell School, Bath.

Carter, G. (ed.) 1985b *The Circus*. Project book. Bell School, Bath (mimeo).

Carter, G. (ed.) 1985c *The Kennet and Avon Canal*. Project book. Bell School, Bath (mimeo).

Carter, G. (ed.) 1986a *Proxemics*. Project book. Bell School, Bath (mimeo).

Carter, G. (ed.) 1986b *The Language of Children's Comics*. Project book. Bell School, Bath (mimeo).

Carter, G. and Cursiter, J. (eds) 1985 *Dear Brown Eyes. Educational Project*. The Bell School, Bath (mimeo).

Carter, G. and Thomas, H. 1986 'Dear Brown Eyes'. Experiential learning in a project-oriented approach. *ELTJ* 40: 196–204.

Carter et al. 1985 *The Circus*. Video film. Bell School, Bath.

Carter et al. 1987 *Jumble Aid*. Video film. Bell School, Bath.

Carter et al. 1988 *Hello is Ciao*. Video film. Bell School, Bath.

Casteel, D. and Stahl, R. 1975 *Value Clarification in the Classroom. A primer.* Santa Monica, CA.

Castillo, G. 1973 *Left-Handed Teaching. Lessons in Affective Education.* Holt, New York, NY (2nd ed. 1978).

Chamot, A. and Kupper, L. 1989 Learner strategies in foreign language instruction. *Foreign Language Annals* 22: 13–24.

Christison, M. and Bassano, S. 1981 *Look Who's Talking.* Alemany Press, San Francisco.

Christison, M. and Bassano, S. 1987a *Look Who's Talking. Activities for Group Interaction.* 2nd ed. Alemany Press, Hayward, CA.

Christison, M. and Bassano, S. 1987b *Purple Cows and Potato Chips. Multi-Sensory Language Acquisition Activities.* Alemany Press, Hayward, CA.

Clark, J. 1987 *Curriculum Renewal in School Foreign Language Learning.* Oxford University Press, Oxford.

Clarke, M. and Silberstein, S. 1988 Problems, prescriptions, and paradoxes in second-language teaching. *TESOL Quarterly* 22: 685–700.

Cohn, R. 1975 *Von der Psychoanalyse zur Themenzentrierten Interaktion. Von der Behandlung einzelner zu einer Pädagogik für alle.* Klett-Cotta, Stuttgart.

Cohn, R. 1979 Ich bin ich. Ein Aberglaube. Ich, das Thema und die anderen. *Psychologie heute* 6/3: 22–33.

Cohn, R. 1984 Gelebte Geschichte der Psychotherapie. Buch II. In Farau, A. and Cohn, R. *Gelebte Geschichte der Psychotherapie. Zwei Perspektiven.* Klett-Cotta, Stuttgart.

Collie, J. and Slater, S. 1987 *Literature in the Language Classroom. A Resource Book of Ideas and Activities.* Cambridge University Press, Cambridge.

CRAC 1986 *Insight into Industry.* Careers Research and Advisory Centre, Cambridge.

Corder, P. 1967 The significance of learners' errors. *IRAL* 5/4: 161–70.

Corder, P. 1973 *Introducing Applied Linguistics.* Penguin, Harmondsworth.

Corder, P. 1986 Talking shop. Pit Corder on language teaching and applied linguistics. *English Language Teaching Journal* 40: 185–90.

Curran, C. 1976 *Counselling Learning in Second Languages.* Apple River Press, Apple River, IL.

Dam, L. 1982 *Beginning English. An Experiment in Learning and Teaching.* Danmarks Laererhojskole (mimeo), Copenhagen.

Dam, L. and Gabrielsen, G. 1988 Developing learner autonomy in a school context. A six-year experiment beginning in the learners' first year of English. In Holec, H. (ed.).

Davies, M. 1987 *Appetite for Adventure.* Video film. Bell School, Bath.

Davies, M. 1989 *An Experiential Approach to Outdoor/Social Education with EFL Students.* Bell Educational Trust, Cambridge.

de Bono, E. 1973 *CoRT Thinking.* Direct Education Services, Blandford.

de Bono, E. 1982 *de Bono's Thinking Course.* British Broadcasting Corporation, London.

de Caluwe, et al. 1988 *School Development: Models and Change.* Acco, Leuven.

De Mille, R. 1974 *Put Your Mother on the Ceiling. Children's Imagination Games.* Penguin, Harmondsworth.

Dennison, G. 1969 *The Lives of Children. The Story of the First Street School.* Vintage, New York, NY.

Dewey, J. 1916 *Democracy and Education*. Macmillan, New York.

Dewey, J. 1963 *Experience and Education*. Macmillan, London.

Dickinson, L. 1987 *Self-Instruction in Language Learning*. Cambridge University Press, Cambridge.

Dietrich, I. 1979a Freinet-Pädagogik im Fremdsprachenunterricht. *Englisch–Amerikanische Studien* 1: 542–63.

Dietrich, I. 1979b *Kommunikation und Mitbestimmung im Fremdsprachenunterricht*, 2nd ed. Scriptor, Kronberg.

Dietrich, I. 1983 Fremdsprachenlernen – Alternativ? In Bolte, H. and Herrlitz, W. (eds).

Dietrich, I. 1984 Wider die Routine im Fremdsprachenunterricht. Eine schrittweise Annäherung an den freien mündlichen Ausdruck und den freien Text. In Schratz, M. (ed.).

Dinsmore, D. 1965 Waiting for Godot in the EFL classroom. *English Language Teaching Journal* 39: 225–34.

Di Pietro, R. 1987 *Strategic Interaction. Learning Languages through Scenarios*. Cambridge University Press, Cambridge.

Doyé, P. 1989 Prüfung der Handlungskompetenz durch pragmatische Tests. In Bach, G. and Timm, J.-P. (eds).

Duckett C. and Hitchin P. 1989 *All in a Word*. Video, VHS, colour, Bell Educational Trust, Cambridge.

Dufeu, B. 1983 Haben und Sein im Fremdsprachenunterricht. In Prengel, A. (ed.).

Edelhoff, C. 1981 Theme-oriented English teaching. Text-varieties, media, skills and project work. In Candlin, C. (ed.).

Edelhoff, C. 1983 Real Language Activities and Projects. Example 'Airport'. *Sproglæreren* (Denmark) 14/1: 16–21.

Edelhoff, C. 1984 Landeskunde zum Anfassen. The Lancaster Outing. Lehrerfortbildung zum Erfahrungen machen. In Schratz, M. (ed.).

Edelhoff, C. 1989 Lehrerfortbildung: Wege zur Handlungskompetenz des Lehrers. In Bach, G. and Timm, J.-P. (eds).

Edelhoff, C. et al. 1990 *Evaluating In-Service Teacher Education and Training. An Interim Report*. Hessisches Institut für Lehrerfortbildung, Fuldatal/Kassel.

Edelhoff, C. and Candlin, C. (eds) 1989 *Verstehen und Verständigung. Zum 60. Geburtstag von Hans-Eberhard Piepho*. Kamp, Bochum.

Edelhoff, C. and Liebau, E. (eds) 1988 *Über die Grenze. Praktisches Lernen im fremdsprachlichen Unterricht*. Belz, Weinheim.

Ellis, G. and Sinclair, B. 1989 *Learning to Learn English. A Course in Learner Training*. Cambridge University Press, Cambridge.

Fauser, P. et al. (eds) 1983 *Lernen mit Kopf und Hand*. Beltz, Weinheim.

Ferragati, M. and Carminati, E. 1984 Airport: An Italian version. *Modern English Teacher* 11/4: 15–17.

Finke, C. 1985 Begegnungen mit englischsprachigen Mitbürgern. Projektorientierter Englischunterricht in der Jahrgangstufe 11. *Praxis des Neusprachlichen Unterrichts* 32: 345–53.

Fischer, A. et al. 1985 *Jugendliche und Erwachsene '85. Generationen im Vergleich*. 5 vols. Leske and Budrich, Opladen.

Fish, S. 1980 *Is there a Text in the Class?* Harvard University Press, Cambridge, MA.

Fleck, M. 1988 Deutsch–amerikanische Partnerschaft. Their life in our country. In Edelhoff, C. and Liebau, E. (eds).

Frank, C. and Rinvolucri, M. 1982 *Grammar in Action. Awareness Activities in the Classroom.* Hueber Verlag, München.

Frey, K. 1982. *Projektmethode.* Beltz, Weinheim.

Fried-Booth, D. (ed.) 1981 *The Good Wheelchair Guide.* Project book. Bell School Bath (mimeo).

Fried-Booth, D. 1982 Project work with advanced classes. *ELTJ* 36: 98–103.

Fried-Booth, D. 1983 *Bath Handicapped.* Video film. Bell School Bath, Bath.

Fried-Booth, D. 1986 *Project Work.* Oxford, Oxford University Press.

FWU (Institut für Film und Bild in Wissenschaft und Unterricht) 1983 *Aktive Schüler lernen besser. Neue Wege im Französisch-Unterricht.* Video film, VHS, colour, 45 min. München-Grünwald, FWU 420349.

FWU 1984 *Schüler organisieren ihren Unterricht selbst. Neue Wege im Französisch-Unterricht.* Video film, VHS, colour, 45 min. München-Grünwald, FWU 420451.

FWU 1987a *Schüler zwischen formaler Sprache und freiem Ausdruck. Neue Wege im Französisch-Unterricht.* Video film, VHS, colour, 59 min. München-Grünwald, FWU 4200745.

FWU 1987b *Paris-Torcy: Schüler erkunden die 'ville nouvelle'. Neue Wege im Französisch-Unterricht.*Video film, VHS, colour, 31 min. München-Grünwald, FWU 4200701.

Galyean, B. 1975 Gestalt therapy: new wine in old skins. Notes from a high-school French teacher's journal. In Brown, G. (ed.).

Galyean, B. 1976 *Language from Within.* Confluent Education Research Center, Santa Barbara, CA.

Galyean, B. 1977 A confluent design for language teaching. *TESOL Quarterly* 11: 143–56.

Galyean B. 1979 A confluent approach to curriculum design. *Foreign Language Annals* 12: 121–8.

Geddes, M. and Sturtridge, G. 1979 *Listening Links.* Heinemann, London.

GGG. Gemeinnützige Gesellschaft der Gesamtschule (ed) 1978 *Bundeskongreß Gesamtschule 1977. Referate, Berichte der Arbeitsgruppen.* GGG mimeo, Ammersbek.

Goethe-Institut et al. (eds) *Triangle 2. Approaches, Methodik, Enseignement.* AUPELF, Paris.

Goodman, K. 1986 *What's Whole in Whole Language.* Heinemann, Portsmouth, NH.

Goodman, P. 1956 *Growing up upsurd.* Problems of youth in organized society. Vintage, New York.

Goodman, P. 1982 *Compulsory miseducation.* Vintage, New York.

Graubard, A. 1972 *Free the Children. Radical Reform and the Free School Movement.* Vintage, New York, NY.

Hadfield, J. 1984 *Elementary Communicative Games.* Nelson, Walton-on-Thames.

Hadfield J. 1987 *Advanced Communicative Games* Nelson, Walton-on-Thames.

Hallam, J. (ed.) 1985 *Bath in the Words of its People*. Project book, (mimeo). Bell School, Bath.

Hebdige, D. 1979 *Subculture: the Making of Style*. London.

Heintel, P. 1978 *Modellbildung in der Fachdidaktik. Eine philosophisch-wissenschaftliche Untersuchung*. Verlag Carinthia, Klagenfurt, Austria.

Heitz, S. 1985 Zigger-Zagger. Die Behandlung und Aufführung eines Dramas im Englischunterricht in einer 10. Gymnasialklasse. In Bredella, L. and Legutke, M. (eds).

Hendricks, G. and Roberts, T. 1977 *The Second Centering Book. More Awareness Activities for Children, Parents and Teachers*. Prentice-Hall, Englewood Cliffs, NJ.

Hendricks, G. and Wills, R. 1975 *The Centering Book. Awareness Activities for Children, Parents and Teachers*. Prentice-Hall, Englewood Cliffs, NJ.

Heron, J. 1989 *The Facilitator's Handbook*. Kogan Page, London.

Hessische Kultusminister, Der (ed.) 1980 *Rahmenrichtlinien. Sekundarstufe I. Neue Sprachen*. Diesterweg, Frankfurt.

Holec, H. 1980 *Autonomy and Foreign Language Learning*. Council of Europe, Strasbourg.

Holec, H. 1987 The learner as manager: managing learning or managing to learn? In Wenden, A. and Rubin, J. (eds).

Holec, H. (ed.) 1988, *Autonomy and Self-Directed Learning: Present Fields of Application*. Council of Europe, Strasbourg.

Holt, J. 1964 *How Children Fail*. Pitman, New York, NY.

Holt, J. 1969 *The Underachieving School*. Pitman, New York, NY.

Hopkins, A. (ed.) 1988 *Bell at IATEFL 1988*. Academic Reports. Bell Educational Trust, Cambridge.

Howatt, A. 1984 *A History of English Language Teaching*. Oxford University Press, Oxford.

Howe, L. and Howe, M. 1975 *Personalizing Education. Value Clarification and Beyond*. Hart, New York, NY.

Humburg, L. et al. 1983 *Airport. Ein Projekt für den Englischunterricht in Klasse 6*. Video film, PAL/VHS, colour, 29 mins. Institut für Film und Bild in Wissenschaft und Unterricht (FWU 420379.), Grünwald.

Hunfeld, H. 1982 *Englischunterricht: Literatur 5–10*. Urban und Schwarzenberg, München.

Hunt, J. and Hitchin, P. 1986, *Creative Reviewing*. Groundwork, Grange-over-Sands.

Illich, I. 1970 *Deschooling Society*. Harper and Row, New York, NY.

Jäger, C. 1984 *Kommunikative Fremdsprachendidaktik: sprachsystem- und sprachhandlungsorientiert*. Peter Lang, Frankfurt.

Johnson, D. 1972 (repr. 1981) *Reaching Out. Interpersonal Effectiveness and Self-Actualisation*. Prentice-Hall, Englewood Cliffs, NJ.

Johnson, D. and Johnson, R. 1987 *Learning Together and Learning Alone*. Prentice-Hall, Englewood Cliffs, NJ.

Johnson, D. and Johnson, R. 1988 *Cooperation in the Classroom*. Rev. ed. Interaction Book Company, Edina, MN.

Johnson, K. and Morrow, K. (eds) 1981 *Communication in the Classroom*. Longman, Harlow.

Johnson, R. (ed.) 1989 *The Second Language Curriculum*. Cambridge University Press, Cambridge.

Jones, B. 1984 Contacts sans voyage. In CILT (ed.) *Using Authentic Resources Teaching French*. CILT, London.

Jones, K. 1982 *Simulations in Language Teaching*. Cambridge University Press, Cambridge.

Jones, N. and Roberts, J. 1987 Street reading ... street talking. Language and cross cultural learning through the environment. *Bulletin of Environmental Education* 195/6: 10–21.

Jong, E. 1980 *Fanny. Being the True History of the Adventures of Fanny Hackabout-Jones*. Granada, London.

Jugendwerk der Deutschen Shell (ed.) 1982 *Jugend '81 Lebensentwürfe, Alltagskulturen, Zukunftsbilder*. Leske and Budrich, Opladen.

Jugendwerk der Deutschen Shell (ed.) 1983 *Näherungsversuche. Jugend '81*. Leske and Budrich, Opladen.

Kaufmann, F. 1977 Lernen in Freiheit – im Fremdsprachenunterricht. *Praxis des Neusprachlichen Unterrichts* 24: 227–36.

Kilpatrick, W. 1918 The project method. *Teachers' College Record* 19/4.

Kleppin, K. and Königs, F. 1987 Was willst du, daß ich tun soll? Überlegungen und Beobachtungen zur Rolle der Erwartungen im Fremdsprachenunterricht. *Zielsprache Deutsch* 18/1: 10–21.

Klippel, F. 1980 *Lernspiele im Englischunterricht mit 50 Spielvorschlägen*. Schönigh, Paderborn.

Klippel, F. 1983 Which games? Ein Überblick über Spielesammlungen für den Englischunterricht. *Praxis des neusprachlichen Unterrichts* 30: 417–25.

Klippel, F. 1984 *Keep Talking. Communicative Fluency Activities for Language Learning*. Cambridge University Press, Cambridge.

Knowles, M. 1970 *The Modern Practice of Adult Education*. Association Press, New York, NY.

Kohonen, V. 1987 *Towards Experiential Learning of Elementary English 1. A Theoretical Outline of an English and Finnish Teaching Experiment in Elementary Learning*. University of Tampere, Tampere.

Kohonen, V. 1989 Experiential language learning – towards second language learning as learner education. *Bilingual Research Group Working Papers*. University of California, Santa Cruz, CA.

Kolb, D. 1984 *Experiential Learning. Experience as the Source of Learning and Develpment*. Prentice-Hall, Englewood Cliffs, NJ.

Kramsch, C. 1984 *Interaction et discours dans la classe de langue*. Hatier-Crédif, Paris.

Kramsch, C. 1985 Literary texts in the classroom: A discourse. *The Modern Language Journal* 69: 356–66.

Lach-Newinsky, P. and Seletzky, M. 1986 *Encounters. Working with Poetry*. Kamp, Bochum.

La Forge, P. 1975 *Research Profiles with Community Language Learning*. Apple River Press, Apple River, IL.

Lambert, V. (ed.) 1989 *Keynsham*. Project book (mimeo). Bell School, Bath.

Legutke, M. 1984 Americans in the Giessen/Frankfurt Area: How They Live. Anmerkungen zu einem landeskundlichen Projekt für Lehrerstudenten. In Bredella, L. (ed.).

Legutke, M. 1984/85 Project Airport. Part 1. *Modern English Teacher* 11/4:

10–14; Part 2, *Modern English Teacher* **12**/1: 28–31.

Legutke, M. 1985 Interactive approaches to poetry. In Bredella, L. and Legutke, M. (eds).

Legutke, M. (ed.) 1986 *American Studies in the Language Classroom. Intercultural Learning and Task-Based Approaches.* Hessisches Institut für Lehrerfortbildung, Fuldatal/Kassel.

Legutke, M. 1988a *Lebendiger Englischunterricht. Kommunikative Aufgaben und Projekte.* Kamp, Bochum.

Legutke, M. 1988b Szenario für ein Textprojekt. J.D. Salinger's *The Catcher in the Rye.* In Edelhoff, C. and Liebau, E. (eds).

Legutke, M. 1989a Projekte im Fremdsprachenunterricht: Bilanz und Perspektiven. In Edelhoff, C. and Candlin, C. (eds).

Legutke, M. 1989b Szenarien für einen handlungsorientierten Fremd-sprachenunterricht. In Bach, G. and Timm, J.-P. (eds).

Legutke, M. (ed.) (forthcoming) *Schüleraktiver Deutschunterricht. Aus der Praxis für die Praxis.* Superintendent of Public Instruction, Olympia, WA.

Legutke, M. and Thiel, W. 1983 *Airport. Ein Projekt für den Englischunterricht in Klasse 6.* Diesterweg, Frankfurt.

Lewis, M. 1981 *Partners.* Language Teaching Publication, Brighton.

Littlejohn, A. 1983 Increasing learner involvement in course management. *TESOL Quarterly* **17**: 495–608.

Littlewood, W. 1981 *Communicative Language Teaching. An Introduction.* Cambridge University Press, Cambridge.

Löffler, R. 1979 *Spiele im Englischunterricht.* Urban und Schwarzenberg, München.

Long, M. 1985 The design of classroom second language acquisition: towards task-based language teaching. In Hyltenstan, K. and Pienemann (eds) *Modelling and Assessing Second Language Development.* Multilingual Matters, Clevedon, Avon.

Long, M. and Porter, P. 1985 Group work, interlanguage talk and second language acquisition. *TESOL Quarterly* **19**: 2.

Maley, A. and Duff, A. 1982 *Drama Techniques in Language Learning. A Resource Book of Communication Activities for Language Teachers,* 2nd edn. Cambridge University Press, Cambridge.

Maley, A. and Moulding, S. 1985 *Poem into Poem. Reading and Writing Poems with Students of English.* Cambridge University Press, Cambridge.

Mares, C. (ed.) 1985 *Our Europe. Environmental Awareness and Language Development through School Exchange.* Brighton (Keep Britain Tidy Group Schools Research Project, Brighton Polytechnic).

Martin, J.-P. 1983 *Aktive Schüler lernen besser. Begleitkarte zur Videokassette* (cf. FWU 1983) Institut für Film und Bild, München-Grünwald.

Martin, J.-P. 1985 *Zum Aufbau didaktischer Teilkompetenzen beim Schüler. Fremdsprachenunterricht auf der lerntheoretischen Basis des Informationsver-arbeitungsansatzes.* Gunter Narr Verlag, Tübingen.

Martin, J.-P. 1986 Für eine Übernahme von Lehrfunktionen durch Schüler. *Praxis des neusprachlichen Unterrichts* **33**: 395–404.

Martin, J.-P. 1988 Schüler in komplexen Lernumwelten. Vorschlag eines kognitionspsychologisch fundierten Curriculums für den Fremdsprachen-unterricht. *Praxis des neusprachlichen Unterrichts* **35**: 294–302.

Martin, J.-P. also see FWU 1983; 1984; 1987a; 1987b.

Maslow, A. 1962 *Towards a Psychology of Being*. D. van Nostrand, Princeton, NJ.

Maslow, A. 1971 *The Farther Reaches of Human Nature*. The Viking Press, New York, NY.

Matthews, A. and Read, C. 1981, *Tandem*. Evans, London.

Maurer, R. (forthcoming) Spurensuche. Deutsche in Salem, Oregon. Ein Projekt mit Schülern der South Salem High School. In Legutke, M.

Maurice, M. 1984 Un réseau vidéo correspondence (RVC.) *Die Neueren Sprachen* 83: 352–58.

Mohammedi-Lange, J. et al. 1989 *The Summer Fête*. Project pamphlet (mimeo). Bell School, Bath.

Montgomery, C. and Eisenstein, M. 1985 Real reality revisited: an experimental communicative course in ESL. *TESOL Quarterly* 19: 317–33.

Morley, J. 1987 Current directions in second language learning and teaching: a state-of-the-art synopsis. *TESOL Newsletter* 21/2: 16–20.

Morrow, K. 1981 Principles of communicative methodology. In Johnson K. and Morrow, K. (eds).

Morrow, K. 1984 Testing performance in oral interaction. In Savignon, S. and Berns, M. (eds).

Morrow, K. (ed) 1989 *Bell at IATEFL 2. Academic Reports*. The Bell Educational Trust, Cambridge.

Moskowitz, G. 1978 *Caring and Sharing in the Foreign Language Class. A Sourcebook on Humanistic Techniques*. Newbury House, Rowley, MS.

Moskowitz, G. 1982 Self-confidence through self-disclosure. The pursuit of meaningful communication. In The British Council (ed.).

Neihardt, J. 1972 *Black Elk Speaks. Being the Life Story of a Holy Man of the Oglala Sioux*. Pocket Books, New York, NY.

Neumann-Zöckler, H. 1980 *Märchenveränderung am Beispiel von 'Little Red Ridinghood'. Szenisches Spiel im Englischunterricht der Sekundarstufe I*. Pädagogisches Zentrum, Berlin.

Neuner, G. et al. (ed.) 1981 *Übungstypologie zum kommunikativen Deutschunterricht*. Langenscheidt, München.

Nossenko, E. and Garkusha, V. 1990 Correspondence. *English Language Teaching Journal* 44: 86.

Nuhn, H.-E. 1982 Schüler organisieren ihr Lernen selbst – Ein Projekt im englischen Anfangsunterricht. *Die Deutsche Schule* 74: 35–43.

Nunan, D. 1987 Communicative language teaching: making it work. *English Language Teaching Journal* 41: 136–45.

Nunan, D. 1988 *The Learner-Centered Curriculum*. Cambridge University Press, Cambridge.

Nunan, D. 1989a *Designing Tasks for the Communicative Classroom*. Cambridge University Press, Cambridge.

Nunan, D. 1989b A client-centred approach to teacher development. *English Language Teaching Journal* 43: 111–18.

Oaklander, V. 1978 *Windows to our Children. A Gestalt Approach to Children and Adolescents*. Real People Press, Moab, Utah.

Oakley, C. 1984 Simulationen in der Hochschule. In Jones, K et al.

Simulationen im Fremdsprachenunterricht. Handbuch für Schule, Hochschule und Lehrerfortbildung. Hueber, München.

Oller, J. and Richard-Amato, P. (eds) 1983 *Methods that Work.* Newbury House, Rowley, Mass.

Olliphant, J. 1986 *Methods that Work* (mimeo). Tacoma Public Schools and University School District, Tacoma, WA.

Oskarsson, M. 1980 *Approaches to Self-Assessment in Foreign Language Learning.* Pergamon Press, Oxford.

Oskarsson, M. 1984 *Self-Assessment of Foreign Language Skills: a Survey of Research and Development Work.* Council of Europe, Strasbourg.

Oxford, R. et al. 1989 Language-learning strategies, the communicative approach, and their classroom implications. *Foreign Language Annals* 22: 29–39.

Paine, D. 1985 *Some Observations on the Role of the Teacher in Project Work* (mimeo). The Bell School, Bath.

Pattison, P. 1987 *Developing Communication Skills.* Cambridge University Press.

Pennycook, A. 1989 The concept of method, interested knowledge, and the politics of language teaching. *TESOL Quarterly* 23: 589–618.

Perls, F. et al. 1951 *Gestalt Therapy. Excitement and Growth in the Human Personality.* Dell Publishing, New York, NY.

Perls, F. 1971 *Gestalt Therapy Verbatim.* Bantam Books, New York, NY.

Petronio, G. 1985 Tours of the Community as Part of the Conversation Class. *Foreign Language Annals* 18: 157–9.

Petzold, H. et al. 1977 Gestaltpädagogik. Konzepte der Integrativen Erziehung. Pfeiffer, München.

Piepho, H.-E. 1974 *Kommunikative Kompetenz als übergeordnetes Lernziel im Englischunterricht.* Frankonius, Limburg.

Piepho, H.-E. 1979 *Kommunikative Didaktik des Englischunterrichts.* Frankonius, Limburg.

Piepho, H.-E. 1981 Establishing objectives in the teaching of English. In Candlin, C. (ed.).

Porter-Ladousse, G. 1983 *Speaking Personally.* Cambridge University Press, Cambridge.

Prabhu, N. 1987 *Second Language Pedagogy.* Oxford University Press, Oxford.

Prengel, A. (ed.) 1983 *Gestaltpädagogik. Therapie, Politik und Selbsterkenntnis in der Schule.* Beltz, Weinheim.

Prokop, M. 1990 *Strategies for Success in Second Language Learning.* Edwin Mellen Press, New York, NY.

Puchta, H. and Schratz, M. 1984 *Handelndes Lernen im Englischunterricht.* 3 vols. Hueber Verlag, München.

Pulverness, A. (ed) 1989 *All in a Word.* Bell Educational Trust.

Pütt, H. 1978 Projekt und Vorhaben. Eine Begriffsgenese. In Stach, R. (ed.).

Reimer, E. 1970 *School is Dead. Alternatives in Education.* Doubleday, Garden City, NY.

Remocker, J. and Storch, E. 1979 *Action Speaks Louder. A Handbook of Non-Verbal Group Techniques.* Churchill Livingstone, Edinburgh.

Richards, J. and Rodgers T. 1982 Method, approach, design, and procedure.

TESOL Quarterly **16**: 153–68.

Richards, J. and Rodgers, T. 1986 *Approaches and Methods in Language Teaching. A Description and Analysis.* Cambridge University Press, Cambridge.

Richards, J. and Schmidt, R. (eds) 1983 *Language and Communication.* Longman, London.

Rinvolucri, M. 1982 Awareness activities for teaching structures. In The British Council (ed.).

Rinvolucri, M. 1980 The Abortion. In Spaventa, L. et al.

Rivers, W. 1983 *Communicating Naturally in a Second Language. Theory and Practice in Language Teaching.* Cambridge University Press, Cambridge.

Roberts, J. 1988a *Cross-Cultural Inset for Language Teachers. Academic Reports.* The Bell Educational Trust, Cambridge.

Roberts, J. (ed) 1988 *Thoughts and poems.* Project book. Bell School Bath, Bath (mimeo).

Rogers, C. 1961 *On Becoming a Person.* Houghton Mifflin, Boston.

Rogers, C. 1969 *Freedom to learn.* Charles E. Merrill, Columbus, OH.

Rogers, C. 1975 Bringing together ideas and feelings in learning. In Read, D. and Simon, S. (eds) *Humanistic Education Sourcebook.* Prentice Hall, Englewood Cliffs, NJ.

Rogers, C. 1983 *Freedom to Learn for the 80s.* Charles E. Merrill, Columbus, OH.

Rosenblatt, L. 1978 *The Reader, the Text, and the Poem. Transactional Theory of the Literary Work.* Southern Illinois University Press, Carbondale, IL.

Roszak, T. 1972 Sources. *An Anthology of Contemporary Materials Useful for Preserving Personal Sanity while Braving the Great Technological Wilderness.* Harper and Row. New York, NY.

Roszak T. 1973 *Where the Wasteland Ends. Politics and Transcendence in Post-Industrial Society.* Doubleday, Garden City, NY.

Royal Society of Arts 1980 *Examinations in the Communicative Use of English as a Foreign Language.* Royal Society of Arts, London.

Royal Society of Arts 1983 *English as a Second Language Pilot Scheme.* Royal Society of Arts, London.

Royal Society of Arts 1988 *English as a Second Language. Dual Certification.* Royal Society of Arts, London.

Royal Society of Arts 1988 *The Communicative Use of English as a Foreign Language.* University of Cambridge, Local Examinations Syndicate, International Examinations, Cambridge.

Rutherford, W. 1987 *Second Language Grammar: Learning and Teaching.* Longman, Harlow.

Salinger, J. 1958 *The Catcher in the Rye.* Penguin, Harmondsworth.

Savignon, S. and Berns, M. (eds) 1984 *Initiatives in Communicative Language Teaching. A Book of Readings.* Addison-Wesley, Reading Mass.

Schiffler, L. 1980 *Interaktiver Fremdsprachenunterricht.* Klett, Stuttgart.

Schratz, M. 1983 Fremdsprachenunterricht als Identitätsstütze. In Solmecke, G. (ed.).

Schratz, M. (ed.) 1984 *Englischunterricht im Gespräch.* Kamp, Bochum.

Schratz, M. et al. 1983 *Lehren und Lernen im Englischunterricht mit Erwachsenen. Kommunikation und Interaktion im Unterrichtsprozeß. Ein Forschungsbericht.* Verband Wiener Volksbildung, Wien.

Schwäbisch, L. and Siems, M. 1974 *Anleitung zum sozialen Lernen für Paare, Gruppen und Erzieher. Kommunikations- und Verhaltenstraining*. Rowohlt, Reinbek.

Schwerdtfeger, I. 1977 *Gruppenarbeit im Fremdsprachenunterricht. Ein adaptives Konzept*. Heidelberg.

Schwerdtfeger, I. 1983 Alternative Methoden der Fremdsprachenvermittlung für Erwachsene. Eine Herausforderung für die Schule. *Neusprachliche Mitteilungen* **36**: 3–14.

Scovel, T. 1978 The effect of affect on foreign language learning. *Language Learning* **28**: 129–42.

Scovel, T. 1983 Current approaches to the teaching of English as a foreign language. Alternative methods *Zielsprache Englisch* **13**: 6–12.

Seidler, K. 1988 Kontakte ohne zu reisen: Video-Letter-Exchange. In Edelhoff, C. and Liebau, E. (eds).

Seletzky, M. 1984 Entwurf einer prozeßorientierten Methodik des Englischunterrichts in der Landeskunde (Output-Input-Model). In Bredella, L. (ed.).

Seletzky, M. 1986 'The Graduate' as a way into the 1960s. In Legutke, M. (ed.).

Seletzky, M. 1989 Teaching the American constitution. In Edelhoff, C. and Candlin C. (eds.).

Seletzky, M. and Thomas, H. 1982 *Job Satisfaction and the Effect of Unemployment*. Hessisches Institut für Lehrerfortbildung, Fuldatal.

Selinker, L. 1972 Interlanguage. *IRAL* **10/3**: 209–31.

Sendzik, J. and Rahlwes, S. Lernort Frankreich: Schüleraustausch und praktisches Lernen. In Edelhoff C. and Liebau (eds).

Sexton, M. and Williams, P. 1984 *Communicative Activities for Advanced Students of English. A Typology*. Langenscheidt, München.

Sheerin, S. 1989 *Self Access*. Oxford University Press, Oxford.

Sheils, J. 1988 *Communication in the Modern Languages Classroom*. Council of Europe, Strasbourg.

Simon, S. et al. 1972 *Values Clarification*. Hart, New York, NY.

Sinclair, J. and Coulthard, R. *Towards an Analysis of Discourse. The English used by Teachers and Pupils*. Oxford University Press, Oxford.

Solmecke, G. (ed.) 1976 *Motivation im Fremdsprachenunterricht*. Schönigh, Paderborn.

Solmecke, G. (ed.) 1983 *Motivation und Motivieren im Fremdsprachenunterricht*. Schöningh, Paderborn.

Solmecke, G. 1984 Lehrer-Schüler Interaktion im Fremdsprachenunterricht. Vorschläge ihrer Änderung. *Englisch* **19**: 14–19.

Spaventa, L. et al. 1980 *Towards the Creative Teaching of English*. George Allen and Unwin, London.

Stach, R. (ed.) 1978 *Projektorientierter Unterricht. Theorie und Praxis*. Kastellaun.

Stankewitz, W. 1977 *Szenisches Spiel als Lernsituation*. Urban und Schwarzenbeck, München.

Stevick, E. 1976a *Memory, Meaning, and Method. Some Psychological Perspectives on Language Learning*. Newbury House, Rowley, Mass.

Stevick, E. 1976b Teaching English as an alien language. In Fanselow et al. (eds) *On Tesol '76*. TESOL, Washington, DC.

Stevick, E. 1980 *Teaching Languages: a Way and Ways*. Newbury House, Rowley, Mass.

Stevick, E. 1982 *Teaching and Learning Languages.* Cambridge University Press, Cambridge.

Struck, P. 1980 *Projektunterricht.* Kohlhammer, Stuttgart.

Suin de Boutemard, B. 1975 *Schule, Projektunterricht und soziale Handlungsperformanz.* Pfeiffer, München.

Suin de Boutemard, B. 1986 Projektunterricht. Geschichte einer Idee, die so alt ist wie unser Jahrhundert. In Bastian, J. and Gudjohns, H. (eds).

Swaffer, J. 1985 Reading in the foreign language classroom. A cognitive model. *Modern Language Journal* 69: 15–34.

Swain, M. 1984 Large-scale communicative language testing: a case study. In Savignon, S. and Berns, M. (eds).

Tarone, E. 1988 *Variations in Interlanguage.* Edward Arnold, London.

Taylor, B. 1983 Teaching ESL: Incorporating a communicative, student-centred component. *TESOL Quarterly* 17: 69–88.

Thiel, W. 1983 Eine Zugfahrt. Lernen in Projekten. Adaption des Beispiels AIRPORT für Deutsch als Fremdsprache. *Sproglæreren* (Denmark) 14/5: 18–26.

Thiel, W. 1984 Wir haben die Schmetterlinge im Bauch gespürt. Was Schüler und Lehrer bei der Verfilmung des Airportprojektes wahrnahmen. In Schratz, M. (ed.).

Thiel, W. 1985 Americans in Frankfurt. In Bredella, L. and Legutke, M. (eds).

Thomas, H. (ed) 1986 *Make Life Easy, Try with a Smile.* Project book (mimeo). Bell School, Bath.

Thomas, H. (ed.) 1987 *Poems.* Project book (mimeo). Bell School, Bath.

Thomas, H. 1989 Soldier's Things. In Pulverness, A. (ed.).

Thomas, H. 1990 *Learner Evaluation of Process and Teacher in Project Work.* Video film. Bell School, Bath.

Thomas, H. and Walters, S. 1988 In-service implications of . . . experiential learning. In Hopkins, A. (ed.).

Thomas, U. 1987 *Alternative Fremdsprachenvermittlungsmethoden. Möglichkeiten und Grenzen.* Berlin.

Tomkins, J. 1980 *Reader-response criticism. From formalism to post-structuralism.* John Hopkins University Press, Baltimore MD.

Tomlinson, B. 1986 *Openings.* Lingual House, London.

Turner, J. (ed.) 1987 *It's Hero Time.* Project book (mimeo). Bell School, Bath.

Underhill, A. 1989 Process in humanistic education. *English Language Teaching Journal* 43: 250–6.

van Ek, J. 1977 *The Threshhold Level for Modern Language Learning in Schools.* Longman, London.

van Ek, J. 1980 *Threshhold Level English in a European Unit/Credit System for Modern Language Learning by Adults.* (1975) Pergamon Press, Oxford.

van Essen, A. 1989 The continental European contribution to EFL, past and present. In Edelhoff, C. and Candlin, C. (eds).

van Lier, L. 1988 *The Classroom and the Language Learner. Ethnography and Second-Language Classroom Research.* Longman, Harlow.

Vester, F. 1978 *Denken, Lernern, Vergessen. Was geht in unserem Kopf vor, wie lernt das Gehirn, und warum läßt es uns im Stich?* Deutscher Taschenbuch Verlag, München.

Vester, F. 1980 *Neuland des Denkens. Vom technokratischen zum kybernetischen Zeitalter.* Stuttgart.

Völker, U. (ed.) 1980 *Humanistische Psychologie. Ansätze einer lebensnahen Wissenschaft vom Menschen.* Beltz, Weinheim.

Vopel, K. 1981 *Interaktionsspiele für Jugendliche.* 4 vols. Isko, Hamburg.

Voss, H. and Weber, I. 1988 Cross-Channel-Swap-Shop. Ein Landeskundeprojekt im Englischunterricht. In Edelhoff, C. and Liebau, E. (eds).

Wagner, A. 1982 *Schülerzentrierter Unterricht.* 2nd edn. Urban und Scharzenberg, München.

Wenden, A. 1986a Helping learners to think about learning. *English Language Teaching Journal* **40**: 3–12.

Wenden, A. 1986b What do L2 learners know about their language learning? A second look at retrospective accounts. *Applied Linguistics* **7**: 186–201.

Wenden, A. 1987 Incorporating learner training in the classroom. In Wenden, A. and Rubin, J. (eds).

Wenden, A. and Rubin, J. (eds) 1987 *Learner Strategies in Language Learning.* Prentice-Hall International, Englewood Cliffs, NJ.

Wicke, M. and Wicke R. 1988 *German Round the Corner – the Whyte Avenue in Edmonton.* Alberta Education Publications, Edmonton.

Widdowson, H. 1978 *Teaching Language as Communication.* Oxford University Press, Oxford.

Williams, A. 1984 *Projects. Skills and Strategies.* Pitman, London.

Winitz, H. (ed.) 1981 *The Comprehension Approach to Foreign Language Instruction.* Newbury House, Rowley, Mass.

Winkel, R. 1974 *Das Ende der Schule.* München.

Wolfe, D. and Howe, L. 1973a Clarifying values through foreign language study. *Hispania* **56**: 404–6.

Wolfe, D. and Howe, L. 1973b Personalizing foreign language instruction. *Foreign Language Annals,* **7**: 81–90.

Wright, A. et al. 1979 *Games for Language Learning.* Cambridge University Press, Cambridge.

Wright, T. 1987a *Roles of Teachers and Learners.* Oxford University Press, Oxford.

Wright, T. 1987b Instructional tasks and discoursal outcome in the L2 classroom. In Candlin, C. and Murphy, D. (eds).

Yeomans, T. 1975a Gestalt theory and practice and the teaching of literature. In Brown, G. (ed.).

Yeomans, T. 1975b Search for a working model: Gestalt, psychosynthesis, and confluent education. In Brown, G. (ed).

Yoshikawa, M. 1982 Language learning methodologies and the nature of the individual: A new definition. *Modern Language Journal* **66**: 391–5.

Zeller, H. 1988 Vier Interviews in der Sowjetunion. Ein Videoprojekt für aktive Landeskunde. In Edelhoff, C. and Liebau, E. (eds).

Zinker, J. 1977 *Creative Process in Gestalt Therapy.* Brunner and Mazel, New York, NY.

Index